Security and Risk Mana

Critical Reflections and Internatio

Volume 1

Edited by

Matthieu Petrigh

Centre for Security Failures Studies

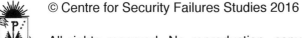

Grateful acknowledgment is due to the following copyright holder:
Gavriel Schneider, "Security Risk Management: the Next Evolution - Applying the Multiplex View to Risk Management", originally published in *Challenging Security Paradigms: Bursting the Assumptions Bubble.* © 2016 Collaborative Publications.

First published in 2016 by
Centre for Security Failures Studies Publishing

The Centre for Security Failures Studies Limited is registered in England and Wales, company number 09662004, 71-75 Shelton Street, Covent Garden, London WC2H 9JQ.

ISBN 978-0-9956270-0-0   Paperback

This book is printed on demand by On-Demand Publishing LLC, an entity part of Amazon Group of companies. Printing quality may vary.

Contents

List of Tables

List of Figures

Acknowledgements

This book has been almost eight months in the making. Over time, I have been helped along the way by many and I would like to take this opportunity to mention a few of them. Firstly, I would like to thank all the authors who responded to my invitation with apparent enthusiasm and gave up their time to support this project. Secondly, I would like to thank Professor Mark Button who has been a source of inspiration and who has accepted to write the foreword of this book despite a rather hectic research agenda. I am also grateful for Doctor Alison Wakefield who has been an immutable source of encouragement and motivation and who has provided me with helpful suggestions and comments during the early stages of this work. The various experts who reviewed this first volume whilst in preparation have been formidable and I also wanted to thank them all. I am also thankful to the two anonymous reviewers for their remarks on the final draft of the manuscript.

Finally, a special thanks to my wife Jurgita and our daughter Kotryna, who provide inspiration and support of the very best kind.

Matthieu Petrigh

List of Contributors

John A. Akerele is currently a professional doctorate researcher in Security Risk Management at the University of Portsmouth. He has previously graduated from the University of Portsmouth with a B.Sc. in Computing and a M.Sc.in Security Management. John is a member of the security institute and an assistant lecturer at the University of Portsmouth. John has worked for top companies within the private security sector and aviation sector in Africa. His research interests include many aspects of the private security sector, terrorism, critical criminology, cyber-crime, aviation security and more.

Dr Gediminas Bučiūnas is lecturer at Mykolas Romeris University Faculty of Public Security, Department of Law, V. Putvinskis str. 70, LT-44211, Kaunas, Lithuania. He is also prosecutor at Kaunas regional prosecution office, organised crime and corruption unit. His areas of academic researches are: pre-trial investigation, methodics on investigation, organised crime, terrorism and public international law (immunities).

Simon de Saint-Claire, PhD is an international police consultant and facilitator. His professional focus centres on security sector reform, international police cooperation, and police engagement – utilising such tools as human terrain analysis, human relations strategies, strategic and intercultural communication, human rights mechanisms, and thematic research. A former New Zealand Army Officer, for over a decade Simon sub-contracted to the United Nations Secretariat providing field-based strategic services, later working in the Private Security Sector. Since 2002 he has provided independent field consultancy, facilitation and research to intergovernmental actors, national police authorities, state development agencies, international police missions, and technical assistance to NGOs (as a Special Consultative Status delegate to UNODC, OHCHR and EU FRA). He currently lectures at the National Police Agency of Japan, Netherlands National Police Agency, and the Hessian Police College, and serves as

Director for International & Interagency Relations for I-NGO "GREAT". Simon has an academic and research background in International Relations, Human Rights, Socio-Cultural Anthropology, Human Relations and Intercultural Communication, Community-Orientated Policing, and Human Trafficking.

Fabiana Maggie Ferraro is an Intelligence professional specialised in Osint and Humint within the law enforcement and government sector, with experience in various fields, including Close Protection. Currently providing consultancy services for Risk Management and private investigation companies in London, she is completing a BSc Security and Risk Management course at the University of Portsmouth, UK.

Dr Nicholas Gilmour is the New Zealand Police Teaching Fellow at Massey University in Wellington responsible for the teaching of Masters Degree papers on intelligence, crime & security, and crime science. Following nearly 10 years in the UK and New Zealand Police working within a number of specialist roles including organised crime and intelligence, Nicholas returned back to the UK in 2008 to work for the National Policing Improvement Agency (NPIA) implementing a strategic business framework before writing practice advice for the UK's 43 police forces. In his final assignment, Nicholas authored a 400 page Association of Chief Police Officer sponsored document on conducting European cross-border investigations. On leaving the NPIA in 2010, Nicholas undertook a four-year term in an advisory position in Abu Dhabi Police working under the direction of His Highness, Deputy Prime Minister and Minister of Interior.

Jerry Hart is the Global Security Risk Manager at SGS SA. He studied for his MSc in Security Risk Management before becoming a Research Officer then Lecturer in Security Management at the University of Leicester. He left academia after nearly ten years to pursue a practitioner career, initially in security consulting then later in security operations and analysis. A near-fluent Spanish speaker, Jerry has conducted security operations, investigations and research work throughout South and Central America, North America, Africa, Asia and

Eastern Europe. He is a former Consultant Advisor to a counter-terrorism unit of the UK police and is currently writing up his doctoral thesis for the Institute for Work-Based Learning at Middlesex University.

Stephen Langley is an accomplished Senior Security Professional and Brand Protection Manager, who has expertise in compliance related investigations. Stephen holds a degree in UK Law (LLB) that he attained from the Open University and a MSc in Security Management that he obtained from the University of Portsmouth and also various Leadership and Management qualifications. Stephen joined the Royal Military Police in 1997 and left in 2010 after a successful career before being employed as the Insider Threat Consultant providing a senior advisory role during the London Olympics and Paralympics 2012, liaising with governmental security departments to deliver safe games. He has over 15 years of experience as a successful senior investigator/ intelligence officer / analyst within the international community (who has worked at international level within The Royal Military Police, G4S, The UK Home Office, Pinkerton and Caterpillar Inc). He is skilled in brand protection investigations covering counterfeit issues, trademark and copyright infringements, as well as supplier diversion issues, supporting and co-ordinating global investigations teams and outside investigator networks.

Matthieu Petrigh is the director of the Centre for Security Failures Studies, a think tank and research centre located in London. He is an advocate and specialist in security risk management and a researcher having a particular interest in security failure analysis, evidence-based security and problem formulation. He holds a BSc in Security and Risk Management from the University of Portsmouth, where he is currently completing a MRes in Security Risk Management.

Dr David Rubens completed his Professional Doctorate at Portsmouth University Department of Security & Risk Management, writing his thesis on 'Beyond Command & Control: Developing a New Paradigm for Incident Command Systems, Critical Decision-Making and 21st

Century Crisis Response'. He hold a MSc in Security and Risk Management from Scarman Centre, Leicester University, where he was subsequently a Visiting Lecturer and Dissertation Supervisor on their Security, Terrorism and Policing programme (2006-12), and was a Visiting Lecturer on the Strategic Leadership Programme run by the Security and Resilience Department, Cranfield University, UK Defence Academy (2009-10), where he lectured on terrorism and public policy, and the management of large-scale, multi-agency programmes. He is a member of the London Gold Command Crisis Management Project academic advisory group, and as a private consultant has worked on large-scale crisis and risk management programmes with global corporations and government agencies around the world.

Dr Gavriel Schneider is the CEO and a founding partner of the Risk 2 Solution Group and the Principal Consultant for the R2S consulting. He has over two decades of experience in the fields of risk management, safety advisory, close protection and high level consulting. Gavriel was the first recipient of both his Doctorate (Criminology) and Master's degree (Security Risk Management) from UNISA (the first in Africa). He is the Author of 'Beyond the Bodyguard: a guide to protective practices success'. He has been interviewed as a subject matter expert by media organisations such as the ABC, CNBC and the Associated Press. Gavriel is an inducted member of the South African Martial Arts Hall of Fame and he is featured in the Israeli Museum of Martial Arts History.

Peter Stiernstedt is pursuing a PhD in Social Sciences on the Perception of Corruption with a fully funded bursary from the University of Portsmouth. Previous academic achievements are a BSc in Physics from the University of Gothenburg in Sweden, followed by an MSc in Security Management from the University of Portsmouth. Prior to the current academic career Peter was working as a consultant providing Strategic Solutions within the realms of risk, security and crisis. Peter is an active member of ISACA, the Security Institute and ASIS International. Personal interests include international politics, particularly the internal and foreign policies of the EU, primarily issues that relate to societal security, such as Anti-Fraud and Corruption efforts as well as the development and results of Crisis Management instruments.

Phillip Wood MBE is the Head of the School of Management and Professional Studies at Buckinghamshire New University in the UK. With a background that includes military service in various roles; the delivery and management of corporate resilience programmes to industry, and his current academic management role, he is committed to the continued development of resilience in organisations and society, against a challenging and dynamic risk and threat background. He has had his work published in journals, industry publications and the media; and his book 'Resilient Thinking: Protecting Organisations in the 21st Century' which was published in 2012, addresses the issues related to human behaviours and their effects on effective resilience planning and response. A strong believer in blending academic theory with the practical applicability of resilience activities and functions, he is currently working on a range of initiatives that are designed to support businesses and organisations in developing effective resilience against the dynamics of global activity and change.

Foreword

Security and risk management have assumed significant prominence in the more risk conscious times we live in. Horrendous terrorist atrocities, sophisticated cyber-attacks to simple staff frauds are just some of the wide range of risks the modern security professional must consider. Unlike other professions which support organisations security managers have been only recent converts to professionalism and the commitment to higher education and research that goes with it. Some might argue many are still not. The last decade has seen a substantial increase in the professionalism of security and risk personnel. The appetite of the most committed to such agendas is often left empty because of the lack of quality research in this field that is published. And it is in this context that this collection of papers in "Security and Risk Management" is welcomed. The book provides an impressive collection of largely research based papers from mostly early career researchers with some link to Portsmouth University. There are some very impressive papers and some of the authors should be noted on the watch list as future star security researchers. I hope you enjoy this collection and I am convinced it will further the research agenda in security and risk, feed the hunger of the growing band of new security professionals and most importantly, offer important insights and knowledge on how to improve security in the very risky times we live in.

Professor Mark Button

Chapter 1

Introduction

Matthieu Petrigh

This is the first volume of *Security and Risk Management: Critical Reflections and International Perspectives.* Until this work appeared, there had been no book containing a blend of studies and researches conducted by students, doctors, PhDs and security professionals. This is therefore an innovation and it is hoped that such an approach to knowledge dissemination will bring some value to the readership. In this volume, experts and students from various fields will attempt to address few problems they thought about or were confronted to and explain how certain aspects of security and risk management should change and the reasons for this. These questions of *what the problem is* and *how to solve it* have been the subject of extensive philosophical pursuits for many years, if not centuries, known to the erudite as ontology (the branch of metaphysics that deals with the nature of being) and epistemology (the study of how we arrive at knowledge).

As the readers will understand, solving problems remains a process. It is therefore an ongoing series of actions without end in itself. On this basis of understanding, the solutions presented in this book should not be considered as definitive answers. They should rather be understood as critical reflections and perspectives on particular subject matters. This book is thus a collection of essays on the broad and evolving subject of security and risk management. It is neither a thesis or a comprehensive textbook. A work of this kind would require a far more competent author and editor, who, in a vast synthesis, would have to follow the development of security and risk management from the days of Clement of Rome, Ignatius of Antioch and Polykarp of Smyrna to Sun Tzu, to the antiquity, to Beccaria, Hobbes, Machiavelli and Morin, Bernstein, Clarke, Gill, Button and many other extremely competent thinkers, to say nothing of the great business strategists of our present

1

time and those philosophers and writers, who, in their own ways, have always known about these security and risk matters and shaped the discipline. But this synthesis of knowledge is not yet achieved and the bridges between the disciplines related to the deep understanding of security and risk management are not yet built. To encapsulate this complex idea that the dimension of security is in its essence polymorph and pluralistic, I would like to perhaps introduce the readers to the terms *security integralism* and *security holism*. This is because it is important to understand that everything in this life is centred on and dependent upon security and risk management and that therefore, all disciplines are concerned with the former and converging towards it.

What unites the contributing authors is their interest in the phenomena and problems attached to the management of security and risk and their willingness to describe them in this work. It will hardly surprise the readers to find that, in spite of their common subject matter, these contributions are like erratic blocks of knowledge, very different in style, length and their degrees of abstraction, and that, when taken as a whole, sometimes contain both unanswered questions and repetitions. After all, these papers have their origin in very different disciplines and cultures and this should be acknowledged by the readers.

The structure of the book

The book contains 12 Chapters, excluding the introduction. All present interesting findings and original contents. They also advance the state of knowledge relative to the discipline of security and risk management to the extent that they bring fresh perspectives and ideas. These contributions are all scholarly papers and most of them have clear practical implications. All but three are written by experts holding doctorates in their respective fields of study and doctoral students.

In the second Chapter, *Dr David Rubens* offers an alternative view to crisis and emergency management, based on the values embodied within High Reliability Organisations (HRO's). Having methodologically and extensively researched some of the problems which are inherent to crisis management failure, David recognises that there is a failure for

2

organisations to effectively learn from rare events. He indeed
that the causes of many of the major threats to our communities
not necessarily the result of external events, but rather due to inher
known organisational weaknesses being systematically ignored. David
concludes his work by making the case that it is possible to transfer the
foundational values that have created HRO's, namely an organisational
mindfulness and commitment to zero-failure reliability, into the chaotic
world of crisis management.

The third Chapter, written by *Dr Gavriel Schneider,* looks at the
notion of silo-thinking and the implications this has upon the security
and risk management organisational capability. Grounding his
reasoning on an extensive study and his own professional experience,
Gavriel argues that security and risk practitioners tend to be too
specialists rather than generalists. This, accordingly, is understood as
being a fundamental problem to address. Consequently, he argues that
the need for security risk managers to become more rounded risk
practitioners is crucial and that a more holistic and wider view to risk
management, which Gavriel terms the "Multiplex View" is more critical
today than ever before.

In the fourth Chapter, *Stephen Langley* advocates that despite the
past and current security efforts made by many organisations to tackle
the problem of insider threat, there is still strong evidence to suggest
that instances of this malevolent activity are becoming more prevalent
and increasing in veracity globally. He argues that current and former
employees, contractors and other organisational "insiders" will continue
to represent a substantial threat to the organisation by virtue of their
knowledge of and access to their employers' IT systems. Recognising
that academics and subject matter experts all too often disagree on
what constitutes an "insider threat", Stephen proposes a rather original
definition of the term to perhaps foster new understandings.

Security fails all the time and very few lessons are being learned by
organisations. There are many reasons for this and the problem should
be addressed. In Chapter 5, *Matthieu Petrigh* seeks to perhaps better
define and conceptualise what is meant by the term "security failure"
and subsequently inform the discussion about how organisations are
analysing, preventing and learning from security failures. Thinking that

d be done at governmental level to address the big
ı then presents the findings of an empirical research
ıcted in which the idea of making the reporting of
United Kingdom a compulsory activity was assessed

... Chapter 6, *Phillip Wood,* by taking a macro-view on the problems attached to organisational resilience and business continuity, argues that our own innate behaviours, ideas, characters and understandings can have a strong impact upon our individual and collective capabilities towards the latter. He recognises that these behavioural and human "pre-conditions" should be addressed and consequently advances the idea that we, as human beings, should make some efforts to overcome our own fixed mindsets and adherence to rigid models, frameworks and structures. In turn, Phillip indeed argues that this "transformation" would be one of the keys to improving organisational resilience.

In the seventh Chapter, *Dr Nicholas Gilmour* seeks to examine the persistent challenges that prevent law enforcement from effectively gaining a comprehensive understanding of organised crime. He indeed identifies those particular challenges as being correlated to the scope of activities; group dynamics; cross border context; and the sharing of intelligence which, in their whole, are comprehended as framing and modelling the (mis)behaviour of law enforcement agencies. During his work, Nicholas clearly demonstrates that organised crime, a composite and shapeless phenomenon, has now become better educated, skilled and resourced than its law enforcement counterparts and subsequently recognises that the big problem should be addressed by refocusing the responses to it. In this regards, Nicholas finally proposes a set of broad solutions having both a strategic appeal and practical implications.

In Chapter 8, *Simon de Saint-Claire PhD* suggests that the Human Terrain System (HTS) - an ethically ambiguous US military intelligence gathering tool and programme utilising social scientists to provide cultural intelligence on the local populace - should be rehabilitated for use in International Police Missions due to its numerous shortcomings and perhaps further revised for domestic policing in civilian settings as a non-invasive engagement tool for operations taking place in diverse and multicultural communities. Grounded on an extensive study of the

4

disciplines and topics related to the full understanding of HTS, Simon's work examines and distinguishes real problems from misconceptions and inconveniences from strategic implications. To conclude, Simon proposes a model of policing multicultural communities adapted from the "Chicago Model" - a people-centred approach to policing.

When ignored or misunderstood, cultural and religious differences can become problems and conflicts facilitators and indeed generate serious security concerns. In Chapter 9, *Dr Gediminas Bučiūnas* examines the communication peculiarities between the believers of Islam and non-Islamic public servants during the process of pre-trial investigation and legal proceedings. Recognising that important "cultural shortcomings" exist among public servants, Gediminas suggests a set of practical recommendations to help reduce friction between public servants who are responsible for maintaining public order and believers of Islam, as well as immigrants from the continents of Africa and Asia.

In Chapter 10, *John Akerele* investigates the public perception of door supervision in the UK night-time economy. By so doing, he presents the findings of a small scale research study he recently conducted and provides valuable insights to academics, officials and policy makers. Drawing upon his research findings, John then recommends important courses of actions which are essentially meant to rebuild what appears to be, in his view, the tarnished reputation of door supervisors. Among the recommendations John makes are the need for a more customer-focused Security Industry Authority's (SIA) training for door supervisors and a better awareness of the improvements recently made within the door supervision's sector by the media.

Fraud and corruption are endemic problems in our modern society. And these are as such for various reasons. In Chapter 11, *Peter Stiernstedt* clearly explains the mechanisms behind such problems. He argues that at a global level and measured in the trillions, fraud and corruption are de facto some of the most costly crimes to society. His view is that such problems must be tackled with consistency and methodologically. Drawing from the latest research findings in the fields of counter-fraud and counter-corruption, Peter justifies and outlines a couple of robust and proven professional approaches aimed at accurately measuring and tackling the problems of fraud and corruption.

In Chapter 12, *Fabiana Maggie Ferraro* critically assesses why the problem of fraud is so difficult to define. Her view is that the efforts in defining the notion of "fraud" have often been hindered by a natural overlap of the theoretical concept of fraud, or deception, and its legal counterpart. Her research starts by distinguishing between the different approaches to fraud from a philosophical perspective and from a legislative point of view with regards to the US and UK key legislations in force. Fabiana then incrementally narrows down her research study and concludes by highlighting the salient discrepancy, yet ambivalence between the theoretical concept of fraud and its legal definition.

In the latest Chapter, *Jerry Hart* argues that despite the fact that the number and range of vocational training and educational programmes made available and given to those wishing to enter the security world have significantly grown over the last decades, the apparent strategy of developing security as a new specialist profession has had a limited impact on improving the management of security within organisations. Reflecting upon this problem, he recognises the nucleus of the matter as being related to the near absence of the subject of "security" from the teaching of mainstream management and other disciplines that shape modern society. To address this shortcoming, Jerry proposes an innovative approach to security and risk management that facilitates interdisciplinary learning and knowledge transfer among professionals operating in different organisational sectors and cultures and sees risks being mapped at process level within the context of a whole system.

Chapter 2

Creating High Reliability Organisations Within Crisis Management

Dr David Rubens

Despite massive levels of investment in terms of time, effort, money and man-power, crisis and emergency management response programmes are often characterised by their failure to deliver their core services at exactly the times that they are needed most. This chapter offers an alternative view to crisis and emergency management, based on the values embodied within High Reliability Organisations (HRO's). Although HROs have been designed to operate within highly-engineered and micro-controlled environments such as nuclear power stations, aircraft carriers and power stations, this chapter makes the case that it is possible to transfer the foundational values that have created those HRO's, namely an organisational mindfulness and commitment to zero-failure reliability, into the chaotic world of crisis management.

Introduction

This chapter examines the concept of High Reliability Organisations (HROs) and demonstrates the relevancy they have to the development of effective crisis management capabilities on an organisational and multi-agency basis. It makes the case that the reason that crisis management often fails is that the situations they respond to are seen as 'rare events' and therefore appropriate capabilities cannot be developed on a 'fail and learn' basis. As an alternative paradigm which allows exactly that sort of learning from rare events, HROs are zero-failure organisations that operate in the highest risk environments but also have to contend with the challenges created by their own organisational limitations.

7

As such, they are organisations that are focussed on identifying weakness in order to prevent failures, rather than responding to failures once they have caused accidents (Flin et al., 2000). The chapter then looks at the difference between efficiency (which is the quality aspired to in centralised ICS) and reliability, which is the ability to deliver the desired service to the desired level. It is a quality that is focussed on 'not failing' rather than 'achieving success'. The chapter concludes by identifying the single most critical quality in developing HROs in high-risk operating environments as being an openness and honesty about organisational weaknesses, and an uncompromising commitment to eradicating those weaknesses on every level of operation. It can therefore be inferred that it is this level of openness and honesty that is the missing component in the current development of effective crisis management capabilities, and without which repeated failures will continue to happen.

The Nature of High Reliability Organisations

HROs are often seen as the supreme embodiment of high-design organizational micro-management, in that by their very nature they have to deliver a high (infallible) level of service delivery in what are often extremely complex operating environments, with the threat of catastrophic consequences for any failure (Mannarelli et al., 1996). As such, despite the fact that they seem to offer a potential model for effective management of high-risk operations, their high-design nature has meant that they have been considered as lacking relevance to the chaotic environment of crisis management. However, a different perspective was offered by Weick and Roberts (1993), who saw HROs as a reflection of a 'mindfulness' rather than a particular design approach. Under this model, the success of HROs was due to the fact that they focussed on reliability rather than efficiency, and on understanding how to avoid failure rather than concentrating on what created success. Efficiency is a quality that is management driven, and that sees subordinate functions as requiring direction, control and standardization.

8

Reliability requires a multitude of approaches, the responsibility to identify faults, and the ability to choose amongst a range of response options. The tension between efficiency and reliability is one based on design-led belief that one can design out problems (and that the world will operate in predictable ways), and operator-led models which accept that even the best designed system will need to have immediate operator input in order to respond to fluctuations in the working environment (Schulman, 2004; Muhren et al., 2007). In its purest terms, efficiency is built on the belief that 'if designed correctly, things will work', whilst reliability is built upon the foundational belief that 'we'd better be ready when things go wrong' (Landau & Chisholm, 1995).

Barry Turner and Nick Pidgeon, in their widely cited investigation of 'Man-Made Disasters' (Turner & Pidgeon, 1997), identified the fact that accidents were not the outcome of some random coincidence of events, but were actually the result of organisational behaviour that had deliberately either ignored or misinterpreted a multitude of warning signs. Effective HROs are those that are open to the fact that there is the need to be adaptive and responsive and therefore are actively aware of the possibilities of the need to look for the causes of potential problems that might lead to the need to respond appropriately. In an organisation where the attempt to identify potential problems is seen as either unproductive or at worst potentially damaging to one's own career, then it is clear that the prevailing culture will be one of ignoring potential (and even actual) threats, and therefore increasing the likelihood of eventual failure.

The report into NASA and the culture associated with the Space Shuttle Challenger disaster (Rogers, 1986) reflected exactly those concerns. A fundamental aspect of the effective HRO is that everyone, whether managers or operators, worries about the possibility of failure, so much so that 'Worries about failure are what give HROs much of their distinctive quality' (Weick & Roberts, 1993, p. 19). This is in distinct contrast to many emergency management programmes, which seem to presume that the event will unroll as predicted in the emergency response plan, and that there is little or no need to take into account the possibility of change or failure (Clarke & Perrow, 1996;

Perry & Lindell, 2003). The main difference between HROs and crisis management is that in HROs, failures are rare events (and management proactively try and bring them as close to zero as practically possible), whilst in emergency management scenarios they are often, even if only in retrospect, seen as inevitable outcomes of known organisational weaknesses. The original HROs, nuclear power stations, were presumed to have been designed and built so effectively, and with so many inbuilt redundancies that created a defence-in-depth against failure, that actual failure could be considered to be so rare a (theoretical) event that it did not need to be taken account of. Once the power station was built and running, it was presumed to just keep on running. It was only when the inevitable failures did arise that it was seen that the complexity of the defence systems were themselves adding to the likelihood of failure, as well as the impact of any failure when it did happen (Carroll, 1998). This is an organisational culture that was mirrored in NASA in the lead-up to the Challenger Space Shuttle disaster, in which the checks and fail-safe systems that had been the foundation of the high-reliability service delivery until then were exactly the components that were removed under the pressure to adhere to artificially imposed political and management time-frames (Vaughan, 1990; Landau & Chisholm, 1995).

Weick and Roberts (1993), set out the five attributes of a mindful organisation as being:

- Preoccupation with failure (in which the possibility of failure is examined at every stage of an operation on a pro-active basis).
- Reluctance to simplify interpretations (so that the inherent complexity of problems, and potential solutions, are accepted as part of the problem-solving process).
- Sensitivity to operations (in which there is the realisation that solutions are only effective if they work within the realities of the operating environment, rather merely existing as paper-based options).
- Commitment to resilience (in that resilience, and the ability to adapt to the widest possible range of challenging environments, is considered as a critical function in any operational plan).

- Under-specification of structures (which means that individuals and teams have the freedom to develop their own working relationships, rather than being forced to adhere to pre-set organisational restrictions).

Whilst the attainment of all of these characteristics to an absolute degree may be more an aspiration than a reality, they are nevertheless accepted as valuable and viable yardsticks for measuring the effectiveness of high-risk operation (Hopkins, 2007). An alternative approach was set out in Cox & Flin's (1998) study of safety cultures in high-risk environments that identified safety as a primary goal, decentralized authority, systems redundancy, organizational learning and senior management commitment as critical factors in creating safe operations.

An organisational culture in which it has become normalised to ignore those issues that seem too big to be dealt with or which would cause political embarrassment if they were acknowledged presumes a high level of 'group think' and a tacit agreement to ignore exactly those issues that are in greatest need of attention (Vaughan, 1997). In effective HROs the culture is exactly the opposite – to go out looking for potential problems or causes of failure points, and to highlight and deal with them at the earliest possible stage – in fact, before they even become problems that can be considered to have the potential to have a negative impact (Schulman, 2004). Just as high-risk systems are designed to have redundancy and multiple fail-safe layers built into them on a technical level, on an organizational basis this is reflected in the quality of scepticism (Weick & Roberts, 1993), which means that the individuals with the knowledge, experience and insight to question official reports, designs and explanations are not only free to do so, but see it as part of their core remit. It is this quality of scepticism that acts as a counter-balance to organisational hubris that leads to the 'drift towards failure' (Woods & Cook, 2002) associated with increased organisational complacency that in turn results in 'managed failure' and an inability to respond to surprises when they do happen. The fact that a report claims that something is true is not accepted until it has been checked and verified, but another person further down the line may well take it upon themselves to doubt that person's findings as well, and to instigate their own checks and verifications. In this way, there is an inbuilt doubt system that acts as a refined, fail-safe mechanism to ensure that what is meant to happen actually has the wherewithal to deliver that service.

Reliability vs Efficiency

As is indicated in its title, the quality of reliability is central to the desired characteristics of an HRO. However, the understanding of reliability has often been misunderstood (Weick et al., 1999). In its generalised usage, reliability has come to mean the standardisation of outcomes, which in itself is dependent upon the delivery of stable operating conditions – whether through standardisation in a production line, or absolute control of all aspects of an operation such as in a nuclear power station. However, even within such highly managed environments, it soon becomes clear that the external operating environment itself is neither constant nor stable – there may be power fluctuations, changes in temperatures, disruption of supply chains or changes in the quality of the raw material, for example. Even within such environments, the ability to adapt and respond is fundamental to maintaining reliable service delivery. A study of US government management procedures pointed out, 'Within a hierarchy-based system, the compulsion to micro manage in the name of efficiency strangles what potential there is for strategic wisdom, operation ingenuity and tactical art' (Luttwak, 1982, p. 20). Rather than being a function of design or systems management, this understanding of reliability is grounded in the cognitive functions that lead to the recognition of change and the acknowledgement of the need to adapt, tied in with the technical capabilities, both individual and organisational, to develop the appropriate responses to the external fluctuations.

The ability to recognise that such fluctuations, and therefore the demands on the organisation and operation flowing from those changes, are an integral aspect of operational management rather than exceptions or outliers, can therefore be regarded as the foundation for the development of reliability. The ability to accept the 'messiness' of operations is part of the development of an HRO, and the desire for management to impose a control structure on that which is inherently unstructured in itself creates the likelihood of failure (Weick & Roberts, 1993). In fact, the more controlling the management structure, the more likely that mistakes in planning or conceptualisation that take place higher up the organisation are to be embedded into all future plans, causing inevitable failure once they cascade down to the operational levels (Schulman, 2004). Given that it is the combination of complexity and the tight-coupling associated with highly complex organisations that causes the inevitability of systems-wide breakdowns, the ability to de-couple different parts of the system so that they can act comparatively autonomously is one of the foundations of the creation of HROs and the avoidance of highly impactful man-made accidents (Perrow, 1999).

Problems and Failures

The characteristics of failures within HROs, as opposed to organizations where the development process of potential problems is more extended, is that problems are considered as being unique and extremely time pressured. Therefore, every problem is accepted as serious, and there is an urgency to find not only a solution to the immediate problem, but to understand the causal chain that led to that situation. Operational failures are not only significant in themselves, but gain significance as indicators of organisational vulnerabilities that allowed those failures to happen. In most organisations, errors are identified as local events that do not reflect or impact on the overall operating framework. By contrast, in well-managed HROs, they are seen as harbingers of potential management weaknesses, and it is recognised that 'causal chains that produced the failure are long and wind deep inside the system' (Weick et al., 2008, p. 89; Carroll, 1998).

The desire to become zero-failure organisations is a fundamental characteristic of HROs, given that they are not able to benefit from a trial and error based learning process, but have to learn significant lessons from what may be limited events (Carroll, 1998). This is in direct contrast to crisis management systems, which are seen to view the possibility of catastrophic failure with alarming nonchalance (Landau & Chisholm, 1995), and for whom the inability to learn from previous disasters is a significant factor (if not the most significant factor) in their continued failures (Donahue & Tuohy, 2006).

If one looks at the failures of supposedly high reliability organisations such as NASA's experience with the Challenger and Columbia failures, or BP with the Deepwater Horizon oil spill, it cannot be claimed that these are 'incompetent organisations'. They were extremely competent, with a high level of expertise at all levels of the operation, and people who were used to taking responsibility for doing their jobs well and properly. Space programmes and oil rigs are not places for people who cannot follow protocols. The problems occur when 'following protocol' is seen as a replacement for 'doing the right thing'. The fundamental issue with crisis events is that they are so rare and so high impact, with such a range of cascading consequences, that it is literally impossible to create realistic plans for dealing with them. Japanese earthquake emergency response plans, for example, are possibly one of the largest 'major event scenarios' one could imagine, and yet both American and Japanese researchers have commented that the plans themselves are built of fantasy data that has no meaning in real life (Geller, 2011; Kawata, 2001). Similarly, following Katrina, the post event report declared that 'Despite the understanding of the Gulf Coast's particular vulnerability to hurricane devastation, officials braced for Katrina with full awareness of critical deficiencies in their plans and gaping holes in their resources' (US Congress, 2006, p. 5).

HROs are built on the belief that the starting point for everything is an acknowledgement of the truth, that is an acceptance of the challenges that any situation might create, as well as the failure points that exist that could lead to an inability to either manage or respond as required to those events. As Weick and Roberts (1993) report, the major determinant of reliability in an organization is not how greatly it values reliability or safety per se over other organizational values, but rather how greatly it disvalues the mis-specification, mis-estimation, and misunderstanding of things. All else being equal, the more things that more members of an organization care about mis-specifying, mis-

14

estimating and misunderstanding, the higher the level of reliability that organization can hope to attain (Weick & Roberts, 1993, p. 104); see also Schulman, 2004, p. ii40). If one were to look at the description of HROs as set out in this chapter, and then to try and develop a framework that was the exact opposite of that, the final version may not be far from what we currently accept as the most appropriate form for crisis and emergency management.

Barry Turner, one of the leading authorities on HROs, was clear as to the underlying cultural assumptions that created the potential for high-impact failures. One of the most dangerous kinds of inadequate management, and one with the greatest potential for disaster, is a situation where senior management have a blinkered, unrealistic view of their organization, its operations, its environment and its vulnerabilities, and use their authority to reinforce this closed view of their world. This condition, which has been called 'groupthink' (Janis, 1982), is particularly dangerous because such a management not only has power to influence events, but is also in a position to appoint staff who reflect its own prejudices and to overrule objections, warnings or complaints originating from those outside the organization who are not under their control (Turner, 1994, p. 217).

Such an approach can be particularly damaging in organisations where the primary objective, at least as far as senior managers are concerned, is no longer the delivery of the organisational or operational objectives, but rather the management of a political agenda. An efficiency based organisation where the underlying condition and functionalities that led to them being an HRO in the first place are gradually eroded, eventually (and often quickly) becomes a prisoner of its own expectations.

The faults within NASA in the run up to the Challenger Space Shuttle disaster were well known, and came about as much through political pressure to maintain a set number of take-offs rather than acknowledging specific maintenance and management requirements (Romzeck & Dubnick, 1987). The attempt to maintain the illusion that everything was OK, while in practice 'It did things that were actually stupid' (Donaghue & Tuohy, 2006), fits Turner's model of groupthink combined with wishful thinking. From a wider perspective, this cultural shift was the result of NASA changing from an organisation that 'deferred to expertise' (i.e. the people who knew how to build a space programme that could get a man on the moon), to one ruled by political bureaucrats who were more concerned with maintaining political and budgetary influence with the decision-makers in Washington (Romzeck & Dubnick, 1987).

Mindfulness as a critical aspect of creating HROs able to respond effectively to changes in the external environment is based as much on the acceptance of the inevitability of failure, and therefore the need to prepare – and actively search – for it, as the ability makes sense out of what is noticed (often based on the realisation of the significance of weak signals (Vaughan, 1986). The lack of mindfulness leads to a situation where the cause of failure is not an inevitable result of complexity and tight coupling, but rather,

> They are alarmingly banal examples of organizational elites not trying very hard.
>
> (Perrow, 1984, p. 305)

In many cases, those failures are not even a result of sloppiness or complacency, but active collusion and malfeasance. As was identified in the US's most serious nuclear disaster,

> Time and again (in the story of Three Mile Island) warnings are ignored, unnecessary risks taken, sloppy work done, deception and down-right lying practiced.
>
> (Perrow, 1984, p. 10)

Conclusion

It is a characteristic of crisis management, as demonstrated through the high-profile, high-impact events that are used at the basis for much crisis management research, that there is a failure to learn from rare events. As a result, the fundamental flaws that are the root cause for major crisis management failures are repeatedly identified as being significant factors in subsequent events. It is as though such failures are themselves seen as being part of crisis management process, and in that fact there is little that can be done to ameliorate them. As an example of an organisational approach in which such failures are considered completely unacceptable, and which is geared towards a total success process, High Reliability Organisations offer a cultural and management template that holds many lessons for crisis management and emergency response planners.

Despite the fact the HROs are associated with some of the most complex and highly-engineered systems in the world, there is an understanding that the ultimate quality is reliability (i.e. objective-focussed) rather than efficiency (i.e. process-focussed). Once the basic capability and service-delivery framework has been established, the efforts of the organisation as a whole, and every subsidiary department within it, is totally focussed on identifying things that could possibly go wrong. As is highlighted in the text, it is this obsession with eliminating failure that is the fundamental characteristic of HROs. As such, all problems, however seemingly minor or innocuous, are treated as signifiers of systemic weaknesses that could have potentially catastrophic impacts.

Under such a regime, all such problems are considered significant and time pressured. If they are known, they should be fixed – and it is someone's responsibility to make sure that they are. It is the culture of non-acceptance of organisational weaknesses, allied to the ownership of that problem by someone who is responsible for ensuring that both the problem and the underlying factors that caused it are identified and resolved, that could be of greatest value in developing a similar culture within crisis management. As has been repeatedly identified in the literature, the causes of many of the major crisis management failures considered to be the greatest threats to our communities are not the result of the external event, but rather due to inherent organisational weaknesses that were known, and systematically ignored. Given the increasing catastrophic impacts of the range of crisis events that we are facing, the failure to accept the responsibility to develop such high-performance crisis management frameworks can in itself be considered a moral and ethical issue.

17

References

Carroll, J. S. (1998). Organizational learning activities in high-hazard industries: the logics underlying self-analysis. *Journal of Management studies*, *35*(6), 699-717.

Clarke, L., & Perrow, C. (1996). Prosaic organizational failure. *American Behavioral Scientist*, *39*(8), 1040-1056.

Cox, S., & Flin, R. (1998). Safety culture: philosopher's stone or man of straw?.*Work & Stress*, *12*(3), 189-201.

Donahue, A., & Tuohy, R. (2006). Lessons we don't learn: A study of the lessons of disasters, why we repeat them, and how we can learn them. *Homeland Security Affairs*, *2*(2).

Flin, R., Mearns, K., O'Connor, P., & Bryden, R. (2000). Measuring safety climate: identifying the common features. *Safety science*, *34*(1), 177-192.

Geller, R. J. (2011). Shake-up time for Japanese seismology. *Nature*, *472*(7344), 407-409.

Hopkins, A. (2007). The problem of defining high reliability organisations. *National Research Center for Occupational Safety and Health Regulation. January*.

Kawata ,Yoshiaka (2001).'Disaster mitigation due to next Nankai earthquake tsunamis occurring in around 2035'. Research Centre for Disaster Reduction Systems, Kyoto.University, Japan. http://nthmp-history.pmel.noaa.gov/its2001/Separate_Papers/1-08_Kawata.pdf (Accessed 12/04/2014).

Landau, M., & Chisholm, D. (1995). The arrogance of optimism: notes on failure-avoidance management. *Journal of Contingencies and Crisis Management*, *3*(2), 67-80.

Luttwak, E. N. (1982). Why we need more waste, fraud and mismanagement in the Pentagon. *Survival*, *24*(3), 117-130.

Mannarelli, T., Roberts, K. H., & Bea, R. G. (1996). Learning how organizations mitigate risk. *Journal of Contingencies and Crisis Management*, *4*(2), 83-92.lk.

Muhren, W. J., Van Den Eede, G., & Van de Walle, B. (2007). Organizational Learning for the Incident Management Process: Lessons from High Reliability Organizations. In *ECIS* (pp. 576-587).

Perrow, C. (1984). *Normal accidents: Living with high-risk technologies.* NY: Basic Books.

Perrow C. (1999). *Normal accidents: Living with high-risk technologies.* Princeton University Press.

Perry, R. W., & Lindell, M. K. (2003). Preparedness for emergency response: guidelines for the emergency planning process. *Disasters, 27*(4), 336-350.

Rogers W. P. (1986). Rogers Commission Report of the presidential commission on the space shuttle challenger accident. Available at http://history.nasa.gov/rogersrep/genindex.htm (Accessed 10/07/2016).

Romzeck, B. S., & Dubnick, M. J. (1987). Accountability in the public sector: Lessons from the Challenger tragedy. *Public Administration Review,* 227-238.

Schulman, P. R. (2004). General attributes of safe organisations. *Quality and Safety in Health Care, 13*(suppl 2), ii39-ii44.

Turner, B. A. Causes of disaster: sloppy management. *British Journal of management* 5.3 (1994): 215-219.

Turner, B. A., & Pidgeon, N. F. (1997). *Man-made disasters.* Butterworth-Heinemann.

United States Congress (2006). Select Bipartisan Committee to Investigate the Preparation for and Response to Hurricane Katrina, & Davis, T. (2006). *A failure of initiative: Final report of the select bipartisan committee to investigate the preparation for and response to Hurricane Katrina.* US Government Printing Office. Available at http://katrina.house.gov/full_katrina_report.htm (Accessed 20/04/2015).

Vaughan D. (1986). *Uncoupling: Turning points in intimate relationship.* New York: Oxford University Press.

Vaughan, D. (1990). Autonomy, interdependence, and social control: NASA and the space shuttle Challenger. *Administrative Science Quarterly,* 225-257.

Vaughan D. (1997). *The Challenger launch decision: Risky technology, culture and deviance at NASA.* University of Chicago Press.

Weick, K. E., & Roberts, K. H. (1993). Collective mind in organizations: Heedful interrelating on flight decks. *Administrative science quarterly,* 357-381.

Weick K. E. Sutcliffe K. M. and Obstfeld D. (2008). Organizing for high reliability: Processes of collective mindfulness. *Crisis Management*, 3(1), pp. 81-123.

Woods, D. D., & Cook, R. I. (2002). Nine Steps to Move Forward from Error.*Cognition, Technology & Work*, *4*, 137-144.

Chapter 3

Security and Risk Management: the Next Evolution - Applying the Multiplex View to Risk Management [1]

Dr Gavriel Schneider

In the ever evolving worlds of safety, security, health and emergency management (SSHE) the regulatory and best practice approaches continue to get more onerous and complex. The evolution of specialist areas within this spectrum has been inevitable. We have also seen a process whereby the areas of the SSHE spectrum, sometimes referred to as 'Hard Risks' (as opposed to soft risks such as currency risk) have become classed as grudge spend areas. This is especially true for the field of security risk management which historically has not had the driver of legislative consequence that the safety sector has had. The requirement for risk and hard risk managers to transcend organisational and psychological barriers to become generalist's practitioners, is an evolutionary change in the way this complex area is dealt. In this day and age, employers demand more from practitioners and require multi-skilled and capable professionals. Many hard risk managers are happy in their specific vocational area of expertise, and whilst their portfolios may include other areas they tend to stay specialists within their comfort zone. The overall risk approach and the need to create security professionals that are also rounded risk practitioners across the SSHE spectrum forms the basis for this paper.

[1]Article originally published in *Challenging Security Paradigms - Bursting the Assumptions Bubble*, 2016, Collaborative Publications, www.c-pubs.com.au and republished with authorisation.

Introduction

There is no doubt that the field of security risk management has evolved to become a vocation more so than a function, and is now widely recognised as a specialist area requiring extensive knowledge, skills and experience by practitioners in order to succeed. Operational settings that, for example, include such scopes as safety, security, emergency response and disaster management invariably require an inherent level of technical expertise by the practitioner, in order to fully understand and thus deal with the risks associated within these environments. As organisations or companies grow we have also seen the evolution of a diverse range of organic organisational and corporate structures. These structures have become so diverse and range from no direct allocation of safety, security, health and emergency management (SSHE) activities to mass duplication. There is the ongoing reality that no one model can be applied across different sized organisations that are in different sectors, operating in vastly differing risk environments. However, in many cases organisations are suffering from wastage due to duplication and inefficiency or intolerably high risk exposure due to lack of resource allocation to 'hard risk' management. In many cases organisations are exposed to both of these realities simultaneously, specifically if they have become silo'd based on size, specialisation, management control or geographic complexity.

Assumption

This paper proposes that the need for Security Risk Managers to become more rounded risk practitioners is crucial and that a more holistic wider view to risk management (referred to as the Multiplex View) is more critical today than ever before.

Context

The harsh consequences of security incidents resulting from crime, (internal and/or external), fraud and terrorism including death, business disruption, reputational damage, fines and jail time are ever-present realities for modern business. The ability to subrogate and de-risk via insurances is no longer as robust as it once was based on the evolution of non-payment clauses for regulatory non-compliance and other complexities. The ability to de-risk via subcontracting has now been legislatively closed off and it is now well established legal precedent that all parties (top to bottom) involved in the supply chain are responsible for the identification, mitigation and management of foreseeable risk in a reasonably practicable manner.

SSHE activities very often include operating areas where physical loss including, death, injury, asset loss, adverse environmental impact, occur. We refer to these as 'hard risk', where outcomes can be measured, and hopefully, forecasted so that elimination, preventative measures and/or mitigation can be achieved. The responsibility for the management of these hard risks were often assigned to a senior manager due to level of accountability associated with it. This has changed over time, and in the current economic climate less senior levels within the organisation have been charged with this responsibility, or this has been assigned as an additional responsibility to an existing role. The core skills of a hard risk practitioner would commonly include appropriate skills, experience and expertise to:

- Identify the potential for internal and external threats and hazards leading to unwanted events;
- Forecast the likelihood of such threats or hazards manifesting into incidents, as well as the potential consequences that may occur as a result;
- Develop and apply management and mitigation systems to eliminate or reduce the likelihood of incidents occurring;
- Design, develop and apply reactive control plans which detail actions to be undertaken to treat threats or hazards prevent incidents, or respond should they occur;
- Monitor, review and update these forecasts, assessments, plans and procedures on an ongoing basis in response to events or reviews.

Hard risk practitioners quite literally save lives as core functions of their roles, and the positive impact of their contribution is often overlooked in the day to day operation of an organisation. The evolution of organisational silo'ing whereby Hard Risk management activities are broken up into various categories as organisations have grown and expanded is now the common reality not the exception. Whilst in principle, silos for large organisations are a necessity, when it comes to managing hard risk the reality of issues such as duplication of activities, denial of incidents and risk exposure, transfer of blame and lack of authority all become potential issues. These issues are highlighted in the various versions of Workplace Health and Safety legislation which in most cases does not differentiate between the employees and subcontractors and places the responsibility at all levels of an organisation (low level worker right up senior executive). The need to move away from the decades old checklist type Hard Risk management approaches utilised by most organisations has reached epidemic proportions.

The Need for a Different Approach

The complex mapping, rating and referencing systems that proliferate through the Hard risk management world have actually reached a point where they are now no longer practical tools for risk management but merely academic routine and/or just another additional non-profit, non-performance enhancing function that organisations "Have To" do. In addition the neglect of Hard Risk education for most of today's business leaders who are often the product of academic education which specialises in conventional modelling and has contributed to two of the biggest issues facing organisations from a hard risk perspective today, namely DENIAL and REACTIVE APPROACHES based on ignorance and negligence. It is human nature to avoid systems that either do not show a direct reward, have a consequence which is deemed harsh enough to force compliance or have an effective 'policing system 'in place to ensure compliance. One only has to look at traffic and road safety and imagine the carnage that would ensue without a set of rules that had harsh enough consequences for non-compliance and no enforcement to apprehend offenders. At various levels I have seen this happening in 100s of organisations we have come across in the last 15 years of business. This is not an unique issue to first world or emerging markets but the focus of hard risk management based on reactivity, sentiment and anecdotal behaviour seems to be the driver. Limitations on the way we view risk continue to be a propagator for reactivity and denial. In many cases this stems from the following core problems:

- Consistent viewing of hard risk management as a grudge spend area.
- Failure to apply proactive budgets based on a dynamic risk based approach.
- Lack of understanding of actual vs perceived risk from a hard risk perspective.
- Inefficient use of internal resources.
- Inefficient use of external expertise.
- Lack of understanding of internal limitations.
- Lack of alignment of hard risk management understanding at senior executive as well as lower levels (middle management mayhem).

These issues are further complicated by two realities:

- The human factor.
- The use of technology (in terms of limitations or over reliance).

While there is no doubt that we have come a long way in improving technology and people management systems we are missing some fundamental principles in the way we make things happen. Unfortunately, I have seen this over and over again where senior executive teams believe an issue has been resolved by creating and attempting to enforce a policy which has no real chance of being embraced at ground level and thus often becoming a purely academic exercise in futility. In fact the organisations may actually make themselves more vulnerable by having a policy but not adhering to it. A side effect of policy setting without effective implementation and take up, results in the executive believing that hard risks are under control, middle managers being frustrated that there are insufficient resources to implement and lower level never even being made aware of issues and or solutions.

Identified Areas of Opportunity

This reality is not new ground and many executives and managers live with this ongoing problem. So what can be done about these issues – here is a brief list of actions and concepts which could each be an article in their own rights:

- Educate at all levels – understanding hard risk management in context at all levels of an organisation is critical as a starting point. One of the simplest ways to do this is get everyone talking the same hard risk language and not get too caught up in silo or specific jargon.
- Assess and understand realties in a dynamic way – we tend to want to ignore bad news and as such it is often hidden from the people that need to know until a crisis occurs. Regular health checks using internal and external resources is critical for more robust discussion making.
- Leverage internal resources – often there is internal expertise and knowledge that is not tapped as a result of corporate segregation and legacy, the creation of internal 'kingdoms' and the biggest problem – lack of internal cross silo forums and structures to leverage capabilities and sharing. This often comes down to HR based limitations tied back to KPI's which sometimes create performance measurements that is silo specific and ignores the core objectives of the organisations on a macro level.
- Leverage external resources – it is important to know when external help is required and how it should be utilised. Not only are external assessments considered to be more impartial but they bring fresh eyes to issues that may have been taken for granted as being 'just the way it is'. The challenge is to act once solutions are identified and not be demotivated by what may appear to be a mountain of issues with no clear start, end and implementation approach.

- Invest in people – the biggest resource for mitigating risk is a 'switched on' staff and contractor base. We need to motivate people using both stick and carrot approaches in a balanced manner to gain their 'buy-in 'otherwise systems will fail and good intentioned solutions will not go anywhere.
- Incorporate technology – it is important to find the balance between human trust and having sufficient checks and balances. We can't forget that the battle ground of the future is in cyber space and organisations face ongoing vulnerability in managing the 'hard risk' realities of data and IP protection along with the physical safety and well-being of their staff.

The requirement for risk and hard risk managers to transcend organisational and psychological barriers to become generalist's practitioners, is an evolutionary change in the way this complex area is dealt. In this day and age, employers demand more from practitioners and require multi-skilled and capable professionals. Many hard risk managers are happy in their specific vocational area of expertise, and whilst their portfolios may include other areas they tend to stay specialists within their comfort zone.

It would be fair to surmise, that organisations want to improve their operational performance with respect to risk management. A potential way to achieve this, is to adopt a 'multiplex' view to the way issues are diagnosed, rated and managed. Even if evaluation tools such as the AS/NZ ISO 3100:2009 Risk Management Guidelines and the numerous other risk matrices are used, a multiplex view is often not applied. It should be noted that we endorse and approve most tools and systems but they should be viewed as exactly that – tools and enablers, not a 'magic bullet' for all that is wrong. Due to the reliance on these tools, they could be seen as barriers to more comprehensive multidimensional approaches.

The Multiplex View

A multiplex approach involves viewing your organisation as a multi-dimensional structure, and evolving methodologies to a broader paradigm aligned to your organisation's key objectives. This will be illustrated and explained below.

Two Level Evaluation

In a traditional risk management system, we would often rate risk hazards and threats using tools such as a 5 x 4 matrix focusing on the core measurement tools of likelihood and consequence which may look like this:

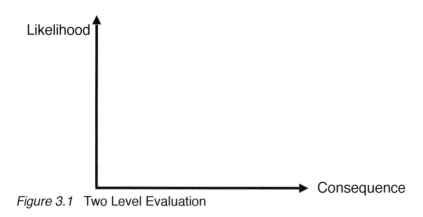

Figure 3.1 Two Level Evaluation

Four Level Evaluation

A more detailed approach may add other variables such as exposure, which may look like this:

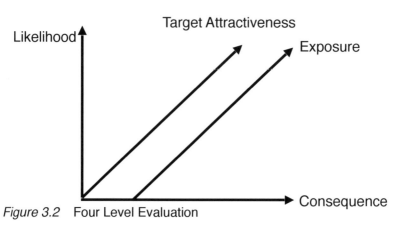

Figure 3.2 Four Level Evaluation

Five Level Evaluation

Once we superimpose variables such as legislative compliance, industry standards and organisational policy the diagram may look like this:

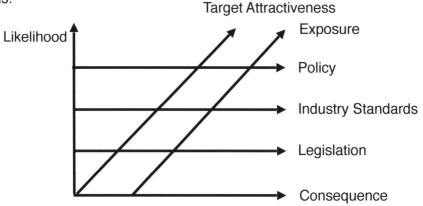

Figure 3.3 Five Level Evaluation

Six Level Evaluation

Then the requirements of understanding the organisation and people itself become issues, these include aspects such as organisational goals, history and culture. The diagram may then look like this:

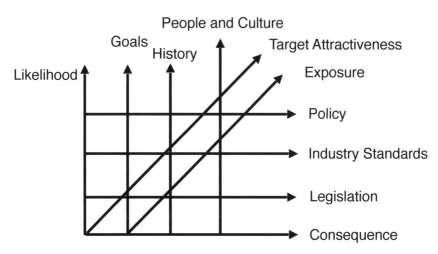

Figure 3.4 Six Level Evaluation

Seven Level Evaluation

The next level has to include some of the unfortunate realities we all live with which pose challenges to any solutions such as resistance to change, limited budget and denial which may make the diagram look like this:

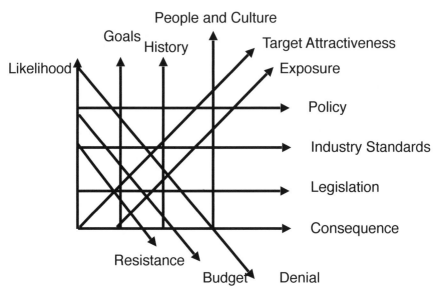

Figure 3.5 Seven Level Evaluation

When risk is being assessed and evaluated on this basis, we are now getting closer to solutions that may actually work, be acceptable and gain budget and traction. However, the next paradigm of reality has to be taken into account which are the limitations of expressing any matrix in two dimension. We need to think of the organisation as a Puzzle Cube. Your goal is to ensure that by moving one piece which makes one side of the cube look great, that it does not destabilise and cause discontinuity on another side. Of course there are also the band aid solutions of taking sticker off and sticking it over the piece that does fit which may work for a while but if the sticker peels off you are back to the same problem.

Summary

In summary, the core ingredients to implement a better security risk management approach stem from striving to eliminate denial via education and ongoing assessment and implementing a proactive approach which requires more than just paperwork and lip service. In essence the driver should be a move to change, improve and sustain an enhanced level of security and safety culture. By aligning hard risk management to culture and core organisational objectives it is truly possible to turn Risk to Opportunity. In order to evolve to this level of thinking we advise hard risk practitioners to embrace some of the following:

- Learn about the organisation that they are working for and its core strategic goals and keep that first and foremost as a fundamental of any activity or solution you scope.
- Align methodology to existing recognised tools and guidelines such as the AS/NZ 31000: 2009 Risk Management Guidelines and apply the multiplex approach.
- Continue to educate themselves so that SSHE practitioners become qualified experts and gain trust and credibility within and without their organisations.
- Practitioners need to know when to ask for help and use external consultants to help them achieve their goals. An unfortunate reality is that when on the inside expertise may be discounted and the only way to achieve real results is to de-risk by using external and credible resources.
- Be flexible and adaptable and learn how to sell ideas in a collaborative and well-structured way up the organisational tree.
- Design solutions based on benefits such as cost saving, risk reduction and strive to apply attribute measurable to solutions.

Whilst in many cases good solutions are the product of all of the above, many other variables interwoven including issues out of your control such as timing and personalities of the role players and stakeholders. The goal of all professionals should be continuous improvement of their own levels of knowledge, skills and experience, with the ultimate goal of adding value to the organisation they work for.

References

Ariely, D. (2008) *Predictably Irrational, The Hidden Forces that Shape our Decisions.* HarperCollins, Melbourne.

Ariely, D. (2012) *The Honest Truth About Dishonesty: How We Lie to Everyone—Especially Ourselves*, Harper Collins. New York.

ASIS Foundation. (2009). Compendium of the ASIS Academic/Practitioner Symposium, 1997-2008. http://www.asisonline.org/foundation/noframe/19972008_CompendiumofProceedingspdf. (Accessed: 15 December 2010).

ASIS International online library. (2015). http://www.asisonline.org/library/glossary/s.pdf. (Accessed: November 2015).

ASQA. (2013). http://www.asqa.gov.au/ (Accessed: 10 November 2015).

Bratton, W. and Kelling, G. (2006). There Are No Cracks in the Broken Windows: Ideological academics are trying to undermine a perfectly good idea. http://old.nationalreview.com/comment/bratton_kelling200602281015.asp. (Accessed: 10 January 2010).

Braunig, M. (1993). *The Executive Protection Bible.* Aspen, CO: ESI Education Development Organisation.

Commonwealth of Australia. (2009). CPP07: Property Services Training Package, version 5. *Australian Department of Employment, Education and Workplace Relations.*

Council of Australian Governments (COAG). (2015). www.coag.gov.au. (Accessed 3 June 2015).
De Nevers, R. (2009). Private Security Companies and the Laws of War. *Security Dialogue*, 40(2). New York: Sage Publications: 169-190.

Department of Justice and the Attorney-General Queensland. (2013). *Refusing or cancelling a security provider's license.* Brisbane: State of Queensland.

Department of Justice and the Attorney-General Queensland. (2013). http://www.justice.qld.gov.au/securityproviders/222.htm. (Accessed: June-August 2013).

Department of Safety and Security, South Africa. (2002). Private Security Industry Regulatory Authority Act No. 56 of 2001. *Government Gazette*, 23051:14 (2002).Pretoria: Government Printers.

Department of Safety and Security, South Africa. (2003). *PSIRA Code of Conduct.* Pretoria. Government Printers.

Department of Safety and Security, South Africa. (2009). Private Security Industry Regulatory Authority Act No. 56 of 2001 amendments. *Government Gazette*, 32670:12(2009). Pretoria: Government Printers.

Kahneman, D. (2011) *Thinking Fast and Slow.* Farrar, Strauss and Giroux. New York.

King, J.A. (2001). *Providing Protective Services.* Shawnee mission: Varro press.

Kotwica, K. (2009). *2009 Security Budget Research Report: Impact of the Economic Downturn.* USA: The Security Executive Council.

Linstead, S. (1997). Abjection and Organization: Men, violence, and management. *Human Relations,* 50(9). September: Wollongong, NSW: The Tavistick Institute.

Maslow, A. (1943). A Theory of Human Motivation, *Psychological Review*, 50(4): 370-96. New York: Philosophical Library.

Mead-Niblo, D. (1995). *Security in the Hospitality Industry.* PhD Dissertation. Melbourne: The University of Melbourne.

Minnaar, A. (1997). *Partnership Policing between the South African Police Service and the South African Private Security Industry.* (Information document prepared for National Policy & Strategy, Division: Management Services, SAPS.) SAPS Research Centre, Pretoria. June.

Minnaar, A. (2004). *Inaugural Lecture: Private-public partnerships: Private security, crime prevention and policing in South Africa.* Florida: Department of Security Risk Management, School of Criminal Justice, College of Law, University of South Africa.

Minnaar, A. (2005). Private-public partnerships: Private security, crime prevention andpolicing in South Africa. *Acta Criminologica: Southern African Journal of Criminology.*18(1): 85-114.

Minnaar, A. (2006). *A comparative review of the regulating of the private security industries in South Africa, Australia and the United Kingdom (UK).* Paper presented to the 6th Biennial International Criminal Justice Conference: Policing in Central and Eastern Europe-Past, present and futures. Ljubljana, Slovenia. 21-23 September 2006.

Minnaar, A. (2007b). Oversight and monitoring of non-state/private policing: The private security practitioners in South Africa. In: S. Gumedze, (Ed.). 2007. Private security in Africa: Manifestation, challenges and regulation. Institute for Security Studies: Brooklyn, Tshwane. *ISS Monograph* No. 139: 127-149.

Minnaar, A. (with a contribution by K. Pillay). (2007c). *A review of the issues andchallenges facing the private security industry in South Africa. Unpublished research report.* Department of Security Risk Management, University of South Africa/Open Society Foundation Society-South Africa.

Minnaar, A. and Ngoveni, P. (2004). The relationship between the South African PoliceService and the private security industry: Any role for outsourcing in the prevention of crime? *Acta Criminologica: Southern African Journal of Criminology.* 17(1): 42-65.

Prenzler, T. (2005). Mapping the Australian Security Industry, *Security Journal.* 18(4), Australia: Palgrave Macmillan: 51-64.

Prenzler, T. (2007). The Human side of security, *Security Journal.* 20. Australia: Palgrave Macmillan: 35-39.

Prenzler, T., Earle, K., & Sarre, R. (2009). Private security in Australia: Trends and key characteristics. *Trends and Issues in Crime and Criminal Justice*, 374, 1-6.

Prenzler, T. and Sarre, R. (1998). *Regulating Private Security in Australia.* Canberra: Australian Institute of Criminology.

Prenzler, T. and Sarre, R. (2000). *The Relationship between Police and Private Security: Models and Future Directions*, Wichita: Wichita State University.

Prenzler, T. and Sarre, R. (2002) 'The policing complex'. In A. Graycar and P. Grabosky (e.d). *The Cambridge Handbook of Australian Criminology.* Melbourne: Cambridge University press. Pp. 52-72.

Prenzler, T. and Sarre, R. (2005). *The Law of Private Security in Australia.* Sydney: Thomson Lawbook Co.

Prenzler, T. and Sarre, R. (2007) 'Private police: partners or rivals?' In M. Mitchell & J. Casey (eds.), *Police Leadership and Management in Australia* (pp. 50-60) Sydney: Federation Press.

Prenzler, T. and Sarre, R. (2009). *The Law of Private Security in Australia.* (2nd edition) Sydney: Thomson Lawbook Co.

Prenzler, T. Sarre, R, and Earle, K. (2008). Developments in the Australian private security industry. *Flinders Journal of Law Reform.* 10:403-417.

Prenzler, T., Sarre, R. and Earle, K. (2009). *Private Security in Australia: Trends and key characteristics.* Canberra: Australian Institute of Criminology.

Sarre, R. and Prenzler, R. (2005). *Policing Corruption: An Australian perspective.* Lexington Books.

Schneider, G. (2005). *An examination of the required operational skills and training standards for a Close Protection Operative in South Africa.* MTech Dissertation. Pretoria: University of South Africa.

Schneider, G. (2009). Know your enemy – the importance of a threat assessment. *Security Focus - The official industry journal for professional risk practitioners: Security, Safety, Health, Environment and Quality Assurance.* January Edition. Security Publications, South Africa: 50.

Schneider, G. (2009). High Risk Close Protection. Security Focus - *The official industry journal for professional risk practitioners: Security, Safety, Health, Environment and Quality Assurance.* April Edition. Security Publications, South Africa: 47.

Schneider, G. (2009). *Beyond the Bodyguard: Proven tactics and dynamic strategies for protective practice success.* Boca Raton, USA: Universal Publishers.

Schneider, G. (2012). *The design and development of the Practical Use of Force Training Model for the private security industry.* Doctoral Dissertation. Pretoria: University of South Africa.

Schneider G. (2012). Close Personal Protection in Action: An analysis of the evacuation of Prime Minister Julia Gillard on Australia day 2012: *Asia Pacific Security Magazine* April/May, My Security Media Pty Ltd: 47-49.

Schneider G. (2012). An Eyes Wide Open Approach in Africa. Asia Pacific Security Magazine, June/July, My Security Media Pty Ltd: 8-10
Schneider G. (2013). The Security Safety Cross Over: How Wide is the Gap. *Asia Pacific Security Magazine*, Issue 45, My Security Media Pty Ltd: 30-31.

Schneider, G. & Minnaar, A. (2013). Business case for safety and security. *Security Focus. The official industry journal for professional risk practitioners: Security, Safety, Health, Environment and Quality Assurance.* Vol 31 No 10. Security Publications, South Africa: 18-20.

Schneider, G. (2015). Business in Emerging Markets – An eyes wide open approach. *Risk Management Today*, Vol 25 No 3. Lexis Nexis: 48-50.

Passfield, N. & Schneider, G. (2015). The multiplex view to Hard Risk Management – time for another dimension. *Risk Management Today*, Vol 25 No 6. Lexis Nexis: 96-99.

Schneider G. (2015). *Security and Risk Management, the next level. Asia Pacific Security Magazine*, Issue 45, My Security Media Pty Ltd: 24-25.

Schneider G. (2015). *Security and Risk Management, the next level. Chief IT Magazine*, Spring 2015 Issue, My Security Media Pty Ltd: 30-31.

Standards Australia. (2009) *AS/NZS ISO 31000:2009 Risk management— Principles and guidelines*.

Standards Australia.   (2010) *Handbook 327: 2010 Communicating and Consulting about Risk*.

Stoddard, A., Harmer, A. and DiDomenico, V. (2008). *The Use of Private Security Providers and Services in Humanitarian Operations*. London: Humanitarian Policy Group.

Strom, K., Berzofsky, M., Shook-sa, B., Barrik, K., Daye, C., Horsteman, N. and Kinsey, S. (2010). *The Private Security Industry: A Review of the Definitions, Available Data Sources, and Paths Moving Forward*. Bureau of Justice Statistics. USA: RTI International.

Swanton, B. (1993). Police and Private Security: Possible Directions. *Trends and Issues in Crime and Criminal Justice*, 42. Canberra: Australian Institute of Criminology.

Winlow. S., Hobbs, D., Lister, S. and Hadfield, P. (2001). Get Ready to Duck: Bouncers and the realities of ethnographic research on violent groups. *British Journal of Criminology* 2001, 4: 536-548. United Kingdom: The Academic Research Library.

Chapter 4

Insider Threat

Stephen Langley

The insider threat is someone on the inside of your business who is stealing or releasing information and/or physical goods to the detriment of your business. Evidence and recent events suggest that instances of insider threat activity are becoming more prevalent and increasing in veracity, therefore various forms of businesses are at risk from this type of threat. Current and former employees, contractors and other organisational "insiders" all pose a substantial threat to the organisation by virtue of their knowledge of and access to their employers' systems and IT databases but also have the ability to bypass existing physical and electronic security measures through legitimate means. Studies often disagree on what constitutes an "insider threat" and it can be seen that numerous definitions have been established and even developed during research; however they all draw a conclusion that it is someone that can cause harm to an organisation. The existing body of literature places most emphasis on cyber insider acts, with relatively little research addressing the issue of a physical attack or the means as to which access was gained to facilitate such an act. These gaps have also made it difficult for organisations to develop a comprehensive understanding of the insider threat and address the issue from an approach that draws on human resources, corporate security and information security perspectives.

Background

The insider threat of crime to organisations is always present and can manifest itself in many ways. This has become more apparent because of the recent social-economic climate change within the UK. Experience has shown over the years that an over-reliance on technology without consideration of other factors can have disastrous results for managing the insider threats. One of the main concerns in relation to this area is that of an individual or individuals that would be aligned to cause illegal activities within the organisation. This has resulted in a large emphasis being placed on the identification of any potential harmful individuals.

Cappelli et al. 2005 identifies insider threats as "current or former employees or contractors who targeted a specific individual or affected the security of the organisation's data, systems and/or daily business operation". There is an emerging risk presented by insiders within organisations. Insider threats exist for all organisations, essentially, this threat lies in the potential that a trusted employee may betray their obligations and allegiance. It is thought that the threat posed by insiders is one most organisations neither understand nor appreciate. During 2008, The National Infrastructure Advisory Council (NIAC) which provides the United States of America's President with advice on the security of the critical infrastructure sectors and their information systems produced a primary goal of to address the assigned tasks to develop policy recommendations to improve their security posture of the Nation's critical infrastructure. NIAC produced a report during which they stated:

> The insider threat [...] is one or more individuals with the access and/or inside knowledge of a company, organization or enterprise that would allow them to exploit the vulnerabilities of that entity's security, systems, services, products or facilities with the intent to cause harm.
>
> (NIAC, 2008, p. 12)

From research that was conducted during 2010 within the United States of America, Catranzos stated:

> All a hostile insider needs to carry out an attack are access to a worthy target, an open door, and a dark corner from which to study and strike.
>
> (Catranzos, 2010)

Insiders are not just employees; they can include contractors, business partners, auditors or individuals that work within the same locations (these present what can be called third party risks). Employees, contractors and even temporary staff are usually provided with the same if not similar access within organisations (NIAC, 2008, p. 12). This access is usually legitimately required to conduct their work that they are being employed to do, but can be taken advantage of to commit 'insider' attacks. There are also individuals whose ambitions are to be employed within an organisation and have the sole purpose of conducting industrial espionage.

Insider threats cannot only destroy the infrastructure of an organisation but can also instil a sense of trepidation. It is an adversary that can provide assurance to the nearest competitor or ally, not only showing any flaws but more importantly highlighting their vulnerabilities. Catranzos deemed it more important since the tragic events of 9/11 and the continuing aftermath during which it has been identified that risk and vulnerability assessments have propelled, with the federal subsidies promoting them, the security focus centred largely on the vulnerability of large populations to attack. Adversaries' have typically been characterised as traditional attackers working as outsiders who generally approach their targets with the determination of succeeding in their objectives. Such high profile insider acts as those at Barings, World-Com and Enron provide examples of what damage can be done. During 2006 an employee of Securitas the security company conducted surveillance whilst carrying out his legitimate role within the depot to facilitate a large scale robbery and kidnap utilising his 'insider knowledge' (BBC News Online, 21st February 2006 Securitas robbery).

Also it was reported that an employee of the Northern Bank based in Belfast, Northern Ireland helped to plan the largest bank robbery within the UK of £26.5 million which was carried out on 20th December 2004. The alleged individual changed the staff duty rota to allow him to be on duty and have access to the vault key. It was stated that during the case the facts could be established to properly infer the robbers had "a high degree of inside knowledge," and that it could only have come from a member of staff (Northern Bank robbery, 20th December 2004).

In a report titled 'Human factors in information security; The insider threat – Who can you trust these days?' written by Carl Colwill (2010) identifies that organisations may not have the effective risk management regimes to deal with the speed and scale of change. Also he states that the lethal consequences of armed insiders turning against their colleagues was demonstrated in November 2009 to UK forces in Afghanistan and US forces at Fort Hood USA, both of these were reported upon by the BBC News in 2009. Certain material was solely based on findings within the cyber-security field and primarily based in the USA. All of the material was used to provide background facts and findings to establish a common trait from the conception to delivery of a solution. It was difficult to exactly identify the material because of the lack of information within the corporate security industry. It is also prevalent that this subject has not been fully reviewed within academic literature such as practitioners discourse, e.g. Papers, conferences, magazines and articles and other identifiable sources. It is recognised that researchers are actively working within the cyber industry, retail loss prevention, fraud research and with government stakeholders to elicit feedback, amass data and experiences and to test new technologies but this has not been introduced into the private sector or corporations.

However, following the initial research the phenomenon that is being investigated appears to have been underestimated or considered within various private departments and organisations within the United Kingdom and more importantly within the corporate security organisations.

Whilst conducting research, policies were identified and highlighted that this is an area that is being controlled within government agencies/ departments by the introduction of the security frameworks such as Her Majesty's Government Security Policy Framework produced by the Cabinet Office. This is also supplemented by the Centre for the Protection of National Infrastructure (CPNI) who are deemed to be the government authority that provides advice on protecting the UK's essential services, facilities and networks from terrorism and other threats. More recently the CPNI provided advice and support to the organisations engaged in planning and running the London 2012 Olympics. One main fact that was established during the initial research and findings was that the impact of insider threats is a costly problem, bedevilling organisations that lack the resources to monitor actions, prevent bad outcomes or avoid harm when data leakages occur. It is the case that in some organisations security is viewed as a 'tick-box' activity meeting audit or regulatory requirements.

Defining the Insider Threat

It can be argued that the lack of a consistent definition of an insider hinders research in the detection of threats from insiders. Many researchers have investigated the area surrounding the problem of insider threat, however most research conducted had failed to precisely define what is an insider threat - instead, it has been assumed that the end user inherently understand their own version of a definition. In 2005, whilst Bishop was employed by British Telecom (BT) to enhance their security package he defined insider threat as:

> A trusted entity that is given the power to violate one or more rules in a given security policy... the insider threat occurs when a trusted entity abuses that power.

> (Bishop, 2005)

This definition identifies that there is a specific need to recognise that an insider must be determined with reference to some set of rules that are part of a security policy.

The term insider threat can refer to harmful acts that trusted insiders might carry out, such as something that causes harm to the organisation or an unauthorised act that benefits the individual, as stated by Greitzer and Hohimer in 2011 whilst they conducted research into the 'Modelling Human Behaviour to Anticipate Insider Attacks' (2011, pp. 25-48). During 2006, The Institute for Information Infrastructure Protection (I3P) worked on a project to acknowledge security must complement, not hamper, business needs and during this they stated:

> The underlying complexities that have been found during the research of this subject 'insider threat', including the very definition of an insider, are poorly understood. Also it was identified that at the same time, protective and mitigative strategies are difficult to implement without the possibility of impairing normal business operations.
>
> (I3P, 2006).

Hanley et al (2011, p. 1) stated that it is hard to give a definition of the insider threat, and that there is debate around whether contractors should be included into the definition as possible insider. Cappelli et al (2006) identifies insider threats as:

> Current or former employees or contractors who targeted a specific individual or affected the security of the organisation's data, systems and/or daily business operation.
>
> (Cappeli et al., 2006)

Hanley et al also include debate around someone who may start as an 'outsider' but through gaining access by unauthorised means would then be deemed an 'insider', for example through hacking into a company network (2011, p. 1). There have been numerous attempts to offer a definition of the term 'insider', with the majority providing various similarities with re-occurring themes.

Whilst conducting the review for established definitions the author identified his own version of an insider threat as:

Anything that is done to jeopardise the proper functioning of an organisation's business whether deliberate or accidental by employees.

This definition was introduced because the author felt that the majority of the insider threats occurred by an individual who had strong ties to an organisation and was intended to cause varying levels of harm to the organisation. For a generalised term, Shaw, Fischer & Rose (2009, p. 1) stated 'the risk that a trusted or authorized person will participate in a behaviour that causes damage to his or her employer', this can be included and found within acts of fraud, terrorism, sabotage, theft, cyber-crime and espionage and also more importantly whether or not the acts where deliberate or accidental.

Plymouth University conducted research into Information Security and produced a research document "Towards an Insider Threat Prediction Specification Language" (Magklareas et al., no date) summarising the picture of the insider threat in IT infrastructure and provided a useful resource for IT security consultants to eradicate their threat. Within this research Magklareas et al., stated:

An insider is a person that has been legitimately given the capability of accessing one or many components of the IT infrastructure, by interacting with one or more authentication mechanisms.

(Magklaras et al., no date)

Pfleeger et al. (2006) defines the term threat in an IT infrastructure context as "a set of circumstances that has the potential to cause loss or harm". Information 'leakage,' espionage, and sabotage involving computers and computer networks are the most notable examples of insider threats, and these acts are among the most pressing cyber-security challenges that threaten not only government but also private sector information infrastructures. A number of Information Atomic

Energy Agency (IAEA) publications deal with physical protection against the unauthorised removal of nuclear material and against sabotage of nuclear material and nuclear facilities. In 2008, the IAEA published 'Preventative and Protective Measures against Insider Threats' within which it stated "threats to nuclear facilities can involve outsiders, insider or both together in collusion".

The term 'threat' is used to describe a likely cause of harm to people, damage to property or harm to the environment by an individual or individuals with the malicious, intention and capability to commit a malicious act. In addition to deliberate malicious insider activity, NIAC (2008, p. 14) and CPNI (2010, p. 22) stated that there can be 'unwitting insiders'; those who are 'manipulated' and 'recruited' specifically by an outsider for information or to facilitate access. When conducting research on the area surrounding insider sabotage cases, Keeney et all (2005, p. 4) also reported 'that insider attacks are under-reported to law enforcement and prosecutors', for possible reasons such as 'insufficient level of damage to warrant prosecution, a lack of evidence or insufficient information to prosecute, and concerns about negative publicity'. Insiders have been identified during research that they are not just employees alone; today they can include contractors, business partners, auditors, ex-employees or more importantly friends, family or family members. Individuals responsible for insider betrayal can be classified as one or more of the following types:

- Psychologically-impaired disgruntled or alienated employees.
- Ideological or religious radicals.
- Criminals.

Moreover, insiders are often very often identifiable by more than one of these classifications. Identifying these different classifications is important in understanding insider actions and developing effective programs to mitigate the insider risks.

Whilst the author was conducting background research into the area surrounding the subject of insider threat it was highlighted that whilst reviewing the literature various current trends/concerns during the present time was due to the recent rise in unemployment and debt, the motivation to commit crime has also increased. Hanley et al. (2011) recognised that 'the insider threat problem has recently been gathering more interest in business and government' (ibid, p. 1). This statement refers to the US and has a strong focus on intellectual property theft, rather than other insider acts but importantly reflects a continuing emergence of the insider threat as an issue. With the rise in perceived or pending unemployment nearly 60% of employees have stored company data in anticipation for their redundancy. Insider threats can take many different forms – some attacks are malicious and some are unintentional. Most importantly is the fear of companies' reputation to enable a brighter future. Reducing the non-malicious accidental threats from employees is difficult because the number of threat actors that could cause a breach equates to everyone in the organisation. Alternatively, it can be assumed that only a tiny proportion of insiders would be motivated and tempted to deliberately perform a malicious or criminal act. It is important that it has also been identified that journalists will utilize any disgruntled individuals to conduct such attacks. The best possible interventions within this area are the aid of various overt and covert investigations and also to employ the expertise of a penetration company. These two pronged attacks would highlight both weakness and major strengths that are being used.

Understanding the Nature of the Insider Threat

Hanley et all further noted that 'insider cases are underreported' (2011, p. 4) and cited the Cybersecurity Watch Survey (by Deloitte, the US SS, CSO Magazine and CERT) which stated that during their research 72 per cent of reported events were investigated internally without any legal or law enforcement involvement, (CSO 2010 cited in Hanley et al., 2011, p. 4). Cappelli et al. (1991) stated within the insider IT misuse their needs to be clarification that separates an IT misuser from a person that uses the available resources in an acceptable way and for an approved purpose.

Insider threat mitigation begins with a complete understanding of potential insider threats. A 2003 survey by the FBI's Computer Security Institute and Ernst and Young showed that nearly 60% of all security threats come from internal sources (Gupta, 2003). Hanley et al. also include debate around someone who may start as an 'outsider' but through gaining access by unauthorised means would then be deemed an 'insider', for example through hacking into a company network (2011, p. 1). As identified earlier by Bishop (2005), an insider must be determined with reference to some set of rules that is part of a security policy and this is primarily represented by the access control rules employed by an organisation. An insider can therefore be defined with regard to two primitive actions:

- Violation of a security policy using legitimate access.
- Violation of an access control policy by obtaining unauthorised access.

In the first instance the insider uses their legitimate access to perform some action that is contrary to the security policy in existence. However, in the second case, the insider uses their authorised access in a manner that not only breaks both the access control and security policies. An individual could be forced to become an insider by coercion or by coercing his family members. Passive insiders are non-violent and limit their participation to providing information that could help adversaries to perform or attempt to perform a malicious act. Active insiders are willing to provide information, perform actions and may be violent or non-violent. Active insiders are willing to open doors or locks, provide hand-on help and aid neutralising response force personnel. Non-violent active insiders are not willing to be identified or risk the chance of engaging response forces and may limit their activities to tampering with accounting and control, and safety and security systems. Violent active insiders may use force regardless of whether it enhances their chances of success; they may act rationally or irrationally. (IAEA, 2008). Shaw et al. (1999) identified six personal characteristics believed to have direct implications for malicious insider risks.

Table 4.1 Six Personal Characteristics - Shaw et al. (1999)

Personal Characteristics	Description
False sense of entitlement	Lack of acknowledgement or status resulting in a desire for revenge
Personal and social frustrations	Anger, alienation, dislike of authority and an inclination for revenge
Computer dependency	Aggressive loners, poor team players, desire to explore networks, break security codes, hack and challenge security professionals
Ethical flexibility	Lacking moral inhibitions that would normally prevent malicious behaviour
Reduced loyalty	Identifying more with their profession or computer speciality than with their employer
Lack of empathy	Disregard or inability to appreciate the impact of behaviour on others

Recent examples from the press and other sources have served to evidence and emphasis this. The Guardian reported on 26th July 2012 and 31st July 2012, that a disgruntled employee of G4S Security was reporting on various aspects of his life during the Olympics, 'The security guard: everything will be fine, until it isn't' and 'The secret security guard: G4S is the Millwall of the Olympics'. Strangely during the findings of Colwill it highlighted that The RSA/IDC findings (Grant, 2009) showed that; most chief security officers (CSO) were more worried about outsider threats rather than insider risks; 82% of respondents responsible for security decisions were unclear on the source of their company's insider risk; In the past year, contractors and temporary employees posed the greatest source of insider threat and outsourcing companies lost nearly $800k because of insider breaches.

Daily Mail published on 8th August 2010, that a Newham council employee who was employed as a fraud investigator was found guilty of a £200,000 fraud. The employee was a trusted employee, made a senior benefits officer, and was later in charge of overseeing payments in the benefits office. His crimes were identified after a three year internal audit uncovered a series of back-dated claims to two local property agents. In Queensland in 2000, a wireless laptop was used to release untreated sewage by a previous employee who 'was apparently taking revenge against former employer's' (Evans, 2005, p. 76). It has been reported (Raywood, 2008) that the placing of moles by criminal gangs, especially in financial institutions is becoming more common. The Department for Business Enterprise and Regulatory Reform (BERR, 2008) concluded that after researching in the UK many organisations are still inapt at protecting themselves and their customers' information: 52% do not carry out any formal security risk assessment; 67% do nothing to prevent confidential data leaving on USB sticks, etc; 78% of companies had computers with unencrypted hard discs stolen. During a recent comment Hay stated:

> One of the key difficulties businesses have is to do with developing an understanding of the risks associated with the environment in which they operate and sometimes recognising the difference between security measures, (which are only a component of risk management), and actual risk management.
>
> (Hay, 2011)

A more simplistic view of risk is that it is "*the combination of the probability of an event and its consequences*" (Institute of Risk Management, 2002, p. 2). Assessment of risk is a normal part of business and, it can be argued, of life. Adams (1995, p. 1) highlights that risk management begins in infancy in the trial and error way in which we learn. Risks need to be identified, analysed and evaluated to allow comparison and direction of any mitigation effort. This sequence, illustrated by the dashed red box in Figure 4.1 below, is common to a wide range of formal and informal risk management processes, each developed separately within particular disciplines, leading to what was described in the Royal Society report as a "*risk archipelago*" (Hood et al, 1992, p. 135). This review supports this view, finding a number of processes and standards.

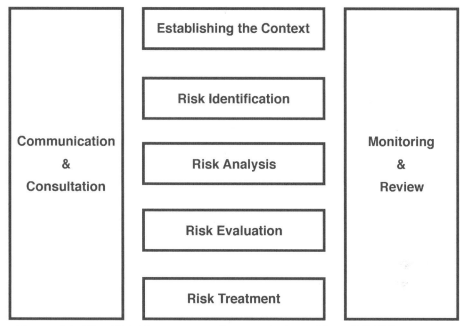

Figure 4.1 The Risk Management Process (adapted from BS ISO 31000:2009)

Research from CERT highlighted various case examples of insider threat incidents:

- 195 illegitimate drivers' licenses are created and sold by a Police Communications Officer who accidentally discovers she can create them.
- A system administrator deletes 18 months of cancer research after being fired since no electronic access controls stood in his way.
- Special function to expedite handling of cases allows two case workers to pocket $32,000 in kickbacks.
- An employee realises there is no oversight in his company's system & business processes, so he works with organised crime to enter & profit from $20 million in fake health insurance claims.
- A foreign currency trader covers up losses of $691 million over a 5 year period by making unauthorised changes to the source code.
- An 18 year old former web developer used his own code to access his former company's network and spam their customers, altering their details and ultimately putting them out of business.

- Project leader for a software project sabotaged his own project rather than admit his inability to meet the deadlines (Cert, 2006).

The emergence of these cases during the research has introduced the term 'White Collar Crime', this is conducted by:

> Persons of the upper socio-economic class who engage in criminal behaviour, that this criminal behaviour differs from the criminal behaviour of the lower socio-economic class' and 'crime committed by a person of respectability and high social status in the course of his occupation.
>
> (Sutherland, 1949, p. 9)

It has been annotated that the majority of the fraudsters see that the rewards available outweigh the potential risks because they are often able to face less questioning regarding decisions they make, have less oversight than junior members and can often adjust figures in order to appear 'legitimate'. White collar crime not only affects a private company's financial results but might also lead to a loss in reputation, shareholder value, customer trust and investor confidence (Zahra, Priem and Rasheed, 2005). The issues raised by crime and corruption practises within the private sector have rarely been highlighted as a topic of interest to the general public domain. This has however changed because some of the huge financial losses that have occurred within some companies have become a matter of interest for the media and the public. The government is a major victim of many forms of economic crime, which indirectly affects all citizens. Offences include:

- Fraud by public servants: Fraudulent claims for expenses and allowances and frauds in relation to income, payroll and creditor payments were found by the Audit Commission (1993) to have led to Local Authorities losing £4.8 million.
- Frauds on the NHS: The Audit Commission (1993) also estimated losses for the NHS of around £5.9 million from frauds on the part of healthcare professionals including doctors, dentist and pharmacists (Johnson and Holub, 2003; Croall, 2005).

Organisations are victims of embezzlement, employee theft and many other frauds are particularly vulnerable to offences involving the financial or technical expertise of employees. For example:

- In one victim survey, Levi (1995) reported that: banks lost £3.2 million; clients or customers lost £1.8 million to 11 white-collar fraudsters; employers lost £1.7 million to 28 employees; suppliers of goods and services lost £1.1 million to 10 white-collar offenders and insurance companies lost £230.000 to 9 white-collar offenders.
- A European Economic Crime Survey by Price Waterhouse Coopers in 2001 found that up to 70 per cent of major companies reported economic crime in the previous two years – a high proportion attributed to employees (Journal of Financial Crime, 2002; (Croall, 2005).

A good example of a fraud triangle in practice is the highly publicised case of the secretary that stole over £4.3 million from her bosses at Coldman Sachs. This case highlighted that the secretary was given free rein to access the accounts and managed to siphon on various amounts over a four year period. Her luck finally ran out when her boss checked his bank balance and noticed how low it was (Various sources including The Guardian, The Times, The Independent and the BBC News).

With all of the recent allegations of fraud being conducted by insiders it has seen the emergence of various risk management practices being implemented within the organisations. These have included the relevant areas associated with fraud prevention, fraud detection and responding to fraud.

Why and How the Threat is Perceived

The National Infrastructure Advisory Council (NIAC) produced a final report 'The Insider Threat to Critical Infrastructures' (2008) during which they highlighted various findings and provided some useful recommendations, some were of little cost and some of more extreme cost to the organisations, this was instructed by the Homeland Security

Michael Chertoff on 16th January 2007. All of these findings were in relation to cyber-crime but this emphasis was still aimed at the insider threat.

> Operators lack an appropriate awareness of the threat insiders pose to their operations. Education and awareness present the biggest potential return for policy by motivating operators and focusing their efforts to address the insider threat [...] preventing all insider threat is neither possible nor economically feasible.
>
> (NIAC, 2008, pp. 12-3)

Companies or organisations that are at the receiving ends on such insider attacks are rarely confident in discussing the attacks because these acts can weaken or destroy public trust, share price value, and financial solvency, all of which are necessary for a company to operate (NIAC, 2008, p. 14). In 2008, Cole stated:

> The insider threat is like a tumor. If you realise there is a problem and address it, you will have short-term suffering but a good chance of recovery. If you ignore it, it will keep getting worse and while you might have short-term enjoyment, it will most likely kill you.
>
> (Cole, 2008)

This not only highlighted the blight of the organisation but also the ignorance of the alleged experts. NIAC also stated:

> Awareness of the insider threat varies greatly among the critical infrastructure sectors. Strong examples include the Banking and Finance as well as Nuclear sectors, which have an excellent awareness of the threat and have a robust risk mitigation approaches to insider sabotage insider fraud. Other sectors have varying levels of awareness and risk mitigation programs.
>
> (NIAC, 2008, p. 18)

Some factors that have been highlighted that appear to be stalling action include greater competition and less cooperation among owner-operators in a sector and less-coordinated and less-cooperative relationships with labour workforces. NIAC further highlighted that among the companies that are not managing insider risks, owner-operator understanding of the threat is the primary problem. In 2007, the Computer Security Institute conducted a Computer Crime and Security Survey which recorded that corporate leadership understands that insider incidents occur, but it appears corporate leadership neither completely appreciates the risk nor realises the potential consequences. As a result, most companies do not actively manage their insider risks. (NIAC, 2008, p. 18). Currently companies that have experienced insider incidents are reluctant to share this information because of the costs involved; insider incidents can cause lost credibility with shareholders, employees and customers, and negatively effect to shareholder values. The Information Systems Security Association with the aid of Secoda Risk Management produced a white paper 'Security and the Growing Insider Threat' (15 February 2010) which stated that various organisations needed to be vigilant when introducing measures to control the risk of the increasing threat of insiders. This paper also stated that the fear of impending redundancies, increasing job competition, outsourcing and mergers are all factors that motivate certain individuals to act in a way that can jeopardize business. The 2007 E-Crime Watch Survey found that in cases where respondents could identify the perpetrator of an electronic crime, 31% were committed by insiders. These impacts can be devastating to the point where one employee working for a manufacturer stole blueprints containing trade secrets worth $100 million, and sold them to a Taiwanese competitor.

It has also been identified that organisations may not have the effective risk management regimes to deal with the scale of change as stated in the recent research 'Human factors in information security; The insider threat – Who can you trust these days?' written by Carl Colwill (2010). Colwill further stated that security policies, controls, guidelines and training are lagging behind changes. Also he states that the lethal consequences of armed insiders turning against their colleagues was demonstrated in November 2009 to UK forces in Afghanistan and US forces at Fort Hood USA, both of these were reported upon by the BBC News in 2009. These stories caused mix feelings because new recruits wishing to join were terrified and then certain individuals used these stories to carry out an act of retaliation. Again it fell to the HM Forces justifying why they were in the war. Also during this paper it was noted that far less investment is made in controls to protect against insider threats. It was indicated that 70% of fraud is perpetrated by insiders rather than external criminals but that 90% of security controls and monitoring are focused on external threats (McCue, 2008). Colwill suggested that he believed that companies may be reluctant to share their experiences of 'insider' acts, even within the same sector, possibly because of the detrimental impact it may have on reputation and share price (2009, p. 189).

What Control Measures are Available to Prevent This

Why is it so hard to intervene and prevent an insider attack? There are several reasons why this can appear to be difficult. There are various whys development and deployment of approaches to addressing insider threats, particularly proactive approaches, are so challenging:

- The lack of sufficient real-world data that has some real truth enabling subsequent verification and validation of proposed solutions;
- The difficulty in distinguishing between malicious insider behaviour and what can be described as normal or legitimate behaviour;
- The potential quantity of data, and the resultant number of 'associations' or relationships that may emerge produce enormous scalability challenges;
- Despite ample evidence suggesting that in a preponderance of cases, the perpetrator exhibited observable 'concerning behaviours' in advance of the exploit (Greitzer and Hohimer, 2011, p. 27).

Research findings highlighted that not all insider attacks can be classified as malicious; the perpetrators may be unknowing pawns of a disgruntled colleague or a poorly-tested system, or similar the unforeseen actions of a careless initiator of an unintended consequence. With this is mind it can be found that as a result, research into the detection of insider threats cannot be accurately assessed nor be necessarily applied to one domain or another as the findings may not be able to be translated between the various domains. Within Colwill's report he stated that in his experience the best course of action is to develop information sharing relations via a trusted 'broker', this has many beneficial results to create new security standards and raise overall levels of protection. Also it is highlighted by Colwill that insider risks need to be moved up in importance and discussed in boardrooms prior to attacks, not just after the compromise.

To help address and overcome the obstacles to reduce the threat it is instrumental that organisations introduce the flowing of shared information between internal and external stakeholders and extremely important with high profile stakeholders with a Single Point of Contact (SPOC). Also this method would enable a detailed understanding of information, experience and problem solving to occur between all stakeholders. To enable this to progress a clear and concise set of guidelines would have to be produced in the arena of intelligence and the best procedures to follow with the flow of intelligence, security, storage and distribution of such.

> To the police intelligence often means nothing more than information by a covert source.
>
> (Hebenton and Thomas, 2001, p. 170)

NIAC stated that organisations should introduce the following recommendations to help mitigate risks to technology infrastructure from an insider attack:

- Operators should establish a priority to maintain current network/IT security best practises.
- Secondary education training on ethics and awareness of the real consequences of cyber actions.

- Improved accountability for virtual crimes through prosecution and equitable punishment for the tangible consequences of cyber-crimes (NIAC, 2008, p. 7).

NIAC recommendations also addressed gaps in information collection, sharing and analysis on insider threats. It is clearly recognised that policy implementation should emphasise recommendations with the potential for a near-term effect. The following recommendations have been identified from various resources to improve information sharing on insider threat, risk and mitigation include the following:

- A clearinghouse resource for owner-operators to assist in the assessment and mitigation of their insider threat risks.
- Establish a mechanism to communicate intelligence agency understanding on insider threats, making use of cleared personnel in each sector and provide periodic, useful briefings on developments about insider threats.
- Develop a mechanism and validated process to share information on national security investigations in order to address a specific information-sharing obstacle between the public, governmental, critical infrastructure and private organisations.
- Each sector should establish a trusted process and mechanism to share incident information on insider threats in a protected manner.

As stipulated within the organisation a corporate security environment should identify, effectively mitigate and manages at an early stage any development that may threaten the resilience and continued survival of a corporation. It is a corporate function that oversees and manages the close coordination of all functions within the company that are concerned with security, continuity and safety. The main area that has stirred an interest is the emergence of the National Intelligence Model (NIM), there has always been a phenomenon on police intelligence and is now a major factor within the law enforcement agencies ever since its introduction. The NIM was introduced to the British Police service by National Criminal Intelligence

Service (NCIS) in 2000 because of a result of vast differences in the collection and collation of intelligence between the various constabularies (NCIS, 2000; Grieve, 2004). Though this approach has been welcomed it was originally utilized to improve the relationship between the police and the community, however critic's claim that the community have been left out of the NIM process (Tilley, 2004; Keane, 2004, personal communication). If an organisation really wanted to introduce technical controls for the threat then organisational information security has long been dominated by the need to keep dangerous outsiders such as hackers, fraudsters and individuals involved in industrial espionage from damaging the systems and itself. Many forms of technology are available to protect information but this is generally applied to identify and restrict outsider access with 'off-the-shelf' products such as firewalls and intrusion detection systems. Outside threat attacks can be easier to detect and defend against, but the tools utilised to protect this are seldom scalable or cost-effective to apply to every employee who require access to the information or assets. The NIAC's recommendations to improve education and awareness include:

- Establish leadership for national insider threat programs within the Executive Office of the President to coordinate government support for CIKR operator education and awareness of insider threats.
- Establish a common baseline understanding of the emergence and dynamic insider threat to critical infrastructures. It should help promote the broad corporate cultural changes needed to elevate internal security and protect against the insider threat.

Key elements of this program should include:

- Leveraging the Executive Office of the President to communicate the issue with executives and partner with companies in each sector to develop pilot programmes;
- Educating executives on key aspects of the insider threat to help in identifying enterprise – level insider threat risks;

- Assisting CIKR operators in developing insider threat education and mitigation programs;
- Identifying and supporting areas for future insider threat research (NIAC, 2008, p. 8).

Education and awareness are needed to, not only generate necessary security investment by all parties but it is also important to create awareness and vigilance among the workforce. Education and awareness programs are a key component that can be utilised to generate an organisational shift needed to change the cultural obstacles that exist to insider threat mitigation. Awareness amongst all senior management of their employees is also beneficial to allow them to understand institutional forces, NIAC recommend that organisations should consider the following preconceptions:

- Unquestioned and unverified trust of employees, after granting employment, especially for long-time employees;
- Poor operator-workforce union relationships;
- Employee expectations of rights and privileges versus obligations;
- Inadequate computer and network ethics education and training;
- Prevailing attitudes about management involvement in workers' personal lives;
- Suspicion for anything that looks like 'big brother is watching' –type monitoring programs;
- Attitudes about corporate sensitivity information (NIAC, 2008, p. 22).

Due to the emergence of newer technology on such a large scale the threat of 'Cyber Threat: State, Radical, Local, Mad Sad', increases in the use of 'smart-phones' mobile telephones with the email capability to the issuing of personal laptops. This is a key area to be considered with the growing number of individuals that could potentially lose unsecured laptops or more importantly by losing memory sticks/ storage devices whether encrypted or not. If this did happen, it could lead to negative media attention. To aid in the prevention of non-technical measures organisations will need to produce with the aid of various departments a comprehensive set of non-technical measures to combat insider threat including: policies, awareness, legal, HR and whistleblowing. Within elements of these combating measures the investigations conduct enquiries into Key Performance Indicator (KPI) failures, and can also be effective if information is received via the whistleblowing line or confidential reporting of matters. Another important mechanism that should be investigated by the organisations is employee screening; this is classified by NIAC as the second most critical area with potential for near-term improvement in insider threat mitigation programs. This program should include access to the best available criminal history records for critical employee risk assessments (NIAC, 2008, p. 6).

Conclusion

Areas of agreement with existing research included that the definition of insider threat is widely distributed but does have the few commonalties that all organisations and/or individuals would agree upon. It also illustrated that various organisations attempt to deal with reported incidents, however, they may chose not to be impartial or more importantly open about their findings or sanctions. Organisations appeared to be fearful of openly discussing what evasive actions or procedures that they have had to instil to prevent the insider threat attacks and more importantly how these are seen by their clients.

It was apparent that all of the organisations employed various forms of assessments but that they did not appear to be of a centralised format or suit. These assessments were originally devised by various employees employed with their respective organisations and deemed to be the 'experts' with the relevant subject knowledge. The use of formal risk assessments was reported although further analysis revealed that in the majority of cases the method used was an in-house development or even that of an outside company being employed to provide these services. This allowed the organisations to apply any recommendations that they wished or even for the clients to disregard what was being suggested. Within a small number of the organisations it was noted that they thrived on themselves being regarded as the professional and world leader in the security industry and wanted potential clients to feel that they could provide the professionalism and expertise required.

References

Adams, J. (1995) *Risk.* Abingdon. Routledge.

Aleman-Meza, B., Burns, P., Eavenson, M., Palaniswami, D., and Sheth, A. (2005) "An Ontological Approach to the Document Access Problem of Insider Threat," (May 2005). IEEE Intl. Conference on Intelligence and Security Informatics.

Anderson, Cappelli, et. Al., (2000) Software Engineering Institute. (February 2004). "Preliminary System Dynamics Maps of the Insider Cyber-threat Problem." PA: Carnegie Mellon University.

Anderson, R., Bozek, T., et. Al. (August, 2000). "Conference Proceedings Research on Mitigating the Insider Threat to Information Systems #2: Workshop Proceedings," DC: National Defense Research Institute.

Anderson, R., and Brackney, R., (2004) RAND Corporation National Security Research Division (March 2004). "Understanding the Insider Threat: Proceedings of a Workshop" CA: RAND Corporation.

Avanesov, E.(2009) *Risk Management in ISO 9000 Series Standards.* [Electronic Version] Paper presented at International Conference on Risk Assessment and Management, 24-25 November 2009, Geneva.

Band, S., Cappelli, D., Fischer, L., Moore, A., Shaw, E., and Trzeciak, R., (2006) Carnegie Mellon University Software Engineering Institute (December 2006). *Comparing Insider IT Sabotage and Espionage: A Model-Based Analysis.* PA: Carnegie Mellon University.

BBC (2007) 'Six more data discs 'are missing', *BBC News Online,* 24 November, http://news.bbc.co.uk/1/hi/7111056.stm
BBC (2008) 'Pension data was on stolen laptop', *BBC News Online,* 10 October, http://news.bbc.co.uk/1/hi/uk/7664274.stm

BBC (2009a). Five British soldiers shot dead, 4/11/09, http://news.bbc.co.uk/1/hi/8341659.stm

BBC (2009b). Deadly shootings at US army base, 6/11/09, http://news.bbc.co.uk/1/hi/8345713.stm

Bell, J. (2010) *Doing Your Research Project (5th ed).* [Electronic Version] Buckingham. Open University Press.

BERR. Department for Business Enterprise and Regulatory Reform (BERR) information security breaches survey 2008, http://66.102.9.132/search? q=cache:LK4aPYKu4gcj:www.berr.gov.uk/files/file45714.pdf+berr +2008+breaches&;cd=2&hl=en&ct=clnk&gl=uk; 2008.

Biggam, J. (2008) *Succeeding with Your Masters Dissertation: A Practical Step-by-Step Handbook* [Electronic Version] Buckingham. Open University Press.

Bishop, M. Gates, C., (2008) *Defining the Insider* Threat. Oak Ridge, Tennessee.

Blakey, R. (2009) PwC auditors 'ignored' Satyam fraud for fees, The Times, 24/4/09, http://business.timesonline.co.uk/tol/business/industry_sectors/ technology/article6154910.ece; 2009.

Cappelli, D., Keeney, M., Kowlaski, E., Moore, A., Randazzo, M.(August 2004). *Insider Threat Study: Illicit Cyber Activity in the Banking and Finance Sector,* PA: Carnegie Mellon University.

Cappelli, D., Moore, A., and Shimeall, T., (2005) "Common Sense Guide to Prevention and Detection of Insider Threats" (2005) DC: US-CERT.

Cappelli, D., Keeney, M., Kowalski, E., Moore, A., Shimeall, T., Rogers, S. (May 2005). *Insider Threat Study: Computer System Sabotage in Critical Infrastructure Sectors.* PA: Carnegie Mellon University.

Capputo, D., Stephens, G., Stephenson, D. and Kim.M. (2009) Human Behavior, Insider Threat, and Awareness An Empirical Study of Insider Threat Behavior, Institute for Information Infrastructure Protection (I3P) research program Research Report No.16, July 2009, Hannover: Dartmouth College, http://www.thei3p.org/docs/publications/134.pdf

Castle, I., (2009) Beware the enemy within, secure computing Magazine, 5/1/09, http://www.scmagazineuk.com/Beware-the-enemy-within/article/ 123505/; 2009.

CERT (2005) 2005 E-Crime Watch survey shows E-Crime fighters making headway: Average Company Loss Estimated at More Than Half Million Dollars, Press release, CERT/CSO, http://www.cert.org/archive/pdf/ ecrime_watch05.pdf

CERT (2010) *Cybersecurity Watch Survey: Cybercrime Increasing Faster Than Some Company Defenses,* CERT Insider Threat Team, Pittsburgh: Carnegie Mellon University, Software Engineering Institute, http://www.cert.org/archive/pdf/ecrimesummary10.pdf (Summaries also available for 2004-2009).

Chinchani, R., Iyer, A., Ngo, H., and Upadhyaya S. (No date) "A Target-Centric Formal Model for Insider Threat and More," NY: State University of New York at Buffalo.

Cole, E., (2008) Addressing the insider threat with NetIQ security and Administration Solutions Dr Eric Cole and NetIQ.

Colwill, C. (2010) Human factors in information security: The insider threat – Who can you trust these days?, Inform. Secur. Tech. Re[. (2010), doi:10.1016/j.istr.2010.04.004

CPNI. (2008) Centre for the protection of national infrastructure (CPNI) ongoing personnel security: a good practice Guide, http://www.cpni.gov.uk/; October 2008.

CPNI. (2009) Insider attacks, http://www.cpni.gov.uk/MethodsOfAttack/insider.aspx; 2009.

Croall, H. (2001) Victims of White-Collar Crime.

Cunningham, W., Ohlhausen, P., Oliver, L., Seamon, T.(2005) of Homeland Security (January 2005). *Enhancing Private Security Officer Surety,* DC: U.S. Government Printing Office.

Cyber-Ark. Snooping about, CIR Magazine; August 2009.

EIU. (2009) Economist intelligence unit: Power to the people? Managing technology democracy in the workplace, http://graphics.eiu.com/marketing/pdf/Technology%20Democracy.pdf; June 2009.

Ellison, R., Moore, A. (March 2003.) "Trustworthy Refinement Through Intrusion-Aware Design (TRIAD)" PA: Carnegie Mellon University Software Engineering Institute.

Falliere, N., Murchu, L. and Chien, E. (2010) 'W32.Stuxnet Dossier: September 2010, version 1.0', *Symantec White Paper,* http://www.symantec.com/content/en/us/enterprise/media/security_response/whitepapers/w32_stuxnet_dossier.pdf

Flinder, K., (2010) Employees will choose their own computers in 2010, Computer Weekly, 18/1/10, http://www.computerweekly.com/Articles/2010/01/19/239999/Employess-will-choose-their-own-computers-in-2010.htm; 2010.

FT (2009) Stanford Scandal, 18/12/09, http://www.ft.com/indepth/stanford-scandal

Government Accountability Office. (2007) "Continuing Attention to Privacy Concerns Is Needed as Programs are Developed" (2007). DC: U.S. Government Printing Office.

Gordon, L., Loeb, M., Lucyshyn, W., and Richardson, R. Computer Security Institute (2006). *CSI/FBI Computer Crime and Security Survey 2006.*

Grant, I., (2009) Insiders cause most IT security breaches, Computer Weekly, 26/8/09, http://www.computerweekly.com/Articles/2009/08/26/237455/insiders-cause-most-it-security-breaches-study-reveals.htm; 2009.

Green, S. (2013) *"An Investigation of current security technology procurement paradigms, and subsequent effects on perceived efficacy".* University of Portsmouth.

Greitzer, F., Hohimer, R. (2011) *Modelling Human Behaviour to Anticipate Insider Attacks* (2011). The Berkeley Electronic Press.

Hayden, C. and Shawyer, A. (2004) *Research Methods and Research Management.* Open Learning Materials. Institute of Criminal Justice Studies. Portsmouth: University of Portsmouth.

Heuer, J., Kramer, L., Crawford, K., (May 2005). *Technological, Social, and Economic Trends That Are Increasing U.S. Vulnerability to Insider Espionage.* CA: PERSEREC.

IAEA (2008) Preventive and Protective Measures Against Insider Threats; Implementing Guide.

Jones, A., Colwill. C., (2008) Dealing with the malicious insider. In: 9th Australian information and Warfare security Conference; December 2008.

Kavanagh, J., (2006) Security special report: the internal threat, Computer Weekly, 25/4/06, http://www.computerweekly.com/Articles/2006/04/25/215621/security-special-report-the-internal-threat.htm; 2006.

Keeney, M., Cappelli, D., Kowalski, E., Moore, A., Shimeall, T. and Rodgers, S. (2005) Insider Threat Study: Computer System Sabotage in Critical Infrastructure Sectors, Pittsburgh, PA Carnegie Mellon University Software Engineering Institute/ United States Secret Service, www.cert.org/archive/pdf/insidercross051105.pdf

LMRMC (2010) *Online Riskiness: Questionnaire Results – Overall,* LM Research & Marketing Consultancy, 20, September (Unpublished).

Mail (2008) 'Military laptop stolen from McDonald's as 'Army captain eats a Big Mac'', Mail Online, 12 April, http://www.dailymail.co.uk/news/article-559178/Military-laptop-stolen-McDonalds-Army-captain-eats-Big-Mac.html#ixzz13NxVuGD0

Mail (2013) 'Jail for the fraud investigator who siphoned off £200,000'', Mail, Online, 08 August http://www.dailymail.co.uk/news/article-1301357/Jail-fraud-investigator-siphoned-200-000.html#ixzz2auqP91ll

Magklaras, G., Furnell, S., Brooke, P., (no date). Towards an Insider Threat Prediction Specification Language, University of Plymouth.

Marsden, R., (2009) Should my employer be allowed to snoop on me online, The Independent, 18/11/09, http://www.independent.co.uk/life-style/gadgets-and-tech/features/rhodri-marsden-should-my-employer-be-allowed-to-snoop-on-me-online-1822277.html; 2009.

McAfee. (2008) Virtual Criminology report, http://resources.mcafee.com/content/NAMcAfeeCriminologyReport; December 2008.

McCue, A., (2008) Beware the insider security threat, CIO Jury 17/4/08, http://www.silicon.com/management/cio-insights/2008/4/17/beware-the-insider-security-threat-39188671/; 2008.

McQuade, S. (2006) *Understanding and Managing Cybercrime,* Boston: Allyn & Bacon.

Mearian (2009) 'Survey: 40% of hard drives bought on eBay hold personal, corporate data: Buyers found data on everything from corporate spreadsheets to e-mails and photos', *Computerworld,* 10 February, http://www.computerworld.com/s/article/9127717/Survey_40_of_hard_drives_bought_on_eBay_hold_personal_corporate_data

Miller, N., (2010) Balancing risk and reward in staff web usage policies, Computer Weekly, 19/1//10, http://www.computerweekly.com/it-management/risk-management/; 2010.

Mohammed, A., (2009) CW security trends for 2009, Computer Weekly, 20/1/09, http://www.computerweekly.com/Articles/2009/01/20/234316/security-trends-for-2009.htm; 2009.

Muncaster, P., (2009) Security experts warn of insider threat timebomb, Enterprise Security Technology, 24/6/09, http://www.v3.co.uk/v3/news/2244699/experts-renew-insider-threat; 2009.

National Infrastructure Advisory Council (NIAC). (2008) Final report and Recommendations: the insider threat to national infrastructures, 8/4/08, http://www.dhs.gov/xlibrary/assets/niac/niac_insider_threat_to_critical_infrastructures_study.pdf; 2008.

Newburn, T., (1999) *"Understanding and preventing police corruption: Lessons from the literature"* Police Research Series Paper 110, London: Home Office, available at http://www.homeoffice.gov.uk/rds/prgpdfs/fprs110.pdf (accessed 1/8/13).

NIAC. (2008) HMG IA standard No. 1, technical risk assessment part 1 (issue 3.2); October 2008.

NCIS (2001) *2001 UK Threat Assessment.* London: National Criminal Intelligence Service.

Oliver Wymann. (2008) Congruence model: a roadmap for understanding organizational performance, http://www.oliverwymann.com/fr/pdf_files/Congruence_Model_INS.pdf; 2008.

Ponemon Institute. (2007) Addressing the insider threat, community Banker, 1/8/07; 2007.

Ponemon (2008) *The Cost of a Lost laptop,* Ponemon Institute, http://www.ponemon.org/local/upload/fckjail/generalcontent/18/file/Cost%20of%20a%20Lost%20Laptop%20White%20Paper%20Final%203.pdf

Ponemon (2009a) *Fourth Annual US Cost of Data Breach Study: Benchmark Study of Companies,* Ponemon Institute, http://www.ponemon.org/local/upload/fckjail/generalcontent/18/file/2008-2009%20US%20Cost%20of%20Data%20Breach%20Report%20Final.pdf

Ponemon (2009b) *Data Loss Risks During Downsizing: As Employees Exit, so does Corporates Data,* Ponemon Institute, http://www4.symantec.com/Vrt/offer?a_id=78695

Ponemon (2010a) *2009 Annual Study: Cost of Data Breach,* Ponemon Institute, http://www.ponemon.org/local/upload/fckjail/generalcontent/18/file/US_Ponemon_CODB_09_012209_sec.pdf

Ponemon (2010b) *2009 Annual Study: UK Cost of a Data Breach,* Ponemon Insitute, http://www.ponemon.org/local/upload/fckjail/generalcontent/18/file/UK_Ponemon_CODB%202009%20v9.pdf

Post, J., Shaw, E., and Ruby, K. (1998) Political Psychology Associates, (June 1998). "The Insider Threat to Information Systems: The Psychology of the Dangerous Insider" *Security Awareness Bulletin.*

Randazzo, M., Keeny, M., Kowalski, E., Cappelli, D., and Moore, A. (2005) *Insider Threat Study: Illicit Cyber Activity in the Banking and Finance Sector,* Philadelphia: Carnegie Mellon University, Software Engineering Institute, http://82.138.248.200/hcs-temp/teaching/GA10/lec4extra/certreprot.pdf

Rasmussen, G. "Insider Risk Management Guide" http://www.gideonrasmussen.com/article-13.html

Raywood, D., (2008) Companies being hit by moles who are employed by gangs steal data. Secure Computing Magazine; 2008. 2/10/08.

Raywood, D. (2009) 'MBNA confirms data loss after laptop containing personal details of thousands of customers was stolen from vendor', *SC Magazine,* 23 December, http://www.scmagazineuk.com/mbna-confirms-data-loss-after-laptop-containing-personal-details-of-thousands-of-cusotmers-was-stolen-from-vendor/article/160217

Raywood, D. (2010) 'Stolen laptop leads to the loss of details of around 13,000 UK dairy farmers', *SC Magazine,* 2 July, http://www.scmagazineuk.com/stolen-laptop-leads-to-the-loss-of-details-of-around-13000-uk-dairy-farmers/article/173843

Royds, J., (2009) Virtual battlefield. CIR Magazine; August 2009.

Sasse, MA., Ashended, D., Lawrence, D., Coles-Kemp, L., Flechais, I., Kearmey, P. (2007) Human vulnerabilities in security systems, human factors working group, Cyber security KTN human factors White Paper; 2007.

Schneier, B. (2003) *Beyond Fear: Thinking Sensibly about Security in an Uncertain World,* New York: Springer.

Shaw, E., Post, J., Ruby, K. (1999) Inside the mind of the insider, security management; 1999.

Shiels, M. (2009) 'Malicious insider attacks to rise', *BBC News Online*, 11 February, http://news.bbc.co.uk/1//hi/technology/7875904.stm

Symantec (2008) *Anatomy of a Data Breach: Why Breaches Happen and What to Do About It,* Mountain View, Symantec, http://eval.symantec.com/mktginfo/enterprise/white_papers/b-anatomy_of_a_data_breach_WP_20049424-1.en-us.pdf

Symantec (2009a) *Internet Security Threat Report Volume XIV:* April, 2009, Symantec, http://www.symantec.com/business/theme.jsp?themeid=threatreport.

Symantec (2009b) SMB Protection Gap: SMB security and data protection: survey shows high concern, less action, Symantec White Paper, http://eva.symantec.com/mktginfo/enterprise/other_resources/b-SMB-Protection-Gap_WP_20094842.en-us.pdf

Symantec (2010) 'The Trojan.Hydraq Incident', *Symantec Security Response Blog,* 18 January, http://www.symantec.com/connect/blogs/trojanhydraq-incident.

Thomson. (2007) HMRC data loss leaves 25 million exposed, ITN News, 22/11/07; 2007.

Thomson, R. (2009) Bosses have their heads in the sand over new technology, Computer Weekly, 29/9/09, http://www.computerweekly.com/Articles/2009/09/29/237920/bosses-have-their-heads-int-the-sand-over-new-technology.htm; 2009.

University of New South Wales (2009) *getting Started on your Literature review,* Sydney: The Learning Centre, University of New South Wales, available at http://www.lc.unsw.edu.au/onlib/litrev3.html (accessed 8/7/13).

U.S. Department of Defense. (September 2007). *Report of the Defense Science Board Task Force on Mission Impact of Foreign Influence on DoD Software. DC; U.S. Government Printing Office.*

U.S. Department of Homeland Security. (2006). *National Infrastructure Protection Plan*. DC: U.S. Government Printing Office.

U.S. Department of Homeland Security, Science and Technology Directorate, (2007) *Domestic Municipal End-to-End Water Architecture Study*. DC: U.S. Government Printing Office.

U.S. Department of Justice, Office of the Inspector General. (March 2008). *Audit of The U.S. Department of Justice Terrorist Watchlist Nomination Processes*. DC: U.S. Government Printing Office.
U.S. Department of Justice. (June 2006). *The Attorney General's Report on Criminal History Background Checks*. DC: U.S. Government Printing Office.

U.S. National Counterintelligence Executive (April 2005). *Annual Report to Congress on Foreign Economic Collection and Industrial Espionage – 2004*. DC: US Government Printing Office.

U.S. National Security Agency: (1999) *The Insider Threats to U.S. Government Information Systems,* (July 1999). DC: U.S. Government Printing Office.

Verizon (2010) *2010 Data Breach Investigation Report,* Verizon, http://www.verizonbusiness.com/resources/reports/rp_2010-data-breach-report_en-xg.pdf

Verton, D. (2002) "Insider Threat to Security May Be Harder to Detect, Experts Say" (April 12, 2002) *Computerworld.*

Wall, D.S. (2007) *Cybercrime: The transformation of crime in the information age,* Cambridge: Polity.

Whitehouse (2003) The National Strategy to Secure Cyberspace, Whitehouse, February, http://www/dhs/gov/xlibrary/assets/National_Cyberspace_Strategy.pdf

Wilding, E. (2007) Insiders are the biggest enemy. Stratcgic Risk magazine; September 2007.

Chapter 5

Understanding, Analysing, Preventing and Learning from Security Failures

Matthieu Petrigh

Security fails all the time. Some security failures involve the human element, in terms of inaction, error or procedural violation. Other failures are more complex, and involve chains of nonlinear interactions, organisational decay, criminal intent, processes and designs flaws and technology malfunction. Many organisations apply safety and security risk management to deal with and learn from this wide spectrum of failures. However, different definitions of the term security failure and divergent understandings of its concept can create confusion and misunderstanding as to what the issue actually is and which form of responses shall address it. Therefore, there needs to be some sort of succinct clarification. By reviewing the existing literature on the correlated topics of security failure, safety failure, human error, disaster, security and risk management, this article firstly seeks to better define and conceptualise what is meant by security failure, and inform the discussion about how organisations are analysing, preventing and learning from security failures. Developing upon this, it then presents and contrasts the findings of the literature review against the findings of an empirical research recently conducted in which 2344 security risk managers were surveyed and twelve others interviewed and subsequently explores the suitability of a strategic solution aimed to minimise such incidences, namely the compulsory reporting of security failures in United Kingdom. All in all, this research produced a number of key findings: (a) there is no agreed definition of the term security failure; (b) organisations tend to analyse security failure in a subjective way; (c) that the structuring of security failure can be patterned and articulated around three common features, namely causal factors, shaping processes and consequentiality; (d) that organisations do not necessarily follow the latest academic developments in terms of failure prevention; (e) that the way organisations are learning from security failures is rather active and mostly experiential and cognitive; (f) that 72% of the organisations having been surveyed seem supporting the idea that the reporting of security failures should be compulsory whilst 78% of those interviewed disagreed with this idea. The main conclusions based on the findings of this research are that current approaches to tackle the problem of security failures are deficient because they fail to embrace a holistic approach to failure prevention, instead opting for an outdated and narrow view of failure prevention; and that further research should be conducted in order to examine in-depth the potential of making the reporting of security failures in UK a compulsory activity. The research argues for a holistic model of doing security adapted from the work of Button (2008) to better minimise and reduce the incidence of security failures and their impacts. One model that effectively takes into account systems dysfunctions, human errors, inaction and ergonomics, technology malfunction, failure analysis, benefactors reliability and proactive learning. It also argues that more research should be conducted in order to ascertain of the need for and utility of the compulsory reporting of security failures in United Kingdom.

Introduction

This paper will examine and critically assess the state of knowledge relative to the conceptual understanding of security failure and outline a hypothetical strategic solution aimed to better reduce the incidence of the latter. First, the term security failure will be clarified. Next, the exploration of various means allowing the analysis of security failures will form the basis of the second section. Then, the abstract structuring of security failure will be explained, altogether with some preventative means associated to it. The different ways organisations are learning from security failure will then be assessed. Finally, the idea of making the compulsory reporting of security failures in UK will be explored.

Clarifying the Term Security Failure

To begin with and in order to better grasp with the term security failure, it is important to comprehend what is actually meant by security and then to consider its lack of success or dysfunction as being what might be termed a security failure. It is also important to note that the term security failure and likewise the one of security will be defined differently from place to place, person to person and will also vary both in scope and definition, depending upon specific viewpoints, conceptualisations and experiences. An example of this could be the consideration of the definition of security presented by Zedner (2003), which appears to be rather broad in itself and the one given by Manunta and Manunta (2006), which antagonistically appears rather narrow. According to Zedner (2003, p. 55), security is a dual concept. It encompasses both a state of being (ie: something is secure) and a means to that end (ie: things are done to secure something). In turn, she argued (ibid), something would be 'security' if and only if (a) threat is not, (b) it is protected from threat and (c) it avoids threat. With that in mind, a security failure would be if and only if (d) threat is, (e) it is unprotected from threat and (f) it is not avoiding threat. Zedner also recognised security as being subjective (ibid). To that end, something would be 'security' if and only if (g) it is felt as being as such and (h) it is not insecure in essence. In that respect, a security failure would be if and only if (i) it is felt as being as such and (j) it is insecure in essence.

Although being relevant to comprehend what is meant by security, such an abstract and broad definition of the term seems perhaps to be problematic, at least for the security practitioner, as for it omits the consideration of few variables inherent to the *functional understanding* of security. This has been partly addressed by Manunta and Manunta (2006, p. 641), whereas they recognised security (S) as being the function (f) of the presence and interaction of a threat (T), a given asset (A), a protector (P) and other structuring variables, what they call, a situation (Si). In turn, they argued (ibid), security could perhaps be understood as follow:

$$S = f (A, P, T) Si$$

This definition is interesting because it encapsulates the concept of security system, whose function is primarily about protecting assets against intelligent actors (as opposed to a safety system concerned with protecting against non-intelligent agents such as fire, water, wind, bacterias, viruses). To that end, a security system unable to protect an asset would be understood as being a security failure, principally because of its dysfunction and lack of success towards achieving its main purpose. Arguably then, it could be extrapolated that:

$$Sf = f (A, T) Si$$

Where Sf is security failure; f the function of; A an asset; T a threat; and Si any given situation.

However original, such a definition of the term security appears to be problematic too, mainly because it fails to address the causality and consequentiality relative to security failure. In turn, this has been justifiably addressed by Button (2008, p. 29), whereas he recognised that 'Security failure *enables an act* that breaches what the security system is designed to prevent' (emphasis added). Consequently, such a view encapsulates the idea that security failures are but consequences or indeed, the resultants of complex chains of events (Reason, 1997) which are in fact converging towards failure. For example, because of multiple factors, a security guard was sleeping whilst on duty in a factory and because the back door of the building was left open, a thief came in and stole an asset. Arguably, it could be hypothesised that *if and only if* N1, N2, ... ,Nn, then Sf whereas:

$$Sf \leftrightarrow \frac{\sum N1, N2, Nn}{T}$$

Where N1, N2 and Nn are the events converging to the security failure Sf; $\leftrightarrow$ the biconditional logical connective if and only if; $\sum$ the sum of; and T the pseudo constant spacetime.

This definition is interesting because it evidences the rationale behind security failure analysis, theme that the next section will indeed explore, and also subtracts the perceptual variable threat, putting rather the focus upon factual events, thereby causality and consequentiality. In that respect, security failure could be prevented *if and only if specific events* are prevented to occur. Nevertheless and as the above has demonstrated, the definition of security failure is subject to much debate and controversy. Central to this assertion is perhaps the idea that security, in essence, is neither objective nor quantifiable (Wood and Shearing, 2007, cited in Button, 2008, p. 3) and that indeed it fails all the time (Button, 2008, p. 29). Indeed, the term security failure appears to be all too often misinterpreted. For instance, some authors would understand it as being security breach, therefore emphasising upon the act which is breaching the security system whereas others would understand it as being a security incident, therefore emphasising upon the consequence of the act which breached the security system. This practice creates confusion and misunderstanding as to what the issue actually is and which form of response shall address it. To that end, security and security failure should not necessarily be dissociated, because after all, they are but one concept. *Security is a risk in itself,* being subject to uncertainty (security is or is not), likelihood (when it is and when it is not) and consequence (what are the resultants from either state).

Analysing Security Failures

By exploring the literature surrounding the topic of security failure, notably the works of Lam (2003), Borodzicz (2005), Toft and Reynolds (2005), Briggs and Edwards (2006), Graham and Kaye (2006), Gill (2006; 2014), Pettinger (2007), Talbot and Jackeman (2009), Carrel (2010), Hopkin (2010), Boyle (2012) and Speight (2012), two broad categories of analysis became apparent, namely (a) *proactive analysis* and (b) *retrospective analysis*. Recognising that security will fail at some point in time, the former aims to assess the likelihood and consequences related to security failure in order to better control the future behaviour of a security enabled environment. To that end, when a proactive analysis is made, security is and indeed, is calculated to remain as such. This sort of analysis is prevalent in the field of risk management and is now applied in most business practices.

On the other hand, retrospective analysis examines security failure once this has manifested and thereby investigates the past. In that respect, when a retrospective analysis is made, security could be but was not. In turn, this sort of analysis prevails in both fields of security management and disaster, recovery and accident management. Either kind of analysis can be of two types indeed, namely (c) *objective analysis* and (d) *subjective analysis*. Objective analysis is formal, scientific and quantitative in approach. Antagonistically, subjective analysis tends to involve value judgement and heuristics and is therefore pseudo-scientific and qualitative in approach. Both types of analysis have advantages and inconveniences. They will serve different security objectives and will allow the analysis of different security problems. Nonetheless, force is to acknowledge that they are but complementary.

Further reviewing the literature, notably the works of Garcia (2006; 2006b; 2008) will reveal that either kind of analysis can be shaped by three sort of logical reasoning, namely (e) *inductive reasoning*, (f) *deductive reasoning* and (g) *abductive reasoning*. In inductive reasoning, the truth of the conclusions relative to the failure analysis is but merely a probability based upon the evidences given (Copil, Cohen and Flage, 2007). It uses a bottom-up approach in which risks are identified at the beginning of the analysis (Garcia, 2006, p. 518). For example, given the preposition that 'if a security failure is true then X, Y and Z are true', then inductive reasoning would suggest that given that X, Y and Z are observed to be true, then security failure should be true too.

On the other hand, deductive reasoning links premises with conclusions in order to ascertain that the latter are true (Eysenck and Keane, 2015, p. 595). To that end, risks are identified as a result of a systematic deductive top-down approach. Considering the previous preposition, a deductive reasoning would suggest that because security failure is true, therefore X, Y and Z are true too.

Lastly, abductive reasoning is a process of deriving logical conclusions from premises known or assumed to be true (often via theorisation), ideally seeking to find the simplest and most likely explanation(s) to security failure (see Tavory and Timmersmans, 2014). To that end, abductive reasoning is a heuristic that eases the cognitive load of making a decision. Examples of such a reasoning could include using a rule of thumb, an educated guess or an intuitive judgment based upon an observation of patterns. In order to perhaps make sense of the above information, Table 5.1, next page, will outline some of the means identified as being relative to security failure analysis.

Table 5.1 Means for Analysing Security Failure

Means Name	Description	Type	Reasoning	Thematic	Reference
Adversary sequence diagram and path analysis	Analysing the potential adversary path to an asset	Proactive Qualitative Quantitative	Deductive	Security	Garcia (2006, p. 521; 2006b, pp. 259-73; 2008, p. 264)
Scenario analysis	Analysing vulnerabilities in a security system	Proactive Qualitative	Inductive	Security	Garcia (2006, p. 521; 2006b, pp. 274-8)
Neutralisation analysis	Analysing the probable effectiveness of a response against attack scenarios	Proactive Qualitative Quantitative	Inductive	Security	Garcia (2006b, p. 265)
Response story board	Analysing the time it will take a response force to fully engage with an adversary and what tactics are appropriate at the different stages of the attack and response	Proactive Qualitative	Inductive Abductive	Security	Garcia (2206b, p. 266)
Security risk analysis	Analysing vulnerabilities in a security system, threats and assets criticality	Proactive Qualitative Quantitative	Inductive Abductive	Security Risk	Norman (2010); Talbot and Jackeman (2009, pp. 141-7); Speight (2012, pp. 62-71)

Table 5.1 Means for Analysing Security Failure (Continued)

Means Name	Description	Type	Reasoning	Thematic	Reference
Risk bow-tie	Analysing potential causes, control measures, recovery measures and potential consequences	Proactive Qualitative Quantitative	Inductive Abductive	Security Risk	Talbot and Jackeman (2009, pp. 158-66)
Threat and vulnerability assessment	Analysing threats against assets vulnerabilities	Proactive Qualitative	Inductive Abductive	Security Risk	Talbot and Jackeman (2009, pp. 286-88)
Conjunction of criminal opportunities	Analysing the immediate causes of criminal events	Proactive Qualitative	Inductive Abductive	Criminology	Elkblom (2014, pp. 503-6)
Cascading decision tree	Analysing employees' security decision-making process	Proactive Qualitative	Deductive	Security	Kirschenbaum (2014, p. 557)
Failure mode and effect analysis (FMEA)	Analysing the various ways a process may fail and determine the effect of different failure modes	Proactive Qualitative Quantitative	Deductive	Disaster	Stamatis (1995)
Reliability block diagrams (RBD)	Analysing how component reliability contributes to the success or failure of a complex system	Proactive Quantitative	Deductive	Disaster	Labib (2014, p. 20, 69, 79, 90, 120, 132)

Table 5.1 Means for Analysing Security Failure (Continued Continued)

Means Name	Description	Type	Reasoning	Thematic	Reference
Schematic report analysis diagram	Analysing the different chains of events built-up during an incident's incubation perioc	Retrospective Qualitative	Deductive	Disaster	Toft and Reynolds (2005, pp. 52-63)
Cause and effect diagram	Analysing the possible causes related to specific symptoms of poor security performance	Retrospective Qualitative	Inductive	Security	Beck, Bilby, Chapman (2005, p. 206-7)
Five whys	Analysing the underlying causes of security problems	Retrospective Qualitative	Deductive	Security	Beck, Bilby, Chapman (2005, p. 207-8)
Fault tree analysis (FTA)	Analysing the relationship between a system and the failure of the components of that system	Retrospective Qualitative Quantitative	Deductive	Security Disaster	Button (2008, p. 130); Labib (2014, p. 20, 69, 79, 90, 102, 132)
Swiss cheese analysis	Analysing security barriers failure and causality	Retrospective Qualitative	Inductive Abductive	Security Human factors	Reason (1990; 1997, pp. 9-20); Talbot and Jackman (2009, pp. 157-9)

Table 5.1 Means for Analysing Security Failure *(Continued Continued Continued)*

Means Name	Description	Type	Reasoning	Thematic	Reference
Maintenance error decision aid (MEDA)	Analysing and investigating maintenance and safety errors	Retrospective Qualitative	Deductive	Safety Human factors	Reason (1997, p. 151)
Tripod-Beta	Analysing incident in parallel with an event investigation	Retrospective Qualitative	Indutive	Safety	Reason (1997, pp. 152-3)
Decision tree	Analysing the culpability of unsafe acts	Retrospective Qualitative	Deductive	Safety Human factors	Reason (1997, p. 209)
Human factor analysis and classification system	Analysing the role of human error in aviation accident by distinguishing between the active failures of unsafe acts, unsafe supervision and organisational influences	Retrospective Qualitative Quantitative	Indutive	Safety Human factors	Shappell and Wiegmann (2000)
Systematic human action reliability procedure (SHARP)	Analysing human reliability with plant logic model development in a probabilistic risk assessment with special focus on the dependencies that exist between human interactions and the specific accident scenario	Retrospective Qualitative Quantitative	Indutive	Safety Human factors	Hollnagel (1993, pp.56-9); EPRI (1992)

Table 5.1 Means for Analysing Security Failure (Continued Continued Continued Continued)

Means Name	Description	Type	Reasoning	Thematic	Reference
A technique for human event analysis (ATHENA)	Analysing and evaluating the probability of human error while performing a specific task	Retrospective Proactive Qualitative Quantitative	Inductive	Safety Human factors	NRC (2000)
Crime pattern analysis	Analysing complex pattern of crimes in order to provide a cognitive structure for crime events understanding	Retrospective Proactive Qualitative Quantitative	Inductive Abductive	Criminology	Brantingham and Brantingham (1984; 2003; 2013)
Crime opportunities analysis	Analysing the opportunities relative to the perpetration of a particular type of crime (aka situational causes of crime)	Retrospective Proactive Qualitative	Inductive Abductive	Criminology	Clarke (1980; 2005; 2013); Clarke and Eck (2005)
Situational precipitators of crime analysis	Analysing the situational precipitators of crimes by focusing on the antecedents of malevolent behaviour	Retrospective Proactive Qualitative	Inductive Abductive	Criminology	Wortley (2001; 2013)
Crime mapping and hot spot analysis	Analysing spacial data and patterns relative to the distribution of crimes (geocoding and geovisualisation)	Proactive Qualitative Quantitative	Inductive Abductive	Criminology	Anselin (1995); Anselin, Griffiths and Tita (2013); Diggle (2014)

Table 5.1 Means for Analysing Security Failure *(Continued Continued Continued Continued)*

Means Name	Description	Type	Reasoning	Thematic	Reference
Repeat victimisation analysis	Analysing spacial data and patterns relative to the distribution of crime and prospective crime mapping	Proactive Qualitative Quantitative	Inductive Abductive	Criminilogy	Farrell (2006); Farrell and Pease (2013)
Human error assessment and reduction technique (HEART)	Analysing task types with their associated nominal error probabilities	Retrospective Quantitative	Deductive	Safety Human factors	Reason (1997, p. 142)
Influence diagram approach (IDA)	Analysing the influences existing at various organisational levels upon adverse outcomes	Retrospective Proactive Qualitative Quantitative	Inductive	Safety Human factors	Reason (1997, p. 146)

As this section has now demonstrated, few means relative to security failure analysis exist. Each of them has advantages and inconveniences and will serve different security needs.

Explaining and Tackling Security Failures

Having defined the term security failure and explored the ways allowing its analysis, this section of the paper will firstly explain the structuring of security failure, thereby the consequentiality and causality related to it and then various strategic means allowing security failure prevention. In that respect, two questions will be answered, namely (a) *how security fails?* and (b) *how to prevent security to fail?*

How security fails

A security failure, like a criminal act or any other event, does not occur randomly, spontaneously or uniformly in both time and space. Its construction follows a set of distinctive patterns (aka failure script or chain of correlated events) and its substance is conditioned by various converging but distinct causal factors (ie: individual, organisational, technological and socio-political – see Borodzicz, 2005; Button, 2008) over a certain period of time (ie: incubation phase, precipitation, event – see Toft and Reynolds, 2005). For example, security can fail because a security guard is sleeping whilst on duty (script element one, individual factor, incubation phase element one), thus allowing a malefactor to break-in (precipitation, script element two) through a door left open due to staff complacency towards security (script element three, organisational factor, incubation phase element two) and steal an asset (script element four, event phase).

It can also fails because a CCTV is faulty (technological factor), thus preventing the cameras operator to detect a crime in progress or because of the weakness of the security industry regulation (socio-political factor - see George and Button, 2000; Button, 2002; 2008), which could, for example, allow criminals to run a security company and infiltrate legitimate businesses in order to carry out their activities.

Furthermore, it will be noted that any security failure script element can be shaped by the consequences emerging from four sorts of process, namely (c) *intentional acts*, (d) *unintentional acts*, (e) i*naction* and (f) *malfunction*. By intentional acts are to be understood acts which are purposefully serving a given security or security failure objective, for example when a security guard decides to follow, or not to do so, a security procedure. These kinds of acts can be either legitimate or criminal indeed. This will depend upon what the frame of reference and objective of the act are. For instance, a security guard deciding not to follow a security procedure in order to steal an asset would be considered an intentional criminal act whereas an employee purposefully bypassing a security protocol in order to become more efficient and productive at work would be an intentional legitimate act.

On the other hand, unintentional acts are, as their name suggests, acts which are not done on purpose and committed either by inadvertence or error. Such erroneous acts can be either due to mistakes or skill-based slips and lapses indeed (Reason, 1997, p. 72; 2008). In that sense, a security guard who forgets to close the backdoor of a warehouse, thus allowing a thief to come in and steal an asset would be considered an unintentional act caused by lapse of memory, for example due to stress, tiredness or lack of focus.

Thirdly, the inaction of an employee or security personnel can also lead to security failure (BBC, 2013). This is what could be termed being complacent vis-à-vis security. For example, when a security manager feeling satisfied by the relative performance of the security system s/he manages does 'nothing' or not much to improve the former could be considered as a case of security complacency. Finally, by malfunction is to be understood the failure of a piece of security equipment to function normally. As the above has demonstrated, security can fail in many ways. Indeed, sometimes it fails without such an incidence being noticed. As demonstrated earlier, security failures can either be anticipated (proactive analysis) or remembered (retrospective analysis). Table 5.2, next page, summarises the findings of this section.

Table 5.2 How Security Fails

Temporal Qualities	Security Failure Script Components		
	Causal Factors	*Shaping Process*	*Consequentiality*
Incubation Phase	Individual	Intentional Acts	Noticed
Precipitating Event	Organisational	Unintentional Acts	Unnoticed
Security Failure	Technological	Inaction	Anticipated
Recovery / Learning	Socio-Political	Malfunction	Remembered

How to prevent security to fail

There are many ways of preventing security failures (Gill, 2006; 2014; Button, 2008; Talbot and Jakeman, 2009), and indeed theories abound (Zimring and Hawkins, 1973; Cornish and Clarke, 1986; Wortley and Mazerolle, 2008; Hopkins Burke, 2009; Tilley, 2009).

However and because of its relevance to this paper (holistic in approach and includes learning from failure in its design), it has been felt important to focus upon the model developed by Button (2008, p. 224) and thereafter to adapt it so as to include elements addressing the three broad security failure script components. Adapted from Button's model and grounded on the findings of the first section, Figure 5.1, next page, outlines a strategic approach to security failure prevention.

**Monitor problem
and effectiveness
of system**
- Regular
  assessment of
  metrics
- Active *and
  proactive* learning
- Tweaking the
  problem and
  system
- *Minimising
  security
  complacency*

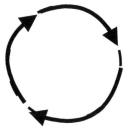

Define the problem
- What needs to be
  protected?
- What are the risks,
  their status and
  consequences?
- Quantify and prioritise
  risks
- Understand
  malefactors' likely
  tactics
- *Understand
  benefactors' likely
  errors*
- *Understand technical
  security components'
  likely malfunctions*

Developing a system tailored to the problem
- Apply metrics
- *Analyse security failures*
- Develop *a converging security* system
- Align system to broader strategy
- Apply ROI where appropriate
- Monitoring and evaluating implementation

**Strategy should be designed with three dimensions in mind
Third dimension**
- Changing malefactors' behaviour
- Refocussing the behaviour of malefactors
- *Improving benefactors' reliability*

Second and First dimensions
- Making the security system effective
- Enhancing the human element

Figure 5.1 Strategic Approach to Security Failure Prevention

As the above figure reveals, seven elements have been added to the model developed by Button, namely (g) understand benefactors' likely errors; (h) understand technical security components' likely malfunctions; (i) analyse security failures; (j) develop a converging security system, (k) minimising security complacency; (l) proactive learning; and (m) improving benefactors' reliability. In turn, Table 5.3 explains why these elements should be included in the model.

Table 5.3 Justification for Expanding Button's Model

Element	Justification	References
Understand benefactors' likely errors	Insider threat is not only about a benefactor who became malefactor or a malefactor pretending to be a benefactor. It is also about a benefactor erring in terms of security/safety	Hollnagel (1993) Wise, Hopkin and Stager (1993) Wiplert and Qvale (1993) Reason (1997; 2008)
Understand technical security components' likely malfunctions	Equipment malfunction can contribute to security system failure	Price (1999) Garcia (2006; 2008) Norman (2010)
Analyse security failures	This is the foundation of learning from security failures	Toft and Reynolds (2005) Stamatis (2014) Labib (2014)
Develop a converging security system	Silo thinking is not compatible with security	Aleem, Wakefield and Button (2013)
Minimising security complacency	Security complacency is a recurring problem and much efforts should be done to minimise its contribution to security failure	BBC (2013) Bunn and Sagan (2014)
Proactive learning	This is the foundation of learning improvement	Flavell (1979)
Improving benefactors' reliability	Should be part of any security strategy so as to mitigate the risk of human error, likewise system failure	Hollnagel (1993) Wise, Hopkin and Stager (1993) Wilpert and Qvale (1993) Reason (1997; 2008)

This section has explained the causality, shaping processes and consequentiality relative to the structuring of security failures. It has also explained how to perhaps better prevent such incidences to manifest. This has been done by complementing the model developed by Button (2008) with relevant safety related features and by increasing the focus upon security failure analysis and learning, the latter being the theme of the next section indeed.

Learning from Security Failures

Learning is a process seeking to improve organisational behaviour (see Argyris and Schon, 1998; Reavans, 1980; Wenger, 1998) via deliberate efforts of adaptation in the face of uncertainty (Rousseau, 1991, originally 1762). To this end, it could be argued that learning is about self-preservation. Consequently and according to Toft and Reynolds (2005), Borodzicz (2005) and Button (2008), learning from security failure appears of vital importance to the organisation. And it is as such because it represents indeed the foundation of security. There are but four broad ways of learning from security failures in general terms, namely (a) *cognitive learning* (see Riding and Rayner, 1998; Myers-Briggs and McCaulley, 1985), (b) *behaviourist learning* (see Pavlov, 1927), (c) *experiential learning* (see Kolb, 1984) and (d) *meta-cognition* (see Flavell, 1979). Cognitive learning is concerned with the development of problem-solving abilities and conscious thoughts. For example, an organisation is learning from security failures because it has decided to do so. According to Button (2008, p. 138), such a learning process can be done either by (e) *cross-organisational isomorphism*, where similar organisations are learning from one another experience, (f) *common mode isomorphisms*, where organisations belonging to different sectors are learning from one another failures because they share common techniques, materials and procedures or (g) *self-isomorphism*, where an organisation is learning from security failure via its constituents. Cognitive learning is an active and thereby planned learning process. Behaviourism is concerned with the development of new behaviours in response to external stimuli. An example of this would be an organisation adapting its security behaviour temporarily following a security failure without analysing the failure itself and according to specific conditions based upon feelings. This is an unplanned and passive learning process to the extent that it only reacts to environmental conditions. Experiential learning, on the other hand, is a process whereby knowledge is created through the transformation of experience. An example of this would be an organisation learning how to better prevent security failure through its own experience, rather than by merely hearing or reading about others' experiences. This is what Professor Button terms event isomorphism (2008, p. 137). Experiential learning is an active process which can be either planned or otherwise. Lastly, meta-cognition is concerned with cognition about cognition, for example when an organisation decides to develop knowledge about when, where and how to use specific learning strategies to better prevent security failures. To this end, it presupposes that an organisation is factually conscious of having learning difficulties with regards to security failure and then decides to engineer a learning process to tackle its own learning deficiencies. In this regard, it is about learning to learn. Meta-cognition is proactive and planned. Table 5.4 summarises the findings of this section.

Table 5.4 Learning from Security Failures

Type of learning	Nature	Condition	Example
Cognitive	Active	Planned	Cross-organisational, self and common-mode isomorphisms
Behaviourism	Passive	Unplanned	Reactions according to stimuli and environmental conditions
Experiential	Active	Planned & Unplanned	Event isomorphism
Meta-Cognition	Proactive	Planned	Knowing that having learning difficulties and developing learning strategies to effectively learn from security failures

This section has assessed how organisations are learning from security failure in general terms. As mentioned earlier, a precondition to effective learning from failures remains analysing. The next section of this paper will therefore explore an idea seeking to increase the 'analysing capability' of organisations, which in turn and by extension, would allow them to perhaps better learn from security failures.

A Hypothetical Strategic Means for Security Failures Prevention

There is much international research on safety failure and on the application of strategic means aimed to better prevent the latter. An example of this would be the consideration of the UK RIDDOR 2013 (Reporting of Injuries, Diseases and Dangerous Occurrences Regulations 2013) and the amount of studies made on this particular subject matter. There is, however, limited research on security failure, especially in terms of strategic preventative means. In addition, there are but very few published studies on security failures which actually draw upon both interviews and survey. This section of the paper bridges both of these gaps providing a focus upon a hypothetical strategic means for security failure prevention, namely the compulsory reporting of security failures, which is based upon an empirical research drawn from a survey of 2344 security managers working in the United Kingdom and twelve interviews.

Method

Researching security failures is a complicated task, mainly because there is scarce information available on the topic and due to the embarrassment security failures could cause to organisations (Button, 2008, p. 27). On that basis of understanding, a mixed-methods approach seeking both qualitative and quantitative data has been chosen so as to increase the likelihood of research success (Tashakkori and Teddie, 2003, p. 14). This reasoning is perhaps contradictory to the position held by Guba (1987, p. 31), who asserted that a mixed-methods approach is doomed to failure because of the inherent philosophical differences underlying each methods used, but it was thought, as argued by Semmens (2011, p. 60), that such an approach will provide better grounds for data triangulation and research validity. In turn, two fundamental aspects of the research will be noted, namely that (a) the purpose of the surveys was to generalise answers with a certain degree of accuracy and that (b) the aim of the interviews was to obtain an in-depth understanding of any given topic researched. Serving two different purposes, these two distinct research methods are indeed complementary (Tashakkori and Teddlie, 2003). For the purpose of research reliability, it has been decided to follow a systematic method to survey sampling and to reduce bias during interviews (Densombe, 2003, p. 267; De Vaus, 2014, p. 69).

Survey Strategy and Data Collection

Because different perspectives wanted to be analysed in order to reduce accidental bias (Davies and Francis, 2011, pp. 102-3), it has been decided to target indiscriminately and randomly 22371 potential research subjects spread across 73 different UK cities. All subjects were security managers working in 22 different industry sectors and their professional experiences were ranging from less than one year to more than ten years. The rationale behind this choice was that such a broad and random selection would better reflect the overall research topic and reduce bias. For convenience purpose, all subjects have been identified and selected on the professional network online platform LinkedIn using the keyword search 'security manager' altogether with the name of a preselected UK city, such as London, Portsmouth or Leeds. Furthermore, cities were selected according to their relative population (the larger the better). Firstly, the total amount of potential subjects has been calculated by summing the LinkedIn members of the 73 preselected cities and inviting them to connect and participate, as outlined in Table 5.5 next page. Then, the sample size required to have a 95% confidence level and a confidence interval of 6% has been calculated using the factorised sample population of 2344 (LinkedIn connections). In that respect, it has been concluded that the required research survey sample size would be 240 subjects. In order to reduce selection bias and because the forecasted response rate was of 10%, every single connected LinkedIn member would be systematically invited to participate to the survey. Each selected member would then be contacted by the researcher using LinkedIn instant message system. In that respect, they would receive a pre-formatted message (invitation to take part in the research study) containing both a brief about the research and a link to the research survey. The invitation process would then stop as soon as the target number of 240 completed surveys would be achieved.

Table 5.5 LinkedIn Members

Cat	Cities, Towns, Districts	Potential	Invited	Connection Ratio
1	London	2000	540	27.00%
2	Birmingham	732	118	16.12%
3	Leeds	424	49	11.56%
4	Glasgow	487	66	13.55%
5	Sheffield	386	59	15.28%
6	Bradford	152	10	6.58%
7	Liverpool	304	42	13.82%
8	Edinburgh	743	90	12.11%
9	Manchester	744	83	11.16%
10	Bristol	572	26	4.55%
11	Wakefield	142	17	11.97%
12	Cardiff	338	46	13.61%
13	Dudley	88	12	13.64%
14	Wigan	99	7	7.07%
15	Coventry	396	31	7.83%
16	Belfast	362	44	12.15%
17	Leicester	285	20	7.02%
18	Sunderland	45	7	15.56%
19	Doncater	177	25	14.12%
20	Stockport	251	38	15.14%
21	Nottingham	449	42	9.35%
22	Newcastle-upon-Tyne	330	9	2.73%
23	Kingston-upon-Hull	433	2	0,46%
24	Bolton	113	8	7.08%
24	Walsall	92	3	3.26%
26	Plymouth	183	14	7.65%
27	Stoke-on-Trent	225	19	8.44%

Table 5.5 LinkedIn Members (continued)

Cat	Cities	Potential	Invited	Connection Ratio
28	Wolverhampton	96	11	11.46%
29	Gloucester	366	36	9.84%
30	Derby	249	20	8.03%
31	Swansea	182	13	7.14%
32	Oldham	106	13	12.26%
33	Aberdeen	189	4	2.12%
34	Southampton	365	16	4.38%
35	Milton Keynes	453	33	7.28%
36	Northampton	370	45	12.16%
37	Portsmouth	480	75	15.63%
38	Warrington	321	32	9.97%
39	Luton	205	22	10.73%
40	York	815	15	1.84%
41	Southend-on-Sea	224	26	11.61%
42	Bath	50	6	12.00%
43	Bornemouth	279	35	12.54%
44	Peterborough	331	25	7.55%
45	Lincoln	7	1	14.29%
46	Chelmsford	357	11	3.08%
47	Brighton	372	2	0,54%
48	Colchester	171	17	9.94%
49	Blackpool	109	10	9.17%
50	Dundee	73	8	10.96%
51	Harrogate	76	9	11.84%
52	Dumfries	12	3	25.00%
53	Rochester	38	38	100.00%
54	Falkirk	99	17	17.17%
55	Reading	1342	61	4.55%
56	Blackburn	3	3	100.00%
57	Oxford	400	36	9.00%
58	Lancaster	75	10	13.33%
59	Newport	134	17	12.69%
60	Canterbury	189	19	10.05%
61	Preston	169	22	13.02%
62	Perth	15	1	6.67%
63	St Alban	180	21	11.67%

Table 5.5 LinkedIn Members (continued continued)

Cat	Cities	Potential	Invited	Connection Ratio
64	Cambridge	293	6	2.05%
65	Norwich	206	30	14.56%
66	Guildford	812	76	9.36%
67	Newcatle-under-Lyme	330	9	2.73%
68	Chester	265	17	6.42%
69	Crewe	13	3	23.08%
70	Ipwich	233	3	1.29%
71	Salisbury	174	4	2.30%
72	Slough	423	4	0,95%
73	Exeter	168	32	19.05%
	Total	*22,371*	*2,344*	*12.46%*

Survey Design

The survey has been designed around the five major themes of this research study, namely clarifying the term security failure; analysing security failure; tackling security failure; learning from security failure; and perspectives on the idea of regulating the reporting of security failure and comported a set of "closed-ended" and "open-ended" questions. Table 5.6 reflects the survey design.

Table 5.6 Survey Questions

Question	Theme	Type
1	Analysing security failure	Closed
2	Analysing security failure	Closed
3	Analysing security failure	Closed
4	Analysing security failure	Closed
5	Tackling security failure	Closed
6	Learning from security failure	Closed
7	Learning from security failure	Closed
8	Perspectives on the topic	Closed
9	Perspectives on the topic	Closed
10	Perspectives on the topic	Open

Interview Strategy and Data Collection

Face-to-face interviews are certainly the gold standard by which other modes of data collection can be compared (De Leeuw and Hox, 2015, p. 22). However, because of the sensitivity and nature of the topic studied, it has been decided that formal and semi-structured interviews should be given in a flexible and convenient way, such as via Skype video call, phone or email, to approachable individuals so as to maximise the likelihood of participation.

On that basis of understanding, six persons known to the researcher would be initially solicited to participate to the empirical research and then six others would be contacted via LinkedIn's message system according to the selection criteria listed in Table 5.7, which here reflects the convenience sampling process.

Table 5.7 Selection Criteria for the Interviews

Cri	Selection criteria by order of priority
1	Should be a former student of the University of Portsmouth
2	Should be member of an association for security professionals
3	Should have a Doctorate in security or risk management
4	Should be senior security manager and working for a large organisation
5	Should be senior risk manager and working for a large organisation
6	Should be senior security consultant and working for a large organisation
7	Should be senior IT security manager and working for a large organisation
8	Should be senior facilities manager and working for a large org.

Against the first criterion, it was thought that former students of the same university than the researcher would be easier to approach than others. This reasoning follows the principles of familiarity and group cohesiveness as outlined by Forsyth (2010, pp. 118-22), both reducing the risk of distrust indeed. The same reasoning was applied to the second criterion, as for the researcher is an active member of the Security Institute. Finally, against the criterion three, it was thought that the wisdom acquired during the course of any doctorate should suffice to increase the relevance and quality of the answers received during the interviews. For convenience purpose, video calls via Skype would firstly be proposed to the participant. Should this be objected to, a more traditional approach would be taken by the researcher, such as by proposing a face-to-face interview, interview over the phone or via emails, or any combination of the above.

A typical face-to-face or phone call interview would last approximately 45 minutes (± 20%), whereas one conducted via Skype would generally last 30 minutes (± 20%). During online (via LinkedIn) and email interviews, questions would be sent electronically to participants and answers would then be collected over a few days period of time and according to the participant's availability and willingness to respond.

Findings

The present section synthesises, analyses and describes the findings of the empirical research in which 2344 security managers working in UK and/or for a UK company were surveyed (response of 10.88%) and another twelve interviewed.

How Organisations are Understanding the Term Security Failure?

Survey findings

Table 5.8 Question 1 - How Would you Understand the Term 'Security Failure'?

A	Description of the answer	Resp	Perc	Conf
1	A security failure is characterised by the lack of success or dysfunction of a security process, system and/or function	161	63.14%	5.59%
2	A security failure is characterised by the breach of a security process, system and/or function	140	54.90%	5.77%
3	A security failure is characterised by the consequences of a security breach	67	26.27%	5.10%
4	None of the above	2	0,78%	N/A
5	I am not sure	1	0,39%	N/A
6	Prefer not to say	0	0.00%	N/A

The findings relative to the Question 1 outline that the definition of security failure is subject to much debate and controversy, oscillating between a lack of success or dysfunction (63%), a breach (55%), the consequences of a breach (26%), or any combination of the previous (multiple answers could be given to the question). This lack of definitional homogeneity creates confusion and misunderstanding as to what the issue actually is and which form of response shall address it.

Interviews findings

Of the twelve interviewees, three-quarters answered that a security failure seemed to be concerned with the lack of success or dysfunction of a security process, system and/or function, whereas the other quarter mentioned that it could either be related to a dysfunction, a breach or the consequences of a breach. Such a confusion is exemplified by the answer given by the Interviewee #4:

> Who determines what is a security failure and will the definition be open to interpretation?
> (Interviewee #4, personal communication, December 7, 2015)

How Organisations are Analysing Security Failures?

Survey findings

Table 5.9 Question 2 - How are Security Failures Analysed?

A	Description of the answer	Resp.	Perc.	Conf.
1	We assess both likelihood and consequence of security failures using scientific means and quantitative tools before it happens	72	28.24%	5.22%
2	We assess both likelihood and consequence of security failures using non scientific means and qualitative tools before it happens	99	38.82%	5.65%
3	We examine security failures using scientific means and quantitative tools once this manifested	38	14.90%	4.13%
4	We examine security failures using non scientific means and qualitative tools once this manifested	69	27.06%	5.15%
5	We analyse security failures systematically	85	33.33%	5.46%
6	We analyse security failures time to time	24	9.41%	3.38%
7	We do not analyse security failures	10	3.92%	2.25%
8	I am not sure	6	2.35%	1.76%
9	Prefer not to say	7	2.75%	1.90%

The above findings suggest that the way organisations analyse security failures is rather proactive (67%) than retrospective (41%), suggesting that the majority of the organisations surveyed have adopted a risk management philosophy whilst managing their security. It will also be noted that a slight preference towards qualitative analysis (66%), as opposed to quantitative one (43%), exists. However, it will be noted that qualitative approaches to analysis have clear limitations, notably in terms of validity and consistency. Furthermore, only one third of the surveyed appears analysing security failures systematically, perhaps demonstrating a lack of constancy and quality towards security failure analysis and certainly revealing gaps within the methodologies and security risk management processes being used.

Table 5.10 Question 3 - Are Human 'Security Related Errors' Analysed?

A	Description of the answer	Resp.	Perc.	Conf.
1	Yes, security related errors are both systematically recorded when they occur and analysed	163	64.17%	5.56%
2	No, security related errors are only systematically recorded when they occur	22	8.66%	3.26%
3	No, security related errors are only systematically analysed when they occur	14	5.51%	2.64%
4	No, security related errors are time to time recorded when they occur and analysed	15	5.91%	2.73%
5	No, security related errors are time to time recorded when they occur	6	2.36%	1.76%
6	No, security related errors are time to time analysed when they occur	8	3.15%	2.02%
7	No	11	4.33%	2.36%
8	I am not sure	7	2.76%	1.90%
9	Prefer not to say	8	3.15%	2.02%

Looking at the findings of Table 5.10 will reveal that two-thirds of the respondents systematically record and analyse security related errors, thereby emphasising the analysis on the human factors aspects of security. This also suggests that the management of security is related to the one of safety and ergonomics to the extent that the former can not be achieved without the consideration of the latter. Interestingly, such an idea is all too often omitted in the specialist literature on the topic of security management. The work of Talbot and Jakeman (2009) is perhaps the unique exception. Furthermore and when compared to the previous findings, evidence shows that organisations are more methodological whilst analysing human errors than security failures. This could indicate that analysing human errors in a systematic way is easier than analysing security failure in a similar one, or that more methods for error analysis have been developed whilst methods for security failures analysis lack. To some extent, it could be suggested, with reserve and according to the above findings, that human security related error are not necessarily considered by organisations whilst analysing security failures.

Table 5.11 Question 4 - Are Near-Miss Security Incidents Analysed?

A	Description of the answer	Resp.	Perc.	Conf.
1	Yes, near-miss security incidents are systematically recorded when they occur and analysed	140	55.56%	5.76%
2	No, near-miss security incidents are only systematically recorded when they occur	15	5.95%	2.74%
3	No, near-miss security incidents are only systematically analysed when they occur	18	7.14%	2.98%
4	No, near-miss security incidents are time to time recorded when they occur and analysed	20	7.94%	3.13%
5	No, near-miss security incidents are time to time recorded when they occur	10	3.97%	2.26%
6	No, near-miss security incidents are time to time analysed when they occur	14	5.56%	2.66%
7	No	24	9.52%	3.40%
8	I am not sure	7	2.78%	1.90%
9	Prefer not to say	4	1.59%	1.45%

Looking at Table 5.11 reveals that approximately half of the respondents (56%) systematically record and analyse near-miss security incidents whilst 10% do not. Similarly to error analysis, it appears that organisations are perhaps more inclined to analyse near-misses systematically than they are as such whilst analysing security failures. In turn, this is also stressing the idea that near-misses are not necessarily considered whilst analysing security failures. It is also important to note that around 17% of the respondents record and/or analyse near-misses sporadically, which could indicate that their approach to analysis is lacking of consistency or that near-miss analysis is subject to specific and predetermined criteria and/or priorities.

Interviews findings

Of the twelve interviewees, half admitted analysing security failures systematically whereas the other half acknowledged not analysing them at all. Furthermore, analysis could be performed either (a) mentally or (b) by using a security incident report (form to complete following a security incident and answering few basic questions such as: what happened, when it did so, how and what has been done to avoid any potential repeat - a brief narrative of the incident resulting from an investigation). This is exemplified by the answer given by Interviewee #3 when asked if he was scientifically analysing security failures in order to find their root cause(s)?

> Yes, I look at it in a logical format: the time of the incident, location, people involved, who done what, for which reasons and so on [...] the incident report forms the basis of the analysis.
>
> (Interviewee #3, personal communication, November 30, 2015)

Of particular relevance perhaps was the answer received from Interviewee #7 who stated that he was, because of the present shortcomings in failure analysis and in the context of his ongoing doctorate degree, developing an advanced model for security incident analysis based on business processes analysis.

How Organisations are Tackling Security Failures?

Survey findings

Table 5.12 Question 5 - Which of the Following Principles are Adhered to?

A	Description of the answer	Resp.	Perc.	Conf.
1	Learning from security failures is part of our organisation's security strategy	188	74.02%	5.08%
2	The reporting of security failures is promoted across our organisation	145	57.09%	5.74%
3	A 'just culture' is promoted across our organisation	95	37.40%	5.61%
4	Information exchange about security failure is promoted across our organisation	107	42.13%	5.72%
5	We exchange data and/or information related to our own security failures with other organisations	54	21.26%	4.74%
6	We know what our security risks are, their status and consequences	122	48.03%	5.79%
7	We quantify and prioritise our security risks	137	53.94%	5.78%
8	We understand malefactors likely tactics	78	30.71%	5.35%
9	We understand employees likely errors	137	53.94%	5.78%
10	We understand technology likely malfunction	126	49.61%	5.79%
11	We apply security metrics where possible	93	36.61%	5.58%
12	Our security system is balanced	54	21.26%	4.74%
13	We apply ROI	61	24.02%	4.95%
14	We regularly assess our security system	130	51.18%	5.79%
15	We use a scientific approach or method to analyse security failures	47	18.50%	4.50%
16	We minimise complacency towards security	101	39.76%	5.67%
17	We follow a converged security approach	44	17.32%	4.39%
18	We consider ergonomics whenever possible	29	11.42%	3.69%
19	We consider the COSO as model when doing security	6	2.36%	1.76%

Table 5.12 Question 5 - Which of the Following Principles are Adhered to? *(Continued)*

A	Description of the answer	Resp.	Perc.	Conf.
20	We consider the ISO/BSI 31000 as model when doing security	39	15.35%	4.18%
21	None of the above	9	3.54%	2.14%
22	I am not sure	4	1.57%	1.44%
23	Prefer not to say	2	79.00%	N/A

The findings presented in Table 5.12 are consistent with the expanded version of Button's model depicted earlier to the extent that organisations seem supporting its design in 43% of the cases, whereas this could be done consciously or otherwise indeed. It is also important to note that whilst 74% of the respondents seem committed at strategical level to learn from security failures, only 2% consider the COSO as a model when doing security. This latter figure perhaps contradicts what Dr Wakefield (2014a) would tend to recommend indeed.

A deeper analysis of the findings versus the model will reveal that organisations tend to be more engaged in problem monitoring (55% in average, A1, A14 and A16), than problem definition (47% in average, A6, A7, A8, A9 and A10), than in solution structuring (29% in average, A2, A3, A4, A5, A11, A12, A13, A15, A17 and A18). In turn, this does not mean that organisations are more effective in one domain or another, but rather that perhaps more commitment towards problem definition and solution structuring should be initiated. An example of this would be the consideration of the fact that only 31% of the respondents admit understanding malefactors likely tactics.

Interviews findings

Of the twelve interviewees, all admitted following risk management principles whilst tackling security risks. However, approaches to security risk management were varied and not necessarily following the expanded version of Button's model. They would rather be adapted from H&S standards or developed in-house. In most cases (60%), risk analyses were not carried out directly by the security managers but rather in collaboration with a specialist or senior executive employed by either the security company providing the security personnel (such as a consultant or a contracts manager) or by the corporation contracting out its security service (such as a senior facility manager). Furthermore, surprise penetration testings were organised regularly by 30% of the interviewees so as to reduce guard force's complacency and find gaps within the security system. Should a vulnerability be found, recommendations will be given to the security buyer for consideration and security policies eventually adapted.

Such an assertion is exemplified by the answer given by the Interviewee #1:

> When a security failure happens, it is systematically reported to our client's facility manager and to the security contract manager. Both security manager and contract manager then act as advisors, explaining to our client what went wrong, why it happened, what has been done and so on. We then wait for our client's approval in terms of implementing a new security procedure or adapting an existing security policy. We propose solutions and they decide.
>
> (Interviewee #1, personal communication, November 16, 2015)

How Organisations are Learning from Security Failures?

Survey findings

Table 5.13 Question 6 - How are you Learning from Security Failures?

A	Description of the answer	Resp.	Perc.	Conf.
1	When a security failure happens in our organisation, we analyse it, review what went wrong and adapt our security processes and/or procedures according to our findings	188	74.31%	5.06%
2	When a security failure happens in an organisation which is similar to us, we analyse it, review what went wrong and look at what the other organisation is doing to respond to the security failure	78	30.83%	5.35%
3	When a security failure happens in any other organisation, we analyse it, review what went wrong and look at what the other organisation is doing to respond to the security failure	47	18.58%	4.51%
4	When a security failure happens in our organisation, we immediately react to it without necessarily taking the time to analyse it or adapt our security processes and/or procedures	38	15.02%	4.14%
5	We are conscious that we are having some learning difficulties with regards to security failure and we are trying to develop new ways of learning from them	25	9.88%	3.46%
6	We listen to the advice of security experts	93	36.76%	5.59%
7	We do not learn from security failures	13	5.14%	2.56%
8	I am not sure	7	2.77%	1.90%
9	Prefer not to say	7	2.77%	1.90%

The findings outlined in Table 5.13 reveal that organisations, whist learning from security failures, tend to prefer experiential learning (74%), than cognitive learning (49%), than behaviourist learning (15%), than meta-cognition (10%). These also suggest that organisations are mostly engaged in active learning than in passive or proactive ones. These figures are consistent with the views expressed in the current specialist literature on the topic of security risk management to the extent that the process of learning is mainly described as being an 'active learning'. Example of this could be the consideration of the works of Toft and Reynolds (2005), Borodzicz (2005) or Button (2008). Here, it will be argued that much more results, thereby security failure prevention, could be achieved by organisations if and only if they were more conscious that they have learning deficiencies (meta-cognition) and dedicate more resources to proactive learning. Such an assertion has serious implications which will be understood by looking at the next Tables and indeed also requires a shift in mentalities.

Table 5.14 Question 7 - Are you Sharing Data About Security Failures?

A	Description of the answer	Resp.	Perc.	Conf.
1	Yes, we systematically share data or information about our own security failures with other organisations	31	12.30%	3.81%
2	Yes, we share time to time data and information about our own security failures with other organisations	28	11.11%	3.64%
3	Yes, we share data and information about our own security failures, but only with our partners	48	19.05%	4.55%
4	Yes, we share data and information about our own security failures, but only when we have to by legal order	22	8.73%	3.27%
5	No	111	44.05%	5.75%
6	I am not sure	23	9.13%	3.34%
7	Prefer not to say	8	3.17%	2.03%

The above findings reveal that the majority of the organisations surveyed (51%) admit sharing their information and/or data about security failures with third parties whilst 44% admit not sharing them. Furthermore, it will be noted that data sharing can be either systematic (12%) or sporadic (11%) and that one-fifth of the organisations surveyed tend to prefer sharing data only with their partners. There is strong evidence to suggest that information sharing, when executed intelligently, is a catalyst to organisational learning, security and resilience.

Interviews findings

Of the twelve interviewees, seven stated that the organisations they were working for were learning from their own security failures, whereas three mentioned they were learning from the security failures committed by others. In most cases learning tended to be both experiential and cognitive. It was cognitive to the extent that monthly meetings were organised for the very purpose of learning from the experiences of others (problems and solutions were exchanged during those meetings) whereas it was experiential to the extent that organisations were primarily learning from their own failures and mistakes.

In turn, this is best exemplified by the input received from the Interviewee #3:

> We are always looking to do the things better. This learning is part of a broader policy which has been developed with our clients. Our clients know that we are organising monthly meetings, sharing intelligence and learning from each other mistakes when these happen.
>
> (Interviewee #3, personal communication, November 30, 2015)

When asked if the sharing of information related to security failures with other organisations could facilitate mutual learning and improve security effectiveness, all interviewees were, to some extent, agreeing with it, whereas in fact only one Interviewee admitted doing it.

This curious reasoning is exemplified by the input received from the Interviewee #1:

> Yes I agree with this statement, but sharing must be internal. This kind of information is sensitive. Sharing information, threat intelligence and so on is something good because we can better learn. However, I am reluctant to share this kind of information with other organisations.
>
> (Interviewee #1, personal communication, November 16, 2015)

What Organisations are Thinking About the Compulsory Reporting of Security Failures in UK?

Survey findings

Table 5.15 Question 8 - 'The RIDDOR is Something Good'

A	Description of the answer	Resp.	Perc.	Conf.
1	I strongly agree with this statement	105	41.34%	5.71%
2	I agree with this statement	107	42.13%	5.72%
3	I neither agree nor disagree with this statement	27	10.63%	3.57%
4	I disagree with this statement	4	1.57%	1.44%
5	I strongly disagree with this statement	2	0,79%	N/A
6	Prefer not to say	9	3.54%	2.14%

The findings outlined in Table 5.15 reveal that 83% of the organisations surveyed tend to recognise that the RIDDOR is good thing to the extent that it allows both organisations and government to learn from health and safety failures. In turn, this is valuing the idea that the compulsory reporting of security failures could also be a good thing. This assumption will be tested in the next question.

Table 5.16 Question 9 - Should Something Like the RIDDOR Exist to Regulate the Statutory Obligation to Report Security Failures in UK?

A	Description of the answer	Resp.	Perc.	Conf.
1	Yes, I think that something similar to the RIDDOR should exist to regulate the statutory obligation to report security failures in UK	156	61.66%	5.64%
2	No, I do not think that something similar to the RIDDOR should exist to regulate the statutory obligation to report security failures in UK	52	20.55%	4.68%
3	I am not sure	37	14.62%	4.09%
4	Prefer not to say	8	3.16%	2.03%

The findings outlined in Table 5.16 reveal that 62% of the organisations surveyed support the idea that the compulsory reporting of security failures in UK should exist whilst 21% disagree with it. Such findings are rather interesting because they corroborate the study's rational and validate its initial assumption.

Based on the interpretation of the answers given to the last question of the survey, the pros and cons attached to very idea of making the reporting of security failures compulsory in UK will in turn be explored.

Figure 5.2 Benefits of Reporting Security Failures

Figure 5.2 reveals that 30% of the security managers having responded to the last question (N=187) tend to think that the compulsory reporting of security failures in UK (CRSFUK) could increase organisational learning in general terms. This is about the principle of leveraging organisational learning through information and/ or data exchange. Secondly, 26% of the respondents seem to support the view that the CRSFUK could indeed facilitate security failure analysis.

For instance, it:

> Could be used to identify and/or improve best practice and provide a constant method for assessing risk.
>
> (Respondent #230)

or

National and strategic reporting would allow organisations the ability to plan risk management strategies based around understanding of reported events.

(Respondent #224)

According to 24% of the respondents, the CRSFUK could also help the United Kingdom and organisations to strengthen their respective security. Example of this could be the consideration of the answer given by Respondent #255 whilst thinking about the opportunities that the CRSFUK could allow organisations:

To strengthen & develop existing policies, procedures and protocols.

(Respondent #255)

For 13% of the respondents, the CRSFUK could also facilitate the benchmarking between similar players, collaboration between organisations in terms of intelligence sharing, and standardisation within the security industry in terms of threat and vulnerabilities analytics. For example, Respondent #164 recognised that :

Collaboration and analytics of common issues would allow us to better identify key issues.

(Respondent #164)

Lastly, 6% of the respondents seem thinking that the CRSFUK could improve their reputation and public trust, whereas 1% that it could facilitate research:

Providing the reporting is conducted professionally, ethically and adeptly, the possibility to have a reliable, robust metric for national security failures cannot be underestimated. There are many opportunities [...] to develop next generation solutions to security problems. Of course the reporting data will also be a significant resource for academic research.

(Respondent #156)

Nonetheless, survey respondents also identified possible caveats which should be considered. Figures 5.3 reveals the findings.

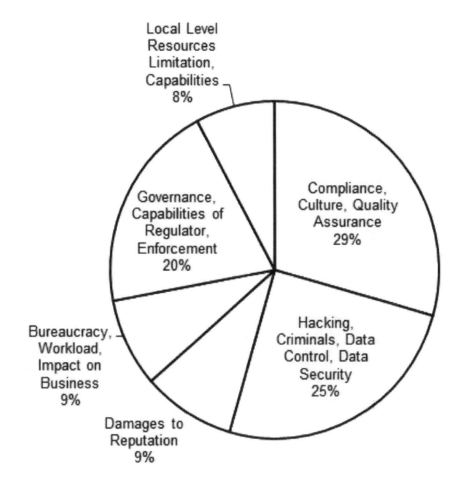

Figure 5.3 Inconveniences of Reporting Security Failures

According to Figure 5.3, 29% of the respondents seem thinking that the lack of compliance (misreporting and/or non-reporting of events), an unadapted organisational culture and/or bad quality assurance mechanisms could undermine the success of the CRSFUK. This is reflected partially in the answers given by Respondents #156:

It depends very much on the quality and quantity of data that is mandated. A poor or incomplete system will produce unusable data.

(Respondent #156)

and Respondent #229:

Honest organisations would be at disadvantage to those who are dishonest not less strict in reporting.

(Respondent #229)

or Respondent #190:

Undercutting security firms paying peanuts will be reluctant to be involved as their systems (& staff) are not fit for purpose.

(Respondent #190)

Furthermore, 25% of the respondents seem advocating the idea that poor data control and data security could undermine the CRSFUK by allowing criminals, competitors and malefactors to access critical data and carry out targeted attacks against organisations. This is reflected in the answers given by Respondents #252:

Alerts potential attackers to be aware of our previous security failures, allowing tactical knowledge.

(Respondent #252)

Respondent #215:

Advertises easy targets.

(Respondent #215)

or Respondent #177:

Wrong people could access the information and it could be used in a negative way towards the company.

(Respondent #177)

According to 20% of the respondents, the poor governance of the organisation which will hypothetically be responsible of the CRSFUK and/or a poor enforcement of the initiative could undermine the viability of the whole scheme. Examples of this could be the answers given by Respondents #148:

> Lack of technical capability from regulator such as the ICO to enforce and assess compliance with proposal.
>
> (Respondent #148)

and Respondent #96:

> No way of policing the adherence to the reporting policy.
>
> (Respondent #96)

Finally, approximatively 10% of the respondents seem advocating the ideas that the effectiveness of the CRSFUK would likely be compromised due to the extra workload it would put upon the companies being subject to it and/or because of the reputational damage that could result from a security breach or public scrutiny. Examples of this could be consideration of the answers given by Respondents #167:

> This could create an enormous amount of bureaucracy for already busy security professionals.
>
> (Respondent #167)

or Respondent #15:

> Bad for company reputation and client perception of an organisation's Infallibility.
>
> (Respondent #15)

Interviews findings

Of the twelve interviewees, nine were asked if whether or not the RIDDOR was something they would consider as being beneficial for both their organisation and the public. Answers were unanimous and all agreed with the concept. However, when asked if something similar to the RIDDOR should exist to regulate the compulsory reporting of security failures in UK, answers were rather negative (78%) and arguments varied. For example, Interviewee #2 explained:

> This is a good idea but because companies are already following ISO 9000 series on quality management and other industry standards such as Investor in People for example, that is not necessary to make the reporting of security failures compulsory. These standards are already allowing organisations to reduce their risk of security failures and to improve their operations. A compulsory reporting of security failures would also be a time consuming exercise for us the security managers and clearly we are already very busy without it. We have to be careful with this.
>
> (Interviewee #2, personal communication, November 23, 2015)

Central to his point of view was therefore that such an exercise would penalise organisations because of the extra workload it could engender and that alternative means already exist to help organisations reducing their risks.

Summary of Findings and Recommendations

This section of the paper will summarise the findings of this research work and offer recommendations based on the findings.

Clarification of what is meant by the term security failure

The findings relative to the survey and interviews corroborated the idea that there is no consensus as to what the term security failure means. It was found that such a practice created confusion and misunderstanding as to what the issue actually was and which form of response shall address it.

On this basis of understanding, the key recommendation to be made is that organisations should define the term security failure properly, such as *security risk* for example. This recommendation should allow organisations to better understand what the problem truly is and articulate the responses to it.

Exploration of the means allowing security failures analysis

The findings of the survey revealed that the ways organisations analysed security failures were rather proactive (67%) than retrospective (41%) and evidenced that organisations preferred using subjective analysis (66%) than objective analysis (43%). Findings also demonstrated that organisations tended to analyse human errors and near-misses systematically and thereby corroborated, to some extent, the literature review findings. The findings of the interviews revealed that organisations tended to use retrospective and subjective means for security failure analysis, such as 'incident reports'. Contrarily to the survey findings, 83% of the interviewees admitted not analysing human error and/or near-misses.

Consequently, the key recommendation to be made is that organisations should use objective, thus scientific, means for failure analysis both retrospectively and proactively. Then that organisations should factorise both human errors and near-misses in their analysis and do it in a systematic way. This recommendation should allow organisations to base their reasonings upon facts, not perceptions. It should also allow them to better understand the failure script and its structuring.

Explanation of security failures and the ways to tackle them

The survey findings revealed that organisations tended to follow the design of the expanded version of Button's model in 43% of the cases (thus corroborating the literature review findings) and also demonstrated that organisations tended to be more engaged in problem monitoring (55% in average), than problem definition (47% in average), than in solution structuring (29% in average). On the other hand, interview findings evidenced that organisations were not necessarily following the principles outlined in the expanded version of Button's model.

On this basis of understanding, the key recommendation to be made is that organisations should follow all the principles outlined in the expanded version of Button's model and put more focus on problem definition and solution structuring. This recommendation should allow organisations to think holistically whilst dealing with their security problems and subsequently reduce their risk of security failure.

Assessment of the ways organisations are learning from security failures

The findings of the survey demonstrated that organisations, whilst learning from security failures, tended to prefer experiential learning (74%), than cognitive learning (49%), than behaviourist learning (15%), than meta-cognition (10%). These figures were found consistent with the current specialist literature on the topic of security risk management to the extent that it remained focussed on active learning (experiential and cognitive). Findings also revealed that 51% of the organisations surveyed admitted sharing data/information related to their security failures with third parties. The findings of the interviews revealed that organisations tended to practice experiential and cognitive learnings. They also revealed that, although recognising the value of data /information sharing, organisations were not sharing their data/information with third parties in 92% of the cases.

Consequently, the key recommendation to be made is that organisations should absolutely reconsider the ways they are learning from security failures, starting by admitting that they have learning deficiencies, thus putting more focus on meta-cognition and then engage more in cognitive learning. This recommendation will stimulate organisations positively and greatly improve their organisational learning capability, thus reducing security failures.

What organisations are thinking about the compulsory reporting of security failures in UK?

The findings of the survey reveal that 62% of the organisations supported the idea that the compulsory reporting of security failures in UK should materialise whilst 21% disagreed with it. It could, according to the findings, increase learning (30%), facilitate analysis (26%), strengthen security and public safety (24%) and facilitate benchmarking and collaboration (13%). On the other hand, findings also revealed that 30% of the respondents were concerned with the idea that the CRSFUK could allow criminals, competitors and malefactors to access critical data and carry out targeted attacks against organisations if the security of the entity collecting and storing the data was weak. Findings also evidenced that 29% of the respondents estimated organisational culture and lack of compliance as being major barriers to such an idea. Finally, findings demonstrated that 20% of the surveyed believed that shortcomings in terms of governance and enforcement would seriously impair the functioning the whole concept. On the other hand, interviews findings revealed that 78% of the participants do not support the idea that the compulsory reporting of security failures in UK would be something good, mainly because of the extra workload this might generate and because alternative preventative means already exist, such as industry standards and best practices.

On this basis of understanding, the key recommendation to be made is that more research should be done in order to determine with certainty if the idea of making the reporting of security failure a compulsory activity in United Kingdom could be more beneficial than problematic. This recommendation should perhaps simulate further research of the topic.

Conclusions

This paper began with the clarification of the term security failure. The fact that much controversy surrounds the latter has been discussed and the reasons for this explained. Next, various means for security failure analysis have been explored. Then, the structuring of security failure has been discussed and various strategic means allowing security failure prevention have been explained. Four broad security failure learning processes were then assessed. Finally, the findings of an empirical research aimed to assess the idea of making the reporting of security failures in UK a compulsory activity have been presented altogether with five key recommendations grounded on the former.

Self-Reflection

Although this research study has achieved its overall objective, it is important to acknowledge that the survey sample is not representative of all security managers working in UK and/or for an UK organisation. Indeed, it is not even representative of all parties which, conceptually speaking, should have been included in the sample, such as business owners, CEOs, regulators and government officials or representatives. This is therefore a deficiency in that this work can not be generalised to be applicable.

References

Aleem A. Wakefield A. and Button M. (2013). 'Addressing the weakest link: implementing converged security', *Security Journal,* 26, pp236-48.

Anselin L. (1995). 'Local indicators of spatial association – LISA', Geographical Analysis, 27:93-115.

Anselin L. Griffiths E. and Tita G. (2013). 'Crime mapping and hot spot analysis' in R. Wortley and L. Mazerolle (eds.) *Environmental criminology and crime analysis.* Oxon: Routledge.

Argyris C. and Schon D.A. (1978). *Organizational learning.* Reading: Addison Wesley.

BBC News (2007). Second Highgrove security breach. Retrieved 24 October 2015, from http://news.bbc.co.uk/1/hi/england/gloucestershire/6521411.stm.

BBC News (2013). Camp Bastion report highlights security 'complacency'. Retrieved 11 November 2014, from http://www.bbc.co.uk/news/uk-24416156.

BBC News (2015). Talk Talk cyber-attack: Website hit by 'significant' breach. Retrieved 24 October 2015, from http://www.bbc.co.uk/news/uk-34611857.

Beck A. Bilby C. and Chapman P. (2005). 'Tackling shrinkage in the fast moving consumer goods supply chain' in M. Gill (ed.) *Managing security.* Basingstone: Palgrave Macmillan.

Bell J. and Waters S. (2014). *Doing your research project: a guide for first-time researchers.* Sixth Edition. Berkshire: Open University Press.

Bernstein P. (1996). *Against the gods: the remarkable story of risk.* New York: John Wiley and Sons.

Borodzicz E. (2005). *Risk, crisis and security management.* Chichester: John Wiley and Sons.

Boyle T. (2012). *Health and safety: risk management.* Oxon: Routledge.

Brantingham P.J. and Brantingham P.L. (1984). *Patterns in crime.* New York: MacMillan.

Brantingham P.J. and Brantingham P.L. (2003). 'Anticipating the displacement of crime using the principles of environmental criminology'. *Crimes Prevention Studies,* vol. 16, pp. 119-48.

Brantingham P.J. and Brantingham P.L. (2013). 'Crime pattern theory' in R. Wortley and L. Mazerolle (ed.) *Environmental criminology and crime analysis.* Oxon: Routledge.

Briggs R. and Edwards C. (2006). *The business of resilience: corporate security for the 21st century.* London: Demos. Retrieved 27 January 2013, from www.demos.co.uk.

British Standards Institution (2010). *BS ISO 31000:2009, Risk management principles and guidelines.* London: BSI.

Bunn M. and Sagan S.D. (2014). *A worst practices guide to insider threats: lessons learned from past mistakes.* Massachusetts: American Academy of Art and Sciences.

Button M. (2002). *Private policing.* Cullompton: Wilan Publishing.

Button M. (2008). *Doing security: critical reflections and an agenda for change.* Basingstone: Palgrave Macmillan.

Carrel P. (2010). *The handbook of risk management: implementing a postcrisis corporate culture.* Chichester: John Wiley and Sons.

Clarke R.V. (1980). 'Situational crime prevention: theory and practice', *British Journal of Criminology,* 20:136-47.

Clarke R. V. (2004). 'Technology, criminology and crime science'. *European Journal on Criminal Policy and Research,* 10: 55-63.

Clarke R.V. (2005). 'Seven misconceptions of situational crime prevention', in N. Tilley (ed.) *Handbook of crime prevention and community safety.* Cullompton: Willan Publishing.

Clarke R.V. and Eck J. (2005). *Crime analysis for problem solvers in 60 small steps.* Washington: US Department of Justice Office of Community Oriented Policing Services.

Clarke R.V. (2013). 'Situational crime prevention', in R. Wortley and L. Mazerolle (eds.) *Environmental criminology and crime analysis.* Oxon: Routledge.

COSO (2004). Enterprise risk management - integrated framework: Executive summary. New York: Committee of Sponsoring Organizations of the Treadway Commission (COSO).

Copil M. Cohen C. and Flage D. (2007). *Essential of logic.* Second Edition. New Jersey: Pearson Education.

Cornish D.B. and Clarke R.V. (1986). *The reasoning criminal.* New York: Springer Verlag now Springer.

Crano W.D. Brewer M.B and Lac A. (2015). *Principles and methods of social research.* Third Edition. Hove: Routledge.

Davies P. and Francis P. (2011). 'Doing criminological research' in P. Davies, P. Francis and V. Jupp (eds.) *Doing criminological research.* Second Edition. London: Sage Publications.

Davies P. Francis P. and Jupp V. (2011). (eds.). *Doing criminological research.* Second Edition. London: Sage Publications.

Dekker S. (2011). *Drift into failure: from hunting broken components to understanding complex systems.* Farnham: Ashgate Publishing.

De Leeuw E.D. and Hox J.J. (2015). 'Survey mode and mode effects', in U. Engel et al. (eds.) *Improving survey methods: lessons from recent research.* Hove: Routledge.

Densombe M. (2003). *Good Research Guide: For Small-Scale Research Projects.* Second Edition. Berkshire. McGraw-Hill Professional Publishing.

De Vaus D. (2014). *Surveys in social research.* Sixth Edition. Oxon: Routledge.

Diggle P. (2014). *Statistical analysis of spatial point patterns.* Third Edition. Boca Raton: CRC Press.

Duffin M. and Gill M. (2007). Staff dishonesty: a report for Procter and Gamble.

Electric Power Research Institute (1992). SHARP1 – A revised systematic human action reliability procedure. Palo Alto: EPRI. Retrieved 17 September 2013, from http://www.epri.com/abstracts/Pages/ProductAbstract.aspx? ProductId=TR-101711-T2.

Elkblom P. (2014). 'Securing the knowledge' in M. Gill (ed.) *The handbook of security.* Second edition. Basingstoke: Palgrave Macmillan.

Engel U. et al. (2015) (eds). *Improving survey methods: lessons from recent research.* Hove: Routledge.

Eysenck M.W. and Keane M.T. (2015). *Cognitive psychology: a student's handbook.* Seventh Edition. Hove: Psychology Press.

Farrell G. (2006). 'Progress and prospects in the prevention of repeat victimisation', in N. Tilley (ed.) *Handbook of crime prevention and community safety.* Cullompton: Willan Publishing.

Farrell G. and Pease K. (2013). 'Repeat victimisation', in R. Wortley and L. Mazerolle (eds.) *Environmental criminology and crime analysis.* Oxon: Routledge.

Flavell J.H. (1979). 'Metacognition and cognition monitoring'. *American Psychologist*, 34(10):906-11.

Forsyth D.R. (2010). *Group Dynamics.* Fifth Edition. Wadsworth: Cengage Learning.

Garcia M.L. (2006). *Vulnerability assessment of physical protection systems.* Burlington: Elsevier ButterworthHeinemann.

Garcia M.L. (2006b). 'Risk management' in M. Gill (ed) *Handbook of security.* Basingstoke: Palgrave Macmillan

Garcia M.L. (2008). T*he design and evaluation of physical protection systems.* Second edition. Burlington: Elsevier ButterworthHeinemann.

George B. and Button M. (2000). *Private security.* Basingstoke: Palgrave.

Gill M. (2006). (ed.). *Handbook of security.* Basingstoke: Palgrave Macmillan.

Gill M. (2014). (ed.). *The handbook of security*. Second edition. Basingstoke: Palgrave Macmillan.

Graham J. and Kaye D. (2006). *A risk management approach to business continuity: aligning business continuity with corporate governance.* Connecticut: Rothstein Associates Publisher.

Guba E.G. (1987). What have we learnt about naturalistic evaluation?, *Evaluation Practices*, 8:22-43.

Hollnagel E. (1993). *Human reliability analysis: context and control.* London: Academic Press.

Hollnagel E. (2004). *Barriers and accident prevention: or how to improve safety by understanding the nature of accidents rather than finding their causes.* Aldershot: Ashgate Publishing.

Hopkin P. (2010). F*undamentals of risk management: understanding, evaluating and implementing effective risk management.* London: Kogan Page.

Hopkins Burke R. (2009). *An introduction to criminological theory.* Third edition. Oxon: Routledge.

Kirschenbaum A. (2014). 'The ethnographic approach and security: the case of airports' in M. Gill (ed.) *The handbook of security.* Second edition. Basingstoke: Palgrave Macmillan.

Kolb D.A. (1984). *Experiential learning: experience as the source of learning and development.* New Jersey: Prentice Hall.

Labib A. (2014). *Learning from failures: decision analysis of major disasters.* Oxford: Elsevier ButterworthHeinemann.

Lam J. (2003). *Enterprise risk management: from incentives to controls.* New Jersey: John Wiley and Sons.

LaPorte T.R (1975). (ed). *Organized social complexity: challenge to politics and policy.* New Jersey: Princeton University Press.

LaPorte T.R. (1991). *Social responses to large technical systems: control and anticipation.* Dordrecht: Kluwer Academic Publishers.

Lund Petersen K. (2014). 'The politics of corporate security and the translation to national security' in Walby K. and Lippert K.R. (eds.) *Corporate security in the 21st century: theory and practice in international perspective*, (pp78-94). Basingstone: Palgrave Macmillan.

Manunta G. Manunta R. (2006). 'Theorizing about security' in Gill M. (ed.) *Handbook of security* (pp. 629-57). Basingstone: Palgrave Macmillan.

Myers-Briggs I. and McCaulley M.H. (1985). *Manual: a guide to the development and use of the MyersBriggs type indicator*. California: Consulting Psychologists Press.

National Regulation Commission (2000). Technical basis and implementation guidelines for A Technique for Human Event Analysis (ATHENA). Washington: US National Regulation Commission.

Norman T.L. (2010). *Risk analysis and security countermeasure selection*. Boca Raton: CRC Press.

Pavlov I.P. (1927). *Conditional reflexes: an investigation of the psychological activity of the cerebral cortex*. London: Oxford University Press.

Pettinger R. (2007). *Introduction to management*. Fourth edition. Basingstone: Palgrave Macmillan.

PKF (2015). The financial cost of fraud 2015: what the latest data from around the world shows. Retrieved 24 October 2015, from http://www.pkf.com/media/31640/ PKF-The-financial-cost-of-fraud-2015.pdf

Prenzler T. (2012). (ed.). *Policing and security in practice: challenges and achievements*. Basingstoke: Palgrave.

Prenzler T. and Sarre R. (2012). 'Public-private crime prevention partnerships' in Prenzler T. (ed.). *Policing and security in practice: challenges and achievements* (pp. 149-67). Basingstoke: Palgrave.

Price G. (1999). T*he interaction between fault tolerance and security*. Technical report number 479. University of Cambridge Computer Laboratory.

PWC (2015). 2015 Information security breaches survey. Retrieved 24 October 2015, from http://www.pwc.co.uk/assets/pdf/2015-isbs-technical-report-bluedigital. pdf.

Rasmussen J. and Svedung I. (2000). *Proactive risk management in a dynamic society*. Karlstad: Swedish Rescue Service Agency.

Reason J. (1991). *Human error.* Cambridge: Cambridge University Press.

Reason J. (1997). *Managing the risk of organizational accident.* Farnham: Ashgate Publishing.

Reason J. (2008). *The human contribution: unsafe acts, accidents and heroic recoveries.* Farnham: Ashgate Publishing.

Reavans R.W. (1980). *Action learning: new techniques for management.* London: Blond and Briggs.

Riding R. and Rayner S. (1998). *Cognitive styles and learning strategies: understanding style differences in learning and behaviour.* London: David Fulton Publishers.

Rousseau J.J. (1991, originally 1762). *The Emile project.* Columbia: Columbia University Press.

Semmens N. (2011). 'Methodological approaches to criminological research', in P. Davies, P. Francis and V. Jupp (eds.) *Doing criminological research.* Second Edition. London: Sage Publications.

Shappell S.A. and Wiegmann D.A. (2000). The human factors analysis and classification system – HFACS. Washington: Office of Aviation Medicine, Federal Aviation Administration. Retrieved 17 September 2013 from https://www.nifc.gov/fireInfo/fireInfo_documents/humanfactors_classAnly.pdf.

Speight P. (2012). *Why security fails: how the academic view of security risk management can be balanced with the realities of operational delivery.* Osset: Protection Publications.

Stamatis D.H. (2003). *Failure mode effect analysis: FMEA from theory to execution.* Second Edition. Milwaukee: American Society for Quality.

Stamatis D.H. (2014). *Introduction to risk and failures: tools and methodologies.* Boca Raton: CRC Press.

Talbot J. and Jakeman M. (2009). *Security risk management: body of knowledge.* New Jersey: John Wiley and Sons.

Taleb N.N. (2007). *The black swan: the impact of the highly improbable.* London: Penguin Books.

Tashakkori A. and Teddlie C. (2003). (eds.). *Handbook of mixed methods in social and behavioural research.* California: Sage Publications.

Tavory I. and Timmersmans S. (2014). *Abductive analysis: therorizing qualitative research.* London: The University of Chicago Press.

Tilley N. (2009). (ed.). *Handbook of crime prevention and community safety.* Cullompton: Willan Publishing.

Toft B. and Reynolds S. (2005). *Learning from disasters: a management approach.* Third edition. Basingstoke: Palgrave MacMillan.

Tropina T. and Callanan C. (2015). *Self- and co- regulation in cybercrime, cybersecurity and national security.* London: Springer.

Wakefield A. (2014a). 'Corporate security and enterprise risk management' in K. Walby and K.R. Lippert (eds.) *Corporate security in the 21st century: theory and practice in international perspective,* (pp235-53). Basingstone: Palgrave Macmillan.

Wakefield A. (2014b). 'Where next for the professionalization of security?' in M. Gill (ed.) *The handbook of security,* Second edition, (pp919-35). Basingstone: Palgrave Macmillan.

Wenger E. (1998). *Communities of practice: learning, meaning and identify.* New York: Cambridge University Press.

White A. (2010). *The politics of private security: regulation, reform and relegitimation.* Basingstoke: Palgrave.

Wilpert B. Qvale T. (1993). (eds). *Reliability and safety in hazardous work systems: approaches to analysis and design.* Hove: Lawrence Erlbaum Associates.

Wise J.A. Hopkin V.D. and Stager P. (1993). (eds). *Verification and validation of complex systems: human factors issues.* New York: Springer Verlag.

Wong R. (2013). *Data security breaches and privacy in Europe.* London: Springer.

Wood J. and Shearing C.D. (2007). *Imagining security.* Cullompton: Willan.

Wortley R. (2001). 'A classification of techniques for controlling situational precipitators of crime', *Security Journal,* 14(4):63-82.

Wortley R. (2013). 'Situational precipitators of crime', in R. Wortley and L. Mazerolle (eds.) *Environmental criminology and crime analysis.* Oxon: Routledge.

Wortley R. and Mazerolle L. (2011). (eds). *Environmental criminology and crime analysis.* Oxon: Routledge.

Zedner L. (2003b). 'The concept of security: an agenda for comparative analysis'. *Legal studies,* 23:153-76.

Zedner L. (2009). *Security.* New York: Routledge.

Zimring F. and Hawkins G. (1973). *Deterrence.* Chicago: University of Chicago.

Chapter 6

Organisations and Management: Inherent Resilience Inabilities

Phillip Wood

The ability of human beings to contribute to organisational effectiveness, and more precisely, organisational resilience is challenged by varied factors. The dynamic nature of threats and the operating environment is a significant issue; however, our own innate behaviours, ideas, characters and understandings can have a strong impact upon our individual and collective capabilities. This chapter argues that our preferences can override more challenging issues, and that the need to overcome our own fixed mindsets and adherence to models, frameworks and structures is key to improved resilience. The importance of organisational learning, of understanding rather than applying our own biases and of a more receptive approach to the risk dynamic, is at the core of a more effective and capable organisational resilience function.

> To swallow and follow, whether old doctrine or new propaganda, is a weakness still dominating the human mind.
>
> (Charlotte Perkins Gilman)

The continuing and increasing resilience challenges that we face in the 21st-century will, it is fair to propose, continue to arise, metamorphose and occupy organisations and individuals as time goes on. Technology brings immense benefits and commensurately immense challenges; the opportunities that our expanding knowledge and capabilities offer can also engender equally expanding difficulties and issues. As our continuing movement towards an interconnected global community takes us towards a future where cultures merge, borders fade and ideas blend, the natural progression towards our communal future also brings communal threats. These threats may come from natural, malicious, intentional on non-intentional risks and impacts. However, there is a possibility that the pace of change is outstripping our ability to keep up with it. While we have the intellectual capacity to design and develop new ideas, we seem to have insufficient capacity to deal with the effects and consequences of them.

In the interconnected world, the consequences of the deliberations and actions of those who shape our society, politics and technology that supports them, can be felt much more quickly than was ever the case in the pre-Internet era. Information flows so quickly, influences are felt rapidly and at all levels of society and the organisations that operate within it. The effect of an innovation, the impact of a political or strategic decision, a societal change, or even a change in the attitudes of our populations and their expectations can be felt; and because of that there is also a need to be able to react accordingly. For example, politicians are much more aware of the power of those who elect them and of the devastating change that social media and the Internet have made not only to their election processes, but also to their electability. The changes that have come (and by inference the changes that will continue to accelerate and increase over the coming years) signify that we need to be able to understand not only what the issues are, but that there is a need to be able to anticipate, respond to and recover from the impacts that may arise. An inability to adapt our thinking and to change the approaches, paradigms and practices that characterise our behaviours and responses to challenges has the potential for the threats to become risks that outstrip our capacity to deal with them.

The threats that we do face, the configuration of our society, and again by inference those organisations that operate within it, means that we should consider having in place, educating and developing, capabilities to be able to build organisational resilience capabilities and capacities at multiple levels. The very fact that risks and impacts are developed and generated before infiltrating society and our organisations at all types of level means that we should be able to develop a commensurate coping capability. The question is that although there is considerable effort and thought applied to the ability to set frameworks and models; and to the development of structures and hierarchies to deliver a capability; are we as human beings able to configure ourselves to effectively meet the issues and deal with them? In the orientation of ourselves and our societies to be able to cope with the developments that we face, do we fall more upon the safety of visualisations and models, of supposed paradigms and ideal types, whilst failing to understand that we should develop in ourselves, paradigms of behaviour and a consideration of ourselves as ideal types who are able to effectively match the development and impact of the threats and issues we face? The consequent limitations that are self-inflicted by our own behaviours, our inability and a willingness to countenance and manage the rapidity and flexibility of thought that are essential for meeting the demands of a rapidly and flexibly developing risk landscape may be significant factors in the inability to prepare for and respond rapidly and appropriately to the impacts that threaten to cause significant damage to us. In this chapter, we will consider whether the basic human condition predicates against the effective adoption and implementation of resilience measures. We will think about how we are able to categorise problems, how we are unable to categorise others, and will posit that we are simply and generically unable to meet the demands that the more fluent and mobile risk landscape places upon us; at least with the mind-sets and approaches that we carry with us.

An Example of Fixedness

The issues related to fixed thought, prejudice and a bloody-minded adherence to what we know (and sometimes what we simply like) can be seen almost everywhere. However in the world of risk and security, these issues can be starkly highlighted. As this is being written, the United Kingdom is embarking upon a significant discussion and governance initiative around the prevention of extremism, which it is considered may sow seeds of terrorism, within young children and students at universities.

The initiative around education is known as Prevent[2], and is part of a wider counterterrorism strategy known as Contest[3]. The initiative's aim is to provide a legal and regulatory mechanism whereby organisations are able to identify and report signs or indications of extremist and ideological issues to responsible and relevant authorities. To the security purist, the strategies may seem to be reasonable. However, Prevent is designed to be implemented in educational establishments, and in universities in particular the concept of reporting on someone who has an ideological view has not been universally well received. Perhaps understandably, there has been a significant resistance to the implementation of Prevent and the current and relevant discussion around its legitimacy and "safety" as a counterterrorism measure is quite vehement.

An example and collection of the sides of the debate is contained in a short article within the Times Higher Education Supplement (2016[4]). It is clear that there are entrenched views, not only in the minds of the extremists that Prevent looks to target, but also in the minds of those who are held accountable for making it happen. In considering the ideas of keeping pace with change and the development of the threat landscape, Prevent provides an interesting case study in the orientation of the human condition to its preferred settings, rather than to dealing with what may or may not be a significant risk development for the future. An assessment of the radicalisation of individuals and the locations for them has yet to be fully made for UK educational institutions. However, there have been cases where students have become radicalised, several of them quite high profile, and the role of education in either facilitating or providing an environment in which groups could discuss and develop extremist ideas have been well (if sensationally) documented. The issues of debate for education and its

---

[2] https://www.gov.uk/government/uploads/system/uploads/attachment_data/file/97976/prevent-strategy-review.pdf

[3] https://www.gov.uk/government/publications/2010-to-2015-government-policy-counter-terrorism/2010-to-2015-government-policy-counter-terrorism

[4] https://www.timeshighereducation.com/features/the-universitys-role-in-counterterrorism-stop-look-and-listen

linkage to Prevent are absolutely clear. Despite the protestations of some, there is probably not a desire by the government of the day to put in place a system, or framework whereby the legitimate and necessary development of free speech is something that is quashed or monitored into extinction. There is probably not a desire to bring in through legislation a "snoopers charter". No legitimate democracy would want to see children and students being reported to the authorities for talking about issues that may affect them, and perhaps that they may have seen on the news. Conversely, we do wish to limit the pernicious influence where it exists, of those who may wish to develop a culture of hatred and adversarialism within our educational system.

The impact of unchallenged extremism is the development of more entrenched, hardened views that may or may not lead to full-blown violent action. However, regardless of which side of the debate that we are on it is worth considering how our own mind-sets may blind us to the issues and concerns which may develop into a much more concrete and serious threat. Free speech is a right, it is hard won in democracy and something that is defended vehemently and vigorously, and absolutely rightly so. In academic circles, as the article identifies, losing the ability to speak freely is significant and damaging. However, there are those who wish to see free speech denied, and those who consider free speech and the expression of contentious thought to be stamped out. It happened on a large scale in the 20th century, and we need look no further than the Charlie Hebdo attacks of 2015 in France to see that the response to free speech and expression can be, and often is violent. The ancient Western democratic right and tradition of free speech for all is far from inalienable to those who would wish to stamp it out.

But how do we, with our motivations, our vehement defence of free speech, actually protect ourselves against the inevitable impacts against us because we espouse it? In what ways does our understandable need to preserve and manage the importance of free speech and research within higher education undermine our ability to be able to understand that the risk of extremism and the development of it into terrorism is no longer a theoretical abstract, but now a reality

131

where the development of an Islamic State, is something that is aspirational for many young people rather than anathema. This has become a first for modern society. For the first time in our 'corporate knowledge', we have an entity that sets itself up as a legitimate cause for which people should be prepared to fight and die, while justifying its means and capabilities on the basis that it needs to conduct asymmetric and terrifying warfare against its adversary as it is outnumbered and out gunned. The link to religion and to the tenets of Islam can be powerfully made to those who wish to listen. In other words, the development of an Islamist iconic group, which is attractive to young people; which is able to disseminate its many messages using the social media and mobile communications that are at the basis of our interactions in modern times, make it a real and significant entrant into our local and environmental shaping forces for the future. This, I would argue, does need to be limited and mitigated for the good of society.

The thinking of those who consider that we should allow dialogue related to Islamist extremism to continue without it being interdicted is not necessarily wrong. However, such thinking does fail to recognise the significant risks that are related to following a route whereby the discussion and spread of extremist views is not effectively challenged. The fault in the thinking is that the ability to challenge such extremist thinking can be by words and dialogue alone; however, this is probably not the sole way in which extremism can be defused. Prevent involves the imposition of measures that restrict discussion; and there will be those who will continue to take the view that this discussion should continue ad infinitum. However, in terms of protecting the organisation and, importantly, those within it, there is a clear potential rationale for allowing our thought processes to catch up with the realities. There is a mismatch: we cannot allow full and free debate and the dissemination of unfettered views concerning the advantages or counters to radicalisation and extremism to continue without there being some degree of payback at some point. This is not an issue of naiveté, more an issue of an inability to grasp changes and unfamiliar views which may have a direct impact upon the way that we think and manage our lives. The idea that the notion of free speech is an inalienable right is challenged by extremists whilst being championed by those who have the greatest power to challenge extremism in its formative years. It seems clear; however, the clarity is clouded by views and ideologies, beliefs and frameworks of thought to which the protagonists cling with alacrity and tenacity.

Where this links to the issues related to human thoughts and behaviours in more detail, is in the idea of keeping pace. If we consider that we are loaded with our own thoughts, views and prejudices and behaviours from an early date, then we should also consider that we need to be able to continue to change as we go forward. The realities are perhaps that we allow our own requirements, perfectly and actually, to override what we may see as the realities that face us. By allowing the frameworks and support structures that we rely on to influence our responses, we build in a lag. With, as previously mentioned, the pace of the change and threat development increasing and quickening, we begin to build in our own vulnerabilities before realising that we have done so. An example would be that in looking at how organisations may be at risk from various criminal activities, we can see that those who use technology and apply flexible thought tend to be the criminals rather than those who are targeted, at least in the early stages. A deterrent or other response will always be exactly that, a response, and therefore will always lag behind the effect or impact felt from the attack in the first place. If we consider manufacturing and retail; when a new 'in-demand' product is developed, for example, a counterfeit will surely follow. The speed with which organisations are able to move to deal with such issues will influence their survival at worst and the viability of their product lines at best. We can illustrate the need to think quickly and flexibly in response to new criminal activities by considering the uniquely 21st Century development of streaming and web available video and media products. With the coming of the Internet, the age of the rentable or purchasable video movie died with amazing speed. The development of a route by which images and content, legally or illegally, could be disseminated, meant that the idea of buying a hardcopy of our favourite film or TV programme was rapidly subsumed by Internet availability and immediacy. In the early years of streaming, the Internet was a playground for those who wish to develop websites, links and other routes for illegally copied material. However, those who were being affected: the commercial providers and movie studios, watched what was going on and realised that net availability would be the next big thing. However, it took time for them to understand that customer demand drove that market growth with the realisation that scale of use overcame legal enforceability; so many were streaming and downloading illegally that prosecution became impossible.

So, the commercial providers moved to counter the problem, leading us to a situation where the market is now becoming dominated by the new media powerhouses such as Netflix who have realised that the market is lucrative, if it can be legally managed and resourced. The only thing that has taken so long for this to happen has been less the legal, or even the technical, issues related to storage and dissemination of information. The initial slowness to respond was in the organisations, and structures who attempted to regulate or legislate out the competition from criminal or other grey market elements. This wasted time (and by implication lost profit), was the result in part of the mental prejudices that considered that this new flexible space was the specific domain of the legal operator. The equal flaw was in the belief that just because a structure for dissemination existed, those who used it as a framework and tool for this dissemination could be held to account in any way. As it has transpired, those who have failed to understand the need to mirror and surpass the techniques used by unregulated elements are those who have fallen behind in the marketplace. The new providers of products and services are those, such as Netflix, Uber and Air BnB, who undercut the less agile and enter the market with vigour and innovation. The fixed and inflexible thinkers are those who are left behind.

It is fairly clear from this example that fixed thinking in business will cost money. Equally, fixed thinking in the development of measures to maintain the resilience of an organisation will also cost money and perhaps much worse. The refusal to countenance, absorb and act upon the clear indicators that there is something that needs to be done can naturally lead to a market or competitive failure in business. If we transpose this limitation in viewpoint towards an organisation that is attempting to protect itself, the stakes may be much higher. The requirement for us to ensure that our people are physically protected and our monetary assets are preserved against loss; that no one who does not need to has access to our assets and sites; that we are able to continue to operate through and beyond a particular problem or crisis needs us to think and operate beyond what may be familiar or recognisable. In terms of what we consider to be not only the threats that may face us, but also what is acceptable are necessary in terms of appropriate response, we limit ourselves. Moreover, the wish to ignore or push aside the recognisable consequences of failure issues by taking a self-centred or naive view of what we are comfortable with in terms of behaviours and even human rights may have considerable impact upon our ability to ensure that those consequences are not mitigated. The important notion is to perhaps consider that we should look at ourselves as organisations that are able to learn. We should perhaps also consider the idea that there is much in terms of behaviour that is self-endorsing and adds to the development of problematic and potentially dangerous situations and consequences.

Organisations and the individuals within them may need to develop the understanding that there is a need to learn and to be able to apply that learning such that they are able to take informed decisions about what they need to do, and when. The concept of overriding the activities that they need to carry out by ingrained thought processes that perhaps informed predecessor or peer behaviour need not necessarily apply when the changing and dynamic views external and internal influences on our integrity and capability begin to impinge and have an impact upon us. The development of organisations that are more capable, more effective and more resilient means requires a shift in focus from the formulaic and familiar to newer territories of thought. And we need to think about learning before we can begin to change our habitual behaviours.

Learning Organisations

The potential for organisations to become more effective in their ability to overcome their hardwired approaches can perhaps be realised by becoming more open to a learning culture. This learning culture, as proposed and discussed by amongst many others, Senge (1990[5]) and Garvin (1993[6]) and Senge (1990) considers that learning organisations and their leadership blend both events, patterns of behaviour and models; Garvin (1993) moves on to develop Senge's ideas further, but still considers organisational learning tools to be considerable contributors to capability. It is difficult to disagree wholly with their views and approaches: the idea of an organisation as a supportive learning environment is important.

However, a reliance on models may framework the organisation and it would be beneficial to consider what the learning and truly flexible organisation may hold as attributes. Apart from the fact that we need to keep pace with the risks and threats that they face is as organisations, we also need to consider the fact that, as organisations ourselves, we should begin to learn and develop a culture of learning so that repeating mistakes does not become an endemic element of our organisational culture. This of course, is an easy thing to say and a difficult and more challenging process to follow. In the context of business development and market conditions, Martenson and Dahlgaard (1999) considered that organisations needed to be able to develop creativity in thought, and as they said:

> So the purpose of the creative organisation is through a conscious and action oriented focus on creativity, to establish a basis for the work with innovation and kaizen will stop.
>
> (Martenson and Dahlgaard, 1999, p. 879[7]).

---

[5] Senge, P. (1990), The fifth discipline: the art and practice of the learning organisation", Doubleday, New York, NY.

[6] Garvin, D. (1993), The learning organisation", Harvard Business Review, July-August, pp. 78-91.

[7] Martensen, A. and Dahlgaard, J.J., (1999). Strategy and planning for innovation management-supported by creative and learning organisations. *International Journal of Quality & Reliability Management*, *16*(9), pp. 878-891.

While the idea of creativity is one element of knowledge, they make the point (ibid, p. 880), that "individual learning does not guarantee organisational learning," as for organisational learning itself, they refer to Senge when they say that team learning, personal mastery, mental models, shared values and systems thinking all contribute to team learning. They also consider Cooper and Garvin and their approaches to the development of learning and capability. The issue does remain however; by considering the Senge concept of models as learning tools, does conditioned thought override true flexibility in approach?

The problem and issue that arises when considering learning organisations is that they should have something that is concrete and manageable to form the basis of learning; that something needs to be defined and clear. Blending historical examples, case studies, ontology and epistemology, paradigms and data and managing to apply those to a learning process that can be further developed into something that prepares the organisation for further occurrences (rather than recurrences) means that the landscape becomes slightly more confusing. Organisational learning, where there is no discernible learning reference point, for example: learning about the need to lessen cost to the bottom line or reduce workplace violence, can be difficult to initiate and manage; and will certainly have unreliable outcomes. More importantly, the construction of frameworks and ideals that perhaps are unable to accommodate the more dynamic future developments that may occur is just one element that may hamper an ability to realistically orientate towards the future. More importantly than that, the concept of adherence to frameworks and ideals which is so reassuring to humans, the ability to pictorialise our thought processes by following models and supposed realisations of abstract concepts is often the most attractive and simplistic option for organisations that have limited economical and intellectual resource.

In his guide to academic study, Grix (2010[8]) discusses models and their limitations; he considers the use of models to be something that gives us a representation, and an abstract view of reality. Importantly, the work of academics in modelling theories and behaviours may be

---

[8] Grix, J., (2010). The foundations of research. Palgrave Macmillan.

less likely to cause fatal (or at least business fatal) issues than their misapplication in the 'real' world. The conflicting views of the effectiveness of models are an interesting area for discussion when we consider the capability or otherwise of organisations to be able to visualise what may be the dynamics that they really face. The use of a model and its interconnecting lines and boxes indicates a particular type of route that is recommended to be followed; and perhaps the setting of such a pictorial view within the mind of an individual allows us to rest upon that model as the definitive source of action to take. Of course, reality doesn't follow models, incidents don't use models to develop into crises and the use of a model or similar reference point or framework for an individual may not necessarily give them the latitude to be able to deal with developing issues. Models such as those of Turner and Toft[9] are commonly quoted as those with which organisations may become familiar in order that they can develop particular views and capabilities. They use processes to inform organisational learning; but what happens when we need to deviate from process?

There are also many risk models and environmental analysis models such as CARVER, SWOT, 'BowTie' and Reason's 'Swiss Cheese'[10] (the list goes on!), all of which provide a useful learning methodology for individuals who are coming to terms with issues related to risk. The danger perhaps lies in the application of those within organisations and workplaces which even under significant threat are unable to move away from the guidance that they are given. The reliance upon models and ideas that are not necessarily our own (and perhaps have some kudos or brand utility) or potentially restrict our ability to think more freely can have significant and disadvantaging impacts upon our ability to continue to operate as resilient organisations.

---

[9] Turner, B.A. and Toft, B., (2006). Organizational learning from disasters. Key readings in crisis management: Systems and structures for prevention and recovery, pp. 191-204

[10] Reason, J. (2000). Human error: models and management. BMJ : British Medical Journal, 320(7237), pp. 768–770.

Not only that, the persuasiveness and ability of our minds to retain pictorial information more clearly than logical or etymological information perhaps disadvantages us; mentally, we will return to an image of a framework or idea that we have learned to use under specific circumstances. This is not particularly helpful when we need to move into nebulous areas of thought, perception and issues related to the consideration of impacts. Where such problems and issues can be fully manifested is when we consider for organisations how they are able to rationalise what they achieve, and aim to achieve. We also, in a complementary manner, should consider who is working against us. We also need to consider and understand the comprehension of individuals who work with us, against the realities that come from the threat scenario and landscape and of the models and frameworks themselves. The gap between understanding and willingness to engage with the nature of risk and the ability to implement a resilience response is something that merits considerable thought. Let us consider the issue of interest. Not everyone is interested in the requirement or need to protect organisations or to maintain their viability – at least it may not be a preoccupation. Whether they do understand or not may be incidental if their personal aims and objectives are at odds with – or do not recognise those of the organisation.

Although the majority of organisations and individuals may make the right noises, or even assign themselves to the appropriate standards; there are probably few who on a day to day basis do not put other priorities first. The lure of self-promotion and self-preservation in competition as opposed to that of constriction and caution may well be attractive. This is especially true when the enticements of reward in terms of increased profit, or for the individual may see increased pay a bonus or similar reward coming into play, focus changes and shifts; moving away quite distinctly from the concepts related to maintaining organisational continuity and more towards focusing upon the endgame and the reward itself. Clearly, from a resilience and asset protection viewpoint, this is a dangerous route to follow. However, it is probably fair to reiterate that this dangerous route and the behaviours and ideas that underpin this type of approach within organisations are probably not unusual or rare. While the behaviours that we have considered here are probably prevalent in the case of normal and routine issues such as information loss, when we return to consider the more dynamic and new developments such as extremism within universities and the ability of those who wish to influence them using our own technology and infrastructure to do so, we then have a different challenge. How much priority do we apply to dealing with a threat when our own selves are more important? The issue begs the question, how do we balance the imperatives, needs and desires of individuals which are more at the forefront of our thinking than they have ever been before, against the more material issues related to the management and continuation of our organisational capability in the face of dynamic and movable threats?

This challenge implies a need to be able to put in place a counter to develop some sort of process whereby we are able to recognise, manage and overcome deficiencies that are caused by our own preloads and ideas. This process would need to be based upon an effective learning strategy, which in the context of resilience means that organisations be able to put in place something that accommodates these behaviours, as they are natural and characteristic. Our strategy also should enable us to maintain the resilience functions that we need as such that the organisation is able to continue along the route that it needs to thrice and survive. While this challenge is a difficult one to meet; it should not be considered to be insurmountable by the organisation that is able to apply or thinking process to its resilience capability. The development of a more analytical approach; the ability to look beyond the prosaic idea that a framework provides explicit guidance; that calling something a Black Swan[11] allows us to identify and prepare for what may come next is a flawed idea, is something that the resilient organisation needs to consider and nurture. And it is a tricky and complicated issue to overcome. In their discussion of

---

[11] Taleb, N.N., (2010). The black swan:: The impact of the highly improbable Random House. Taleb's expression of the unknown and unpredictable has become a touchstone for those who use the word but do not really understand how to build the capability to absorb the impacts.

"megatrends"[12], Naisbitt and Cracknell considered a series of what they called "new directions" that would transform our lives.

Some of them were more prescient than others, for example the discussion concerning the transformation from an industrial to an information society was one that whilst identifying the direction, probably did not realise with enough clarity that the birth of the digital native would allow the shift to move much more quickly than perhaps was anticipated. Therefore, the understanding that what lies ahead, whilst it can be predictable, is something that we should encompass within our planning and thought processes; we should not perhaps be tied to the frameworks that guide our thoughts. By referencing what we know, in this case that the industrial age was what we knew and the information age was not, we measure our future capabilities (and by inference our capability to respond to change) by that on which we can mentally and psychologically rely. It is probably worth conjecturing that the more adaptive organisation is truly thinking forward; and using less the points of reference that it already has, and more those that may require a little more extension of thought and imagination.

Those who are inclined towards looking into academic theories might want to spend some time thinking about concepts and ideas related to 'Groupthink' and 'Communities of Practice'. In his work on Groupthink, Janis (1982[13]) considered that there have been multiple incorrect decisions made by groups of highly capable people who as an entity convince themselves that those decisions are correct. In effect, self-persuasion, self-affirmation and other more base instincts overcome what would be common-sense managerial decision making processes. It may be familiar to many of us; and the really important issue is that the overriding view of the many (and certainly the more powerful), in human behaviour terms, will always marginalise those

---

[12] Naisbitt, John, and J. Cracknell. (1984). Megatrends: Ten new directions transforming our lives. No. 04; HN59. 2, N3. New York: Warner Books.

[13] Janis, I.L., (1982). Groupthink: Psychological studies of policy decisions and fiascoes, 2nd ed., (p. 349). Boston: Houghton Mifflin.

with the right thing to say – but without the voice to say it. Eckert (2006[14]) defines 'Communities of Practice' as:

> A collection of people who engage on an ongoing basis in some common endeavor. Communities of practice emerge in response to common interest or position, and play an important role in forming their members' participation in, and orientation to, the world around them.
>
> (Eckert, 2006)

This is based on hypotheses by Wenger (1999[15]) and others such as Lave (1991[16]) who see the positive outcomes quite clearly in the context of educational settings and in the development of effective and efficient teams. Functionally, this probably makes sense; however, when we have collective decision making that is one issue; good or bad. When we have both flawed and incorrect decision making underpinned by misunderstandings and the application of flawed ideas. Where, in the discussions of which element of organisational resilience does the Groupthink happen? When do the communities of practice self-endorse their concepts, ideas and prejudices into the standards, guidance and organisational behaviours that blight static and poorly or partially resilient organisations? Consensus can be powerful, agreement can be beneficial; but the outcomes may not always (or often) be the most beneficial for the organisation. The discussion around this is not confined to groups and organisations; Thompson, Ellis and Wildavsky (1990[17]) considered that there are multiple theories, contributing levels of influence, perspectives, issues, concepts and approaches that shape ideas and cultures, and further

---

[14] Eckert, P., (2006). Communities of practice. Encyclopedia of language and linguistics, 2(2006), pp. 683-685.

[15] Wenger, E., (1999). Communities of practice: Learning, meaning, and identity. Cambridge university press.

[16] Lave, J., (1991). Situating learning in communities of practice. Perspectives on socially shared cognition, 2, pp. 63-82.

[17] Thompson, M., Ellis, R. and Wildavsky, A., (1990). Cultural theory. Westview Press

complicate any linear idea of what may be considered to be straightforward problems, raising straightforward issues, and requiring straightforward solutions. The complications of reality; of the ways that we are – affect our ability to think and act in automatic logic.

So, where does this leave us? The culture and imbued human behaviour which means that we tend to look for the crutches and support systems that give us the familiarity and guidance that we need to develop a capability is important. We all need a point of reference. However, where the situation around risk and resilience can move quickly and dynamically, we need to be able to consider where the next challenges will come from; and in these cases fixed mind-sets will not have the necessary latitude and capability to make a good fit. Also, if we accept, or at least consider that the issues that we are raising here are to an extent general human traits, then we also need to accept that there is a significant challenge involved in developing change in those human traits. It is by no means a simple task to re-educate individuals to move away from "hardwired" thought processes and behavioural patterns. However, if we also consider and perhaps accept that those thought processes and behavioural patterns may allow or offer some sort of gateway for risks and threats to impact upon an organisation, then we do need to consider that there is a requirement for some methodologies that allow us to change those behaviours. This change in approach is by no means simple, and it is by no means guaranteed that the theoretical discussion that we are having here can be applied in any significant way towards the organisation that is looking to improve security or resilience. What we can do is to look to examples and case studies where we have seen the effectiveness of cultural change within organisations; they may not necessarily be linked to security or resilience processes, but the ability to overcome embedded and entrenched viewpoints and opinions may be something that could be applied in a different way to the particular challenges of asset protection and organisational continuity development. If we consider any number of organisations that have risen to the challenge of change management, we do need to be sure that we do not create a new model in itself. We do need to be careful, if we are cautioning against a reliance upon ideas and models that allow us to prop up our own belief set; we should also caution against a reliance on case studies as the placebo that cures all but changes nothing.

The feeling that something has happened to change the organisation because we have made it happen does not necessarily mean that it has been effective. Change processes and the development of an imbued attitudinal shift would need to be validated and tested in some depth in order to ensure that whatever the organisation has undertaken and accepted in terms of developing processes and ideas to overcome deficiencies have become equally effective in managing the risk issues. In thinking about where this discussion may take us; the consideration of our weaknesses as well as our strengths is an important component of successful and resilience-orientated organisations. Charlotte Perkins Gilman, whose quotation leads this chapter, also had another quotation which is appropriate to the discussion:

> The softest, freest, most pliable and changeful living substance is the brain - the hardest and most iron-bound as well.
>
> (Charlotte Perkins Gilman)

Miss Gilman was not a resilience expert; but clearly she had some significant insight into the difficulties with which human beings are able to adapt their thoughts and reactions to what goes on around them. In the resilience context, the effect of such difficulties can be clearly felt. The idea that we are fixed in our views, and that our views and preconceptions can sometimes override and overrule the important and sensible decisions that we may need to take become stark when we consider the Prevent issue that was discussed in this paper. The idea that technology can be a source of competitive advantage rather than something to be resisted is grasped at various levels by various types of people; however, the resistance to change that technology brings can cause significant issues if the resistance (and the sense of it) overrides the understanding of beneficial effect. Organisations do need to become learning organisations, where they are not already so. Also, the individuals who build the systems and comprise the components of these organisations need to become learning individuals. There is a requirement to move away from the fixedness of vision that models can bring; unless there is a significant understanding that the value of a model is basic; they need to think and develop ideas upon it and around it is advanced, and the ability to develop the organisational resilience capability that is required goes beyond the advanced. This is in recognition of the fact that the dynamics of threat and risk are also advanced, and moving in ways that can impact upon the unprepared and unable to consider the advantages and disadvantages of change acceptance. The idea of predictability and of reliance upon trend analysis is something that requires thought. The evidence of academic study is quite clear; prediction and forecasting rely upon something more than guesswork and simply looking ahead and are dependent upon the multiple variables that we as human beings bring to the overall equation. The idea that the voice of the many is more persuasive than others is important to understand; it is also important to understand that the voice of the many may not necessarily be the truest or firmest basis for the development of organisational capability and not only in terms of resilience. The overall result of failure to overcome our own instinctive responses will be failure. The approaches to the development of more flexibility in thought and response are something that any organisation that aspires to resilience should consider carefully. The future threat landscape and the ability of organisations to operate within that landscape are fundamentally change based; a lack of adaptability will increase the risks exponentially.

Chapter 7

Understanding Organised Crime: A Rationalized and Modern Perspective for Law Enforcement

Dr Nicholas Gilmour

The term 'organised crime' inspires lengthy discussion throughout academic and practitioner environments. Still, what do we really know about the underlying activities associated with organised crime and how do we know law enforcements comprehension of organised crime is correct? It seems likely, based on current comprehension of organised crime that many of the discussions stem from historical data and wide-ranging perceptions by law enforcement personnel. In particular instances, all-purpose observations have formed the foundation of explicit discussions determining law enforcement and preventative activities. This review seeks to examine the persistent challenges that prevent law enforcement from gaining a comprehensive understanding of organised crime. To conclude, the review considers how persistent challenges are likely to continue to influence the future of law enforcement driven activities against organised crime.

Introduction

A structured group of three or more persons, existing for a period of time and acting in concert with the aim of committing one or more serious offences [...] in order to obtain, directly or indirectly, a financial or other material benefit.

(United Nations Convention against Transnational Organised Crime)

Organised Crime – Defining the Basic Premise

Such is the diversity of organised criminal activities that no single definition illustrating the true nature of organised crime remains one of the biggest hazards for those involved in the development of policies associated with the prevention and investigation of organised criminal activities. Countless groups, agencies, and law enforcement organisations have attempted through intellectual debate to define organised crime, yet intuitively the term organised crime has led us to think of crimes and not of criminals. According to Grabosky (2013), approximately 150 accepted definitions of organised crime exist in security literature – aiming to represent a phenomenon that has existed since international trade commenced and the forming of national governments. The term 'organised crime' has become synonymous with the organisation of loose networks, motivated by profit, no longer bound by the constraints of state borders (Senior, 2010; Fourie et al., 2014; Green, 2013). However, as debates continue on the definition of organised, the business comparable enterprise that organised crime outwardly represents introduces further debate as to how 'organised' organised crime really is.

Conversely, theorists and decision makers have grappled with two competing definitions, those that focus on groups of people (Cressey, 1969; Finckenauer, 2005) (see also Levi and Maguire, 2004), and those that focus on types of crime (UNODC, 2010). Although both schools of thought provide useful points of view, neither describes sufficiently the reality of the contemporary global environment in which organised crime exists or what defines the term 'organised'. Nardo (2008) argues that modern society has 'almost fatally' chosen to define organised crime, yet Gilmour (2008) suggests the term 'organised crime' intuitively focuses discussion towards crimes types – not the criminals themselves. Furthermore, Gilmour describes crime types such as money laundering and human trafficking, claiming that it is perhaps easier to frame in the imagination than the (arguably) loose networks of people that control these illicit trades.

Similarly, definitions of organised crime fail to confirm whether a contextual understanding is required of the term 'organisation' and its relevance to facilitating certain serious criminal activities (Levi and Maguire, 2004). Although academic literature frequently questions how 'organised' organised crime actually is, highlighting scenarios which involve 'autonomously acting offenders that may or may not be cooperating with other offenders on a continuous basis' (von Lampe 2012b, p. 183), it is now accepted organised criminals are brought together in 'networks' rather than 'organisations' (see Bruinsma & Bernasco, 2004; Kenney, 2007; Williams, 2001). This amalgamation of organised crime practices incorporates, according to research by Kleemans and Van de Bunt (2008), 'interfaces' between legal and illegal actors that routinely convene allowing for occupations, work relations and work settings to provide opportunities for organised criminal activities. Interaction created by organised crime related to work, social ties, international contacts and travel movements then facilitate the creation of organised networks. Consequently, organised criminal groups no longer solely exist as hierarchical structures, recognised instead by loose sprawling networks where criminals work together to exploit new market opportunities — locally within their 'home surroundings' and internationally. To facilitate transnational opportunities, criminals have increased their incidence of temporary alliances among criminal groups by utilising 'service providers' such as lawyers, accountants and business owners.

The diversity of crimes in which 'organised crime' is actively involved allows networks to work 'two-fold' to increase profit, reduce risk and establish working opportunities through a 'supply and demand' aligned business structure. The clear preoccupation with generating the greatest available profit has meant resources, skills and knowledge have driven the exposure for international opportunities and activities. By seizing on new technologies, organised crime has improved horizontal network structures that despite the best efforts of law enforcement agencies indicate most crimes remain difficult to detect and prevent. In the growing industry, accountants, lawyers, financial advisers, bankers, and chemists profoundly support such organised criminal activities (See for example: Europol, 2013; ACC, 2013b), making the identification, monitoring, and disruption of such groups a momentous challenge.

Understanding Organised Crime – the Enduring Challenges

Organised crime has developed at an exceptional rate, outperforming international corporations for global coverage — allowing it to operate effectively across international borders, enlarge activities and capitalise on opportunities in a range of illicit markets (Ganapathy & Broadhurst, 2008). Organised crime is no longer a domestic or local problem. Established as borderless in nature by Godson and Williams (2001), the persuasiveness of organised crime has continued to undermine traditional methods of law enforcement, forcing criminal justice agencies to routinely reassess their competence in tackling organised crime (Findlay 1995; see also Harfield, 2008b).

According to Jesperson (2014, p. 150), although 'governments, the EU and UN have renewed their commitment to address organised crime, they are not equipped with the knowledge to adequately and consistently understand the changing dynamics of organised crime or even the scale, impact and costs of criminal activity'. Hence, law enforcement agencies and other bodies focused on the fight against organised crime have continued to play 'second fiddle' to the organised criminal who remains better resourced and free to move beyond sovereign borders. This ability of the organised criminal has led to law enforcement agencies focusing on illicit markets rather than organised criminal groups (Ratcliffe, et al., 2014) an approach which has caused governments and policy makers to frame conceivable notions of drug importation, money laundering, and human trafficking instead of identifying the true nature of events that involve loose networks controlling illicit trades. Clearly, this has caused concern, as Gilmour (2008, p.20) suggests that where a law enforcement service is intelligence-led, 'it is the criminal who ought to be our focus, not the crime'. However, the challenge for law enforcement has always been the need to gather data detailed enough to support a factual understanding of organised crime (Albanese, 2001).

A number of persistent challenges preventing law enforcement from gaining a comprehensive understanding of organised crime exist. Several of these challenges are now examined.

Scope of Activities

Organised criminal activities are, according to Albanese (2004) (see also Levi and Maguire, 2004), generally portrayed through three specific types: the provision of illicit goods (e.g. sale and distribution of illicit drugs and sale of stolen property); the provision of illicit services (e.g. loansharking, people smuggling and prostitution) and the infiltration or abuse of legitimate business (e.g. labour racketeering and protectionism). Consistently, this scope in activities falls outside the scope of any one agency (as discussed in Savona et al., 2005) and beyond the competence of traditional investigative agencies' within the criminal justice sector (Findlay, 1995, p. 282; see also Sheptycki, 2007a). Furthermore, increased wealth gaps, uneven income, and expanding urban populations are intensifying criminal economies and encouraging demand for cheaper contraband goods, indicating how the scale of activities is likely to develop even further.

In seeking out the skills, knowledge and support from professionals to penetrate new markets and earn greater profit, organised crime has become better educated, skilled and resourced than its law enforcement counterparts. Partially constrained and occasionally isolated by preventative measures, the activities involving organised crime remain, unsurprisingly, hard to track (Wainwright and Waites, 2014). A distinct trend is the approach taken by organised crime towards changes in world markets and global regulation — responding pro-actively to exploit new opportunities in emerging markets with speed and intensity. Through the emergent phenomena of illegal markets (Reuter, 1983; Van Duyne, 1995) and the positioning of groups and individuals across networks to support offender networking (Morselli, 2009; Malm et al., 2011), organised crime continues to diversify its activities to defeat sovereign restrained preventative and investigative actions by law enforcement.

Group Dynamics

Hierarchical structured groups comprising of close associates and/or family members, some of whom are based overseas do still exist, although in many instances structure is irrelevant, lessened by the importance of trust and reputation. Today, criminal markets provide network-based systems that perform through the discreet behaviour of independent players in what is, according to Nardo (2008) a flexible and general regulatory framework. Although recognised as willing to develop partnerships benefiting criminal activities, organised criminals tend to stay away from tarnished reputations. Whilst new and untested criminal associates remain slow to be embraced, the challenges associated with various cultures and languages remains a consistent problem for law enforcement agencies. Silverstone (2011) recognises this problem by highlighting how, in Chinese language newspapers, illegal employment opportunities remain openly advertised. Likewise, social ties in activities associated with cyber crime complicate the structure of organised criminal groups that operate in loose networks (Bullock et al., 2013) where individuals, pairs or small groups bring associates and contacts together to work on particular enterprises across multiple crime types.

Whilst opportunities for criminally engaged activities continue, understanding of group and partnership formation has become all too common in an effort to decipher the complexities of organised crime. Co-offending between criminal enterprises (Malm, et al., 2011) is becoming more evident as law enforcement begins to understand the benefits of network analysis (Schwarts and Rouselle, 2009). While concepts of network analysis suggest approaches to criminal network formation and function (Mackensie and Hamilton-Smith, 2011), the typical problem is that once a person is removed (through arrest or death), another person takes their place in the network.

Cross Border Context

Group dynamics amidst the activities in which organised crime are involved, have driven the cross border element of organised crime. Although, according to von Lampe (2012a) this is not always with such ease, as political borders, legal, cultural and language barriers pose substantial challenges for criminals. Globalisation has nevertheless reshaped the threats associated with organised crime at the transnational level (Ayling and Mann, 2012). Today, people and goods have greater freedom and greater ability to move, spawned by decreases in the costs associated with international travel, the transportation of goods, and the removal of visa requirements. It follows therefore, that the diversity of organised criminal activities has meant organised crime groups transcend local authority, policing and national boundaries (Harfield, 2008a). Hence, the nature of organised criminality has led to organised crime groups operating on an international scale, seeking out lucrative opportunities for crime and sanctuaries in which to evade prosecution (see Victoroff, 2005). Third world and transition countries with weak or acquiescent governments and inappropriate domestic legislation (Savona, et al., 2005) have further assisted organised crime by providing 'safe havens' in which to operate (see Williams and Godson, 2002; Wagley, 2006).

Sharing of Intelligence

Law enforcement continues to rely heavily on data sharing across international borders. However, uncertainty, risk, and fear of reputation, have amplified the challenges surrounding the sharing of intelligence in the fight against organised crime. While countries such as the United Kingdom seek to "maintain a comprehensive intelligence picture of the threats, harm and risks to the United Kingdom from organised criminals" (Home Office, 2011, p. 13), the overarching frameworks underpinning cross border sharing of information and intelligence are overshadowed by many external issues. These include those sitting alongside human rights, divergent legal systems, traditions, and the administrative capacity of agencies (Block, 2008), in addition to many basic challenges aligned to the lawful collection of intelligence from foreign nationals and the need for translation (Lacsko and Thompson, 2000).

The Implications of Such Challenges on Preventative and Investigative Activities

Time and competing priorities remain on going issues for law enforcement agencies around the globe, with recent cutbacks and austerity measures implemented by national governments having forced a realignment of policing priorities. Prosecution costs are expensive and not always successful, while at the same time organised crime has access to vast financial capital — something law enforcement has not always been able to rely on. Equally, organised crime actively reinvests profits to ensure future success. The challenges these factors place upon law enforcement agencies was publically identified in 2015 by the UK Home Secretary Theresa May during the introduction of the Serious Crime Bill that created new powers to seize assets and money from crime gangs:

> Crime is changing and the criminal justice system is still not keeping up. The challenge from serious crime is increasing, not falling and more needs to be done. Violent crime is increasing yet fewer violent crimes are being prosecuted or convicted. More sexual offences are being reported but fewer are reaching conviction. Reported rapes and domestic violence are increasing yet fewer are reaching conviction. Far fewer drugs are being seized on their way into this country, online crime is escalating exponentially, and police are not equipped to keep up. So the problem is getting worse and not better.
>
> (Daily Mail, 2015)

In recognising the enduring challenges inhibiting a comprehensive understanding of organised crime, it is appropriate to acknowledge the pressure such challenges then create in fighting organised crime. Organised crime has become a major policy issue across the Western world since the middle of 1990's, employed by political elites as a tool for promoting their vision of political and social order. Agencies such as the Australian Crime Commission (ACC) have nevertheless recognised the need to understand organised crime by responding purposefully to threats such as cybercrime and financial crime. By working with 'other partners, such as policy makers, private industry and international agencies to develop understanding and a response …from serious and organised crime' (ACC, 2013a, 18:1), the ACC has sought to gain a national intelligence picture on current and emerging threats. This approach — similar to other strategies across law enforcement agencies worldwide — recognises the need to understand organised crime and the practices that lie behind the illicit activities commonly associated with organised criminals. However, the challenges which organised crime presents, as discussed in the previous section, influence agencies in understanding organised crime. This section of the review examines how persistent challenges will continue to influence the future of law enforcement driven activities against organised crime.

Accuracy of Knowledge

While limitations in research opportunities and capabilities have distorted understanding of organised crime, the level of inaccuracy associated with such practices influence the processes adopted to investigate and prevent organised crime. As von Lampe (2012b) identifies, data collection typically consists of three separate means: observations, interviews, and the retrieval of documentation. Although data sources are combined to provide satisfactory details, the focus on participant observations has been limited due to the inherent risks and the clandestine nature of organised crime. This suggests organised crime is likely to be enormously different from the formal criteria presented by international law enforcement agencies. While it is feasible to overcome the fact there is no single definition, the challenges created by activities, group dynamics and the cross border context of organised crime, suggest the accuracy of the data held by law enforcement agencies is also ill defined. Clearly, organised crime participants do not wish to provide any insight into their activities — especially activities considered far removed from organised criminality. As Dean et al., (2008) and Fahsing et al., (2007) reveal, fighting organised crime requires accurate knowledge concerning the criminal organisation, including the scale, impacts, costs and victims to form a semi-structured benchmark in status. This includes the various enablers that lie behind the organised criminality. Examining crimes as a separate illegal market only seeks to highlight the lack of comparisons across space and time, the problem of congruence and compatibility of data (Borum, 2004) therefore highlighting how changes to organised crime are typically no longer noticeable.

Understanding organised crime is therefore not a static process. Although case studies provide indicators for good/best practice in a range of fields and remain popular discussion points for determining methods through which to stop organised crime, in practical terms they set unhelpful benchmarks in terms of overall success — presenting only a 'snap shot' of a particular criminal landscape. Analysis therefore requires an approach that is sensitive to the changes taking place — especially those influencing illicit activities and criminal formations (Albanese, 2000). Criminals seek out new opportunities, prioritise, and change frequently as group dynamics transform to overcome law enforcement activities. Appropriately, law enforcement is beginning to now recognise the complexity of organised crime embedded in diaspora communities (see Beare, 1996; Kleemans and Van de Bunt, 2008; Borum, 2004; Victoroff, 2005) and the challenges this brings to investigations.

Accuracy of knowledge primarily derives from successful intelligence led activities (HM Govt., 2004), meaning high quality intelligence can simultaneously drive the fight against organised crime. Understanding the scale and importance of the threats posed by individuals allows law enforcement to prioritise targets. The challenge here within law enforcement, is that new challenges are typically deemed uncountable, instead seen as speculative and hypothetical — therefore not always receiving the timely and proactive attention by law enforcement which they deserve.

Strategic Direction

Strategies aligned to the prevention and detection of organised crime are widespread, yet inherently such strategies are based only on the visible activities organised crime is involved in. According to Jasperson (2014, p. 151), 'the 2011 European Police Chiefs conference highlighted limited capacity for anticipating new trends amongst law enforcement agencies, particularly in relation to crimes not already considered a priority'. Likewise, as already reviewed, research limitations and the accuracy of knowledge held by law enforcement agencies have duly created an illusion that existing strategic priorities remain applicable.

Typically, strategic direction towards fighting organised crime has been driven by threat assessments depicting a narrow focus — despite their compilation by intelligence experts and crime analysts. Although strategies routinely describe the need and willingness to reduce the harm of organised crime, such strategies have become, in real terms unworkable, as ground level understanding of the capabilities of organised crime disappears in the consequences of modern policing, government priorities, and austerity measures. In operational terms, this equates to general assessments simply advising priority-setting processes in relation to out dated or inaccurate organised crime related issues or criminal networks. To be effective, objectives must instead align to accurate descriptive analysis and factual evidence as opposed to existing knowledge driving strategy development and later driving knowledge collection.

Although this 'cycle' may create clarity and an easy to follow process, it suppresses opportunities to step outside the known environment, to establish clarity of intelligence and question current understanding. This cylindrical process linking strategies and knowledge collection together indicates, somewhat awkwardly, that the organisation of organised crime policing is ill organised and compounded by insufficient accountability across police structures (Sheptycki, 2002; Desroches, 2005).

Threat Determination

The determination of threat in relation to organised crime is inherently difficult for law enforcement to establish, with previous assessments having become self-fulfilling prophecies (Sheptycki, 2007b; Mittelman & Johnston, 1999; Ridley, 2008). Research on organised crime is difficult to conduct and the accuracy of data difficult to corroborate. Consequently, knowledge and intelligence to support priority setting can become misaligned, especially if knowledge and intelligence collection do not focus on real world activities. Disturbingly, organised crime remains something recognised only when seen first-hand (Le, et al. 2013, p. 74) and therefore limiting the accuracy of assessments that seek to identify risks associated with different types of organised crime activities, markets and enterprises (Van der Beken, 2004). Importantly, studies on the consequences of organised crime remain surpassed by the focus on threat (Borum, 2004) and solidity across organised crime investigations. However, organised crime is not typically viewed as an integral part of society, portrayed instead as an external threat to peaceful and law-abiding institutions. This perception indicates how opportunities to introduce preventative measures can quickly evaporate, allowing overt investigative techniques to become less significant.

To what extent political impetus influences the setting of priorities or the selection of threats is difficult to define. Organised crime seldom registers involvement in licit and illicit activates, therefore, evidence becomes essential in creating accurate assessments of its impact on society. The challenge, however, in determining the greatest threat becomes one of finding sufficient points of reference, before attempting to connect them together in a meaningful manner. The question that then arises is whether threat determination can, based on the occurrence of change to the threats posed, actually play into the hands of the embryonic organised criminal.

Discussion

Gaining an accurate appreciation of the strengths and weaknesses of each organised crime group has developed into a central activity for many law enforcement agencies across the globe (Ratcliffe, et al., 2014). Nevertheless, it remains notoriously difficult to develop a clear picture regarding the scale of the overall problem — meaning reliable global assessments are difficult to produce. Furthermore, the global promotion of the war on organised crime has promoted preventative measures that seek to ambitiously prevent the entire scope of organised criminal activities. Yet, the narrow focus by law enforcement in addressing organised crime has created a number of shortcomings, including inconsistencies in legislation, preventative capability, and the willingness to act.

Capable of blending into international commerce, the challenges fostered by legal appearing criminal activities has escalated beyond the generic capacity of law enforcement (Williams, 2001), with recent developments in technology having grown beyond the knowledge base of many in law enforcement. Similarly, the use of the Internet to facilitate organised criminal acts is a threat to law enforcement. This progressively positive aptitude amongst organised crime has enabled [it] to remain several steps ahead of law enforcement. Technology, the Internet, and secret communication — supported by encryption — has further enabled organised criminals to surf open and hidden networks anonymously. Despite having remained efficient 'stand alone' problem solvers, organised crime has begun to purchase the expertise and knowledge of generation Z to maximise opportunities at a rate almost impossible for law enforcement to match — complicating the development of accurate strategies which seek to 'detect, disrupt, prevent, and investigate them' (Saitch, 2002, p. 1).

Asset recovery has altered the approach by law enforcement to tackling organised crime, cultivating a scenario primarily driven by financial benefit alongside a belief the approach is effective and preventative in nature. While this may be appropriate where the definition of organised crime is that which is aligned to those organised criminal activities committed for profit, asset recovery practices have created inaccurate and problematic performance measures. The significant reliance on the notion that seizing criminal assets prevents further criminal activities and discourages others from becoming involved in predicate criminal offences has distorted law enforcements perception of organised crime. Such suggestions have also discouraged law enforcement from recognising the shrewdness criminals actually take in hiding illicitly derived funds and assets and how they survive despite the preventative measures in place — such as asset recover — and the attention their activities frequently generate.

159

Strategic prioritisation also remains a constant challenge for governments and law enforcement. The reality for law enforcement, due to the current generic approach, is that it is almost impossible to accurately understand threats and emerging organised crime trends in such a way as to predict the correct response. Although knowledge of organised crime does exist, as this paper emphasises, it is difficult to establish the true accuracy of such knowledge based on — at the best of times — widely adopted and generic methodologies. Despite the need to gain detailed understanding of organised crime and to determine priority setting, the current amalgamation has failed to create a process in which knowledge assists in creating flexible strategies as opposed to the cylindrical process in which strategy drives knowledge collection and knowledge supports the strategy. This alternative single step process for understanding organised crime purposefully incites the need to collect diverse, consistent data relevant to law enforcement. As discovered, preventing organised crime can no longer be deciphered in a single strategic — long-term plan whilst organised crime remains flexible, adaptive, and willing (without hesitation) to alter direction.

Where a strategy must exist, is around the collection of information on criminals and their responses to interventions. By measuring the performance of preventative activities — not simply based on single case study assessments — it is possible to establish what is happening and what actually works to limit illegal activities. Increasing involvement towards understanding organised crime would assist in overcoming, according to the United Nations Office for Drugs and Crime (2012, p. 54); 'domestic policy and general strategic attitudes including (a) lack of willingness to get involved in a crime that occurred in another country (your crime is not my crime); (b) lack of understanding of local criminal phenomena (c) insufficient crime awareness; (d) non-compliance with international legal instruments; and (e) conflicting perceptions of priority issues at the global and regional level'. This far wider, potentially holistic approach to understanding organised crime supersedes present responses that frequently respond to single criminal activities while failing to recognise the association between criminal groups and criminal practices.

Reducing the growth and development of organised criminal groups also requires understanding their underlying routines, behaviours, and activities. Understanding of organised crime cannot be simplified, simply acknowledging who is involved is not the way forward, as understandably they too fluctuate amidst law enforcement operations. Stepping back, listening, contemplating and asking questions 'how does this undesirable situation persist' and 'what is required to change it' achieves more than the basic research queries relating to generic assessments on perpetrators, structures, methods and the financing of organised criminal groups. When such practices are not incorporated, the result is the creation of subjective and interpretive intelligence products built upon soft intelligence that fails to improve crime detection or provide a deeper understanding of criminal markets. Reducing the complexity of organised crime further ill informs those responsible for challenging preventative models. Money laundering, for example, is not simply placement, layering and integration; it is a complicated process involving many facets that when ignored fail to broaden understanding of *how* and *why* particular methods are chosen (Gilmour, 2014).

No doubt, the complexities of policing organised crime are further complicated by organised crimes ability to discourage law enforcement from understanding the practices it is involved in and the lack of a single definition defining organised crime. On the strength of current understanding surrounding activities associated with organised crime it seems apparent successes to date suggest enforcement agencies, policy makers and governments are incorrectly aligned in the approach they are taking. Still, activities and perceptions can be changed — encouraged by the potential for identifying additional criminal assets, clearer opportunities to limit social harm and the chance to reduce the harm caused by organised crime on society.

Conclusion

The intention of this review was to highlight from a law enforcement perspective the problems associated with understanding activities connected to organised crime. The review sought to examine the persistent challenges that prevent law enforcement from gaining a comprehensive understanding of organised crime — not suggest law enforcement had no future capacity for understanding organised crime. The review identified several major themes and summarised key issues, yet it identified that the single most important challenge facing law enforcement is trying to make up ground on organised crime without reliable data to guide meaningful and purposeful preventative and investigative activities. Bridging the gap between what law enforcement understands and reality may in fact sit uncomfortably with many involved in policy development and law enforcement. As Christiane Kesper – Head of Division at International Development Cooperation declared in 2013 to conference delegates, 'tackling organised crime in a sustainable manner requires the development and implementation of intelligent, multidimensional approaches to untangle networks and address the incentive structures and enabling factors of the various business models' (Rriedrich, 2013, p. 4). As findings on organised crime tend to be alarmist or trigger complacency from those who remain cautious, policy agendas continue to restrict important research necessities.

Such paralysis has clearly established a reluctance to extend generic methodologies — such as those used in money laundering, fraud, human trafficking, and cybercrime. Only by exiling traditional ways of thinking will a truly comprehensive picture of the activities pertaining from organised crime be possible. Simple risk assessments of known organised criminal activities are simply no longer sufficient (Sheptycki, 2007b; Harfield, 2008a). In parallel, a 'bottom-up' approach to data gathering and analysis is necessary to assist in placing value or judgments against particular enterprise based crimes — thus recognising such activities as 'organised'. After all, the present fight against organised crime represents a game of hide and seeks, in which those who are seeking (law enforcement), are doing so while blindfolded.

References

Albanese J. S. (2000). The causes of Organised Crime. Do criminals Organise Around Opportunities for Crime or Do Criminal Opportunities Create New Offenders? *Journal of Contemporary Criminal Justice* 16(4): 409-423.

Albanese J. S. (2001). The prediction and control of organised crime: A risk assessment instrument for targeting law enforcement efforts. *Trends in Organised Crime.* 6(3-4): 4-29.

Albanese J. S. (2004). The prediction and control of organised crime: a risk assessment instrument for targeting law enforcement efforts. In: J.O. Finckenauer and J.L. Schrock, (eds). *Prediction and control of organised crime: the experience of post-Soviet Ukraine.* New Brunswick, NJ: Transaction Publishers, 11-41.

Australian Crime Commission (2013). Strategic Plan 2013–18 Retrieved from https://www.crimecommission.gov.au/sites/default/files/strategic-plan-2013-18.pdf.

Australian Crime Commission (2013a). Organised Crime in Australia 2015 Retrieved from https://www.crimecommission.gov.au/publications/intelligence-products/organised-crime-australia/organised-crime-australia-2015.

Australian Crime Commission (2013b). Organised Crime Groups Fact Sheet. Retrieved from https://www.crimecommission.gov.au/publications/intelligence-products/crime-profile-fact-sheets/organised-crime-groups.

Ayling J. & Mann M. (2012). Capturing organised crime in Australian law. (D. Delaforce, Ed.) Briefing Paper (19). Retrieved from http://www.ceps.edu.au/CMS/Uploads/file/Mann_Ayling%20issue%2019WEB.pdf.

Beare M. E. (1996). *Criminal Conspiracies, Organised Crime in Canada,* Nelson Canada 1996.

Block L. (2008). Combating Organised Crime in Europe: Practicalities of Police Cooperation. *Policing* 2(1): 74-81.

Borum R. (2004). Psychology of terrorism. Tampa: University of South Florida. Retrieved from https://www.ncjrs.gov/pdffiles1/nij/grants/208552.pdf?q=psychology-of-terrorism.

Bruinsma G. & Bernasco W. (2004). Criminal groups and transnational illegal markets: a more detailed examination on the basis of Social Network Theory. *Crime, Law and Social Change,* 41(1): 79–94.

Bruns M. (2015). A network approach to organised crime by the Dutch public sector, *Police Practice and Research: An International Journal* 16:2 161-174.

Bullock R., Clarke R.V. & Tilley N. (2013) *Situational Prevention of Organised Crimes.* Edited by Bullock, R., Clarke, R., and Tilley, N. Crime Science Series. Willan Publishing.

Cressey D. R. (1969). *Theft of the nation: the structure and operations of organised crime in America.* New York: Harper and Row.

Daily Mail (2015). May launches Serious Crime Bill. Retrieved from http://www.dailymail.co.uk/wires/pa/article-2897940/May-launches-Serious-Crime-Bill.html.

Dean G., Fahsing I. A. & Gottschalk P. & Solli-Sæther H. (2008). 'Investigative thinking and creativity: an empirical study of police detectives in Norway', *Int. J. Innovation and Learning,* 5(2): 170–185.

Desroches F. J. (2005). *The crime that pays: Drug trafficking and organised crime in Canada.* Toronto: Canadian Scholars' Press.

European Parliament (2013). The EU response to organised crime. Retrieved from http://www.europarl.europa.eu/RegData/bibliotheque/briefing/2013/130625/LDM_BRI(2013)130625_REV1_EN.pdf.

Europol (2013). SOCTA 2013 EU Serious and Organised Crime Threat Assessment. Retrieved from https://www.europol.europa.eu/sites/default/files/publications/socta2013.pdf.

Fahsing I.A., Filstad C. & Gottschalk P. (2007). 'Research propositions for the use of role models in law enforcement: the case of newcomers in police investigations', *Int. J. Innovation and Learning,* 4(5): 501–515.

Finckenauer J. O. (2005). Problems of definition: what is organised crime? *Trends in Organised Crime,* 8(3): 63-83.

Findlay M. (1995). International Rights and Australian Adaptations: Recent Developments in Criminal Investigation. *Sydney Law Review* 17(2): 278-297.

Fourie L., Sarrafsadeh A., Pang S., Kingston T., Hettema H/ & Watters P. (2014). *The Global Cyber Security Workforce – An On going Human Capital Crisis.* Global Business and Technology Association. Retrieved from http://unitec.researchbank.ac.ns/handle/10652/2457.

Ganapathy, N. & Broadhurst, R. (2008). Organised Crime in Asia: A Review of Problems and Progress. *Asian Journal of Criminology,* 3(1), pp. 1-12.

Gilmour N. (2014). *Understanding Money Laundering – A crime script approach.* European Review of Organised Crime (EROC).

Gilmour S. (2008). Understanding Organised Crime: A Local Perspective *Policing* 2 (1): 18-27.

Godson R. & Williams P. (2001) Strengthening Cooperation against Transnational Crime: A New Security Imperative. In *Combating Transnational Crime: Concepts, Activities and Responses*, edited by Dimitri Vlassis and Phil Williams, 321-355. Oxfordshire: Frank Cass Publishers.

Grabosky P. (2013). Organised crime and the Internet: Implications for national security. *The RUSI Journal* 158 (5): 18-25.

Green A. (2013). Regulatory Impact Statement: All of government response to Organised Crime. Ministry of Justice. Retrieved from http://www.justice.govt.ns/publications/global-publications/r/regulatory-impact-statement-all-of-government-response-to-organised-crime.

Harfield C. (2008a). `Paradigms, Pathologies, and Practicalities-Policing Organised Crime in England and Wales', *Policing: A Journal of Policy and Practice* 2(1): 63-73.

Harfield, C. (2008b). The organisation of 'organised crime policing' and its international context *Criminology & Criminal Justice.* 8(4): 483–507.

HM Govt (2004). One Step Ahead - A 21st Century Strategy to Defeat Organised Crime. Retrieved from https://www.gov.uk/government/uploads/system/uploads/attachment_data/file/251075/6167.pdf.

Home Office (2011). The National Crime Agency A plan for the creation of a national crime-fighting capability. https://www.gov.uk/government/publications/national-crime-agency-a-plan-for-the-creation-of-a-national-crime-fighting-capability .

Home Office (2013). Understanding organised crime: estimating the scale and the social and economic costs. Research Report 73 Retrieved from https://www.gov.uk/government/publications/understanding-organised-crime-estimating-the-scale-and-the-social-and-economic-costs.

Jesperson S. (2014). Bridging the Research and Policy Divide on Organised Crime. *The European Review of Organised Crime* 1(2): 147-157.

Kenney M. (2007). The architecture of drug trafficking: network forms of organisation in the Colombian cocaine trade. *Global Crime*, 8(3): 233–259.

Kleemans E. R. & Van de Bunt H. G. (2008). Organised crime, occupations and opportunity. *Global Crime*, 9(3): 185–197.

Lacsko F. & Thompson D. (eds.) (2000). *Migrant Trafficking and Human Smuggling in Europe: A review of the evidence with case studies from Hungary, Poland and Ukraine Geneva,* International Organisation for Migration.

Le V., Bell P. & Lauchs M. (2013). Elements of best practice in policing transnational organised crime: critical success factors for international cooperation. *International Journal of Management and Administrative Sciences.* 2(3): 24-34.

Levi M. & Maguire M. (2004). Reducing and preventing organised crime: An evidence-based critique. *Crime, Law and Social Change.* 41: 397–469.

Mackensie S. & Hamilton-Smith N. (2011). 'Measuring police impact on organised crime', *Policing: An International Journal of Police Strategies & Management,* 34(1): 7–30.

Malm A., Bichler G. & Nash R. (2011). Co-offending between criminal enterprise groups pages. *Global Crime* 12(2): 112-128.

Mittelman J. H. & Johnston R. (1999). The globalisation of organised crime the courtesan state and the corruption of civil society'. *Global Governance,* 5(1): 103–126.

Morselli C. (2009). *Inside criminal networks.* New York: Springer.

Nardo M. (2008). Organised crime and networking economy: models, features, dynamics and related approaches. *Journal of Money Laundering Control* 11(2): 172-178.

Ratcliffe J. H., Strang S. J. and Taylor R. B. (2014). 'Assessing the success factors of organised crime groups: Intelligence challenges for strategic thinking', *Policing: An International Journal of Police Strategies & Management,* 37(1): 206 – 227.

Reuter (1983). Disorganised Crime: The Economics of the Visible Hand. *Michigan Law Review* 82(4): 1127-1131.

Ridley N. (2008). 'Pan-European Law Enforcement Strategic Analysis: Trendsand Concerns', pp. 131–45 in C. Harfield, A. MacVean, J. Grieve and D. Phillips (eds) *Handbook of Intelligent Policing,* pp. 131–45. Oxford: Oxford University Press.

Rriedrich E. S. (2013). *Being tough is not enough – Curbing Transnational Organised Crime.* Conference Notes. Retrieved from http://www.globalinitiative.net/wpfb-file/fes-being-tough-is-not-enough-curbing-toc-2013-pdf.

Saitch D. (2002). *Trafficking cocaine: Colombian drug entrepreneurs in the Netherlands.* The Hague: Kluwer Law International.

Savona E., Lewis C. & Vettori B. (eds.) (2005). *EUSTOC – Developing an EU Statistical Apparatus for Measuring Organised Crime, Assessing its Risk and Evaluating Organised Crime Policies* (2003 AGIS programme).

Schwarts D. M. & Rouselle T. (2009). 'Using Social Network Analysis to Target Criminal Networks.' *Trends in Organised Crime.* 12(2): 188–207.

Senior A. (2010). *Organised Crime: Combating an Elusive Transnational Threat.* Waikato University.

Sheptycki J. (2002). 'Accountability Across the Policing Field: Towards a General Cartography of Accountability for Post-Modern Policing', *Policing and Society.* 12(4): 323–38.

Sheptycki J. (2007a). 'High Policing in the Security Control Society', *Policing: A Journal of Policy and Practice.* 1(1): 70–9.

Sheptycki J. (2007b). 'Police Ethnography in the House of Serious and Organised Crime', in A. Henry and D. Smith (eds) T*ransformations of Policing*, pp. 51–77. Aldershot: Ashgate.

Silverstone D. (2011). From Triads to snakeheads: organised crime and illegal migration within Britain's Chinese community. *Global Crime* 12(2): 93-111.

United Nations (2012). Digest of organised crime cases. Retrieved from http://www.unodc.org/documents/organised-crime/EnglishDigest_Final301012_30102012.pdf.

UNODC (2010). The globalisation of crime: a transnational organised crime threat assessment. Retrieved from https://www.unodc.org/documents/.../TOCTA_Report_2010_low_res.pdf.

Van der Beken T. (2004). Risky business: A risk-based methodology to measure organised crime. Crime, Law & Social Change 41: 471–516.

van Duyne P. C. (1995). *The Phantom and Threat of Organised Crime.* SDU, The Hague.

Victoroff J. (2005). The mind of the terrorist: A review and critique of psychological approaches. *Journal of Conflict Resolution*, 49(1), 3–42.

von Lampe K. (2012a). chapter in book – *handbook of transnational organised crime*. Edited by Felia and Gilmour.

von Lampe K (2012b). Transnational organised crime challenges for future research. *Crime, Law and Social Change* September 2012b, 58(2): 179-194.

Wagley J. R. (2006). *Transnational organised crime: Principal threats and U.S. responses*. Washington: Congressional Research Service.

Wainwright R. & Waites B. (2014). The Changing Face of Organised Crime: Can Europol keep up? *Organised Crime, Corruption and Crime* Prevention S. Caneppele, F. Calderoni (eds.), Springer International Publishing Switserland.

Williams P. (2001). Transnational criminal networks. In J. Arquilla & D. F. Ronfeldt (Eds.), *Networks and netwars: The future of terror, crime, and militancy* (pp. 61–97). Santa Monica: Rand.

Williams P. & Godson R. (2002). Anticipating organised and transnational crime. Crime, *Law & Social Change*, 37(4): 311–355.

Chapter 8

The Human Dimension: Rehabilitating the Human Terrain System - A People-Centred Approach to Policing Diverse Communities

Simon de Saint-Claire, PhD

In 2006 the US Army introduced the world to the Human Terrain System (HTS) – a programme utilising social scientists, in theatre, to provide much needed cultural intelligence on the local populace. From the outset HTS faced controversy over the [mis]use of academic practice for military application, as well as general criticism over programme effectiveness. Phased out in late 2014, a question mark still remains as to whether shuttering the programme was a wise move, and whether the "cultural knowledge" concept could be revisited for use in non-combat environments, such as humanitarian intervention and post-conflict reconstruction. As a logical progression, this discourse suggests that the Human Terrain System could be rehabilitated for use in International Police Missions - as an aid to Security Sector Reform (SSR) acceptance - and further revised for domestic policing as a non-invasive engagement tool in diverse and multicultural communities. Police authorities[1] already employ a range of mechanisms to engage with society, the most common of which is known as Community-orientated Policing, however Community Policing lacks consensus on model, methodology and definition. Therefore, this contribution further discusses how a socio-cultural approach could provide police authorities with a universal process for dialogue, understanding,

---

[1] For the purpose of this contribution, "police" is used as the all-encompassing term for law enforcement: agencies and functions (i.e. public order, security, prevention, reduction and investigation of crime etc.).

and cooperation within multicultural, disaffected, and marginalised communities.

In the consideration of context, the cultural and historical features of a situation or operation area are perhaps most important of all. Culture and Human Terrain (MOD-UK, JDN 4/13, September 2013)

Part One: Backgrounder

Culture: From "Knowledge" to "Intelligence"

Broadly speaking, culture can be thought of as,

> A shared way of life, customs, beliefs, ideas, social behaviour, patterns and structures of a particular group or people. It is shaped by the political, social, and environmental circumstances in which we live.

Often based on tradition, culture is learned and passed on: it influences our views, beliefs, practices, sense of identity, as well as the way in which we relate to and interact with people from within that culture, external cultures and peoples from other geographic regions.

Before the days of globalisation, affordable travel, the internet, and smartphones, geography (in terms of distance, natural barriers, climate, resources etc.) played a determining role in the formation of language, culture and identity, the results of which can still be seen today through those living in comparative geographic, ethnic and cultural stasis, who have a tendency – conscious or otherwise – towards 'ethnocentrism',

> Seeing and judging other cultures from the perspective of one's own culture; using the culture of one's own group as a standard for the judgement of others....
>
> (Shusta et al., 2015)

The exploration of the above mentioned relationship between people and their physical environment is known as Human Geography, whereas Anthropology examines humans – past and present. Of relevance are the sub-disciplines social anthropology and cultural anthropology, which describe societies and cultural variation around the world, and linguistic anthropology, which investigates the influence of language in social life.

However, these fields have a disposition for academic distance - the "eye of God" - lacking interpersonal engagement. This contrasts with the interactivity of Cultural Intelligence (CQ), which relates to,

> A person's capability to adapt as s/he interacts with others from different cultural regions.
>
> (Earley, 2002)

Cultural Intelligence refers to and measures the perceptive, motivational, and behavioural ability to understand and effectively respond to the beliefs, values, attitudes, and behaviours of groups - and individuals - under complex and changing circumstances in order to influence change (Earley, 2002). Often used in business and diplomacy, CQ can be viewed as a collective utilisation of anthropology, strategic communication, psychology, sociology, geo-politics, and history to make informed decisions. In layman's terms, CQ can be described as a measuring stick of application, rather than the tool itself.

In the context of the aforementioned interdisciplinary fields, the "Human Terrain" refers to a target population within a designated area. The "Human Terrain System" was the US Military application of Human Terrain analysis (research, data collection and analysis), specifically for intelligence purposes.

The Human Terrain System

First conceived by Montgomery McFate[2] and Andrea Jackson[3] as the "Pentagon Office of Operational Cultural Knowledge" (2005[4]), the Human Terrain System (HTS) was a United States Army programme[5] aimed at identifying socio-cultural knowledge deficiencies in the military's understanding of local populations within a deployment area - as witnessed during the US-led invasion and subsequent occupation of Afghanistan and Iraq, where communities were inadvertently alienated due to cultural ambivalence and ignorance.

HTS teams were comprised of social scientists from the mixed disciplines of anthropology, ethnology, sociology, political science, theology, and area studies as a means for military commanders to gain a clearer understanding of the "human terrain" (i.e. the local populace), thus providing an intelligence enabling insight within a given area of operation, for eventual use in the Military Decision Making Process (MDMP[6]). Similar to the aims of Psychological Operations (PSYOPS), and to a lesser extent Civil-Military Cooperation (CIMIC[7]), HTS could be effectively used as a non-kinetic tool to counter insurgency... to "win hearts and minds", through bridge-building, mutual understanding, developing trust and cooperation – something digestible to sceptical academia.

Or it could be used as a Military Intelligence tool – and all that implies.

---

[2] Dr. Montgomery McFate Profile: http://montgomerymcfate.com/bio/ (accessed 18 April 2016).

[3] Ms. Andrea Jackson is a US military cultural training and intelligence specialist.

[4] *"An Organizational Solution for DOD's Cultural Knowledge Needs"*, http://www.au.af.mil/au/awc/awcgate/milreview/mcfate2.pdf (accessed 18 April 2016).

[5] Under the auspices of the United States Army Training and Doctrine Command (TRADOC).

[6] 7-step process for military decision making, linked to Troop Leading Procedures and Operations orders.

[7] Specifically *"Support to the Force"* and *"Support to Civil Actors and their Environment"*, NATO Allied Joint Doctrine for Civil-Military Cooperation, Chapter 2: CIMIC in Mission Theatres and Operations (pp. 4-5).

Launched in February 2007, HTS quickly became the subject of controversy, drawing heavy criticism from journalists, military officials, [former] HTS personnel, and most notably the Executive Board of the American Anthropological Association (AAA), which claimed the programme contravened its Code of Ethics, betraying,

> Basic ethical standards for protecting the interests and well-being of studied populations.

> (Price, 2011)

The 74-page "Final Report on the Army's Human Terrain Proof-of-Concept System", concluding that,

> When ethnographic investigation is determined by military missions, not subject to external review, where data collection occurs in the context of war, integrated into the goals of counterinsurgency, and in a potentially coercive environment – all characteristic features of the HTS concept and its application – it can no longer be considered a legitimate professional exercise of anthropology.[8]

Academic social research relies on ethical impartiality; HTS arguably misused an academic discipline as a means for strategic intelligence gathering, essentially weaponising Anthropology [et al] as a tool to manipulate, exploit weakness and dominate.

Controversy aside, with the ending of combat operations in Afghanistan and Iraq, HTS teams were withdrawn and the programme was effectively mothballed in September 2014.

Although polarising, HTS went on to inspire similar though broader programmes, such as the Department of Defense's Minerva Initiative[9].

---

[8] CEAUSSIC Releases Final Report on Army HTS Program (http://www.americananthro.org/issues/policy-advocacy/statement-on-HTS.cfm - accessed 18 April 2016).

[9] Minerva Initiative Program History & Overview (http://minerva.dtic.mil/overview.html - accessed 18 April 2016).

New but Old – "Reinventing the Wheel"

Despite its recent prominence in military circles, the concept of the Human Terrain System – utilising socio-cultural knowledge for strategic purposes – is nothing new. In their book "Science Goes to War: The Human Terrain System in Iraq and Afghanistan" (2015), Dr. Montgomery McFate and Dr. Janice H. Lawrence highlight this very point by quoting Chinese military strategist Sun Tzu,

> If you know the enemy and know yourself, you need not fear the result of a hundred battles. If you know yourself but not the enemy, for every victory gained you will also suffer a defeat. If you know neither the enemy nor yourself, you will succumb in every battle.
>
> (Chapter III - Strategic Attack, Art of War)

Perhaps Sun Tzu himself had been inspired by an older Chinese proverb,

> Those who understand others as well as themselves will be granted success in a thousand encounters.
>
> (Schmidt, 2007, Preface XIV)

Even so, the concept of utilising anthropological theory as a military asset was already well established throughout the period of colonisation (Whitehead, 2009), whilst the term Human Terrain first surfaced in the late 1960's in relation to counter-insurgency during the Vietnam War, and later applied to the Black Panther movement in the USA (for similar reasons).

Britannia: Culture and Human Terrain

> Knowledge is power.
> Sir Francis Bacon (Meditationes Sacræ. De Hæresibus, 1597)

By the end of Queen Victoria's rule, the British Empire had colonised as much as 40% of the world. It's no secret that they did so through domination of the seas, and the superior use of land forces. Culture, however, played an equally vital role in the building and securing of their vast empire.

The British Military have had a long tradition of utilising cultural knowledge as an intelligence tool. One need only look at the colonial strategy of "divide and conquer"[10], utilising the principle of the "enemy of mine enemy is my friend"[11] as effectively demonstrated in India through the East India Company, and much later in Kenya as a tool of repression during the Mau Mau Uprising (1952-1959)[12].

Although aims and methodology changed, the British learned well their lessons of cultural knowledge, brought home from the 'battle fields' of North Ireland (McFate, 2014), as discussed in the UK Ministry of Defence's Joint Doctrine Publication 04 "Understanding",

> By the early-1980s, however, through a process of learning and adapting, the military forces understood better the dynamics of the theatre in terms of the roles played by individual and group actors, including paramilitary groups.

From the late-1980's, unlike their US counterparts[13], the UK military developed a comprehensive pre-deployment training programme. Ministry of Defence (MOD-UK) correspondence[14] states that,

> In any given mission area, every All Ranks Briefing (ARB) will contain presentations from various Subject Matter Experts (SMEs) to provide an understanding of the geo-political situation there. Units would then begin their own preparations, including a

---

[10] The British manipulated and used rival tribes (by allying with one) to fight against each other as a means to weaken them both, thus strengthening the British position.

[11] Kautilya: The Arthashastra (4th century BC).

[12] The British effectively used rival tribes against each other as a means to weaken them both, whilst strengthening the British position.

[13] The US Armed Forces initiated pre-deployment orientation training in 2003.

[14] In personal correspondence, received under the Freedom of Information Act (2000) on 4 July 2016.

conceptual cadre, and these will draw in experts from across a range of national and international agencies to develop the understanding of the country, the politics and the history.

In all operations they utilise the services of,

A Cultural Advisor (CULAD) to deliver country specific advice and guidance. This takes the form of a one to one briefing with the commander, and a more generic brief to the ARB audience. During individual Mission Specific Training (iMST), nominated individuals will receive varying levels of language training and during the ARB we cover basic phrases as well as issuing language cards as appropriate and where available.

This approach is reflected in the current Joint Doctrine Note 4/13 "Culture and Human Terrain" (JDN 4/13, September 2013), which states its purpose as,

Contribut[ing] to wider policies and training aimed at strengthening cultural capability, and should inspire cultural thinking in everything we do.

Under "Context" the JDN 4/13 continues,
All conflict is about people; their behaviours, attitudes, fears, social structures, family and ideological ties and narratives. Understanding the human dimensions of conflict is therefore a critical determinant in preventing conflict, shaping it and influencing the actors involved. It contributes to our strategic awareness, our ability to plan[…], and it helps us identify threats and opportunities. It enables us to enhance relations with our existing allies, friends and strategic partners, and to nurture emerging relationships.

It is perhaps because of this approach that the UK Military did not suffer the professional and academic backlash that beset the Human Terrain System.

That is not to say that the UK's field implementation proved superior. In fact, a 2015 study on the British Army's Afghanistan Campaign (HERRICK) reached the conclusion that raw intelligence feeds tended to fixate, ignoring other in-field aspects, and stove-pipe information, leading to the poor execution of Human Terrain Analysis (HTA). Despite the UK's long history of cultural knowledge implementation, it was US HTS civilian contractors (social scientists) who provided the only usable (and sophisticated) 'in-theatre' strategic HTA capability[15].

Methodology and Utilisation

Based on well-honed academic research methodology, HTS effectively mapped the human terrain in areas where the military were deployed by creating databases of information concerning local leaders, tribes and ethnic groups, social groups, disputes and tensions (historic, political, territorial), economic issues, and social problems. This information – obtained through observation, monitoring, interviews and surveys - was compiled and analysed, the results of which were used to provide on-the-spot advice to the military. The data was then archived, for future access by military and government agencies.

Even under the cloud of controversy - and facing internal obstacles - the Human Terrain System proved its worth, achieving programme goals and changing the way the US Military approached future foreign deployments.

However, to further tap the potential of HTS, the military could have learned much from the business sector, which had already fully embraced the importance of intercultural knowledge from the mid-1960's, spawning Organisational Culture and Communication, Intercultural Communication, Cultural Intelligence, and Social Intelligence.

Seen as Intercultural Studies pioneers, social scientists Geert Hofstede and Edward T. Hall proposed several frameworks pertaining to perceptions on how individuals, groups, and societies, organise, perceive, and communicate.

---

[15] "*Human Terrain Understanding*" (5.3.11-12), in "*Operation HERRICK Campaign Study*" (MOD-UK, 2015).

Hofstede[16] developed the seminal "Dimensions of Work-Related Values" (1967-1973), which by 1980 had been developed into a model that identified four primary dimensions in differentiating cultures:

- Individualism-collectivism.
- Power distance.
- Uncertainty avoidance.
- Masculinity-femininity.

to which he later added,

- Short and long-term orientation.

Although perhaps superseded by later works, Hofstede's research is still held equally valid in today's world.

Edward Hall[17] (1916-2009), seen as the 'the Godfather of Intercultural Studies', developed the concept of social cohesion - describing how people behave, react and communicate in different types of culturally defined spaces. His conclusion was,

> Context is everything. The information that surrounds an event is inextricably bound up with the meaning of that event.

Part Two: International Civilian Crisis Management

International Police Missions

Clearly compatible and valuable to both the military and business sectors, Cultural Knowledge would seem equally viable and important for International Civilian Crisis Management and Peace Support

---

[16] Dutch social psychologist, well known for his pioneering research on cross-cultural groups and organisations..

[17] An American anthropologist and cross-cultural researcher, most well-known for the Anthropology of Space.

Operations[18], in their respective roles within State capacity building. Although applicable to all international actors, the focus here being International Police Missions (IPM), and their role in the reformation of Host Nation law enforcement bodies.

On the topic of United Nations Policing, Secretary-General Ban Ki-Moon states that,

> In addition to protecting individuals, they [UN Police] help society as a whole by redefining the role of policing in countries emerging from conflict, forging trust in uniformed police, establishing faith in national justice systems and fostering confidence in peace processes.[19]

In terms of winning over the local populace, Deputy Secretary-General Jan Eliasson adds,

> In societies emerging from war, citizens often fear local law enforcement, who may have been associated with the conflict. Deploying to these communities, International Police must do more than help rebuild damaged infrastructure - they must repair broken faith in the authorities.[20]

Police officers have been seconded and deployed by the United Nations, and later the European Union and the Organisation for Security and Cooperation in Europe (OSCE), since the 1960s.

Up until the end of the Cold War, the police mandate within peacekeeping operations was limited to monitoring, observing and reporting. However, the fall of the Soviet Union - and subsequent civil conflicts in the Balkans and Central Africa - altered the entire approach

---

[18] Through such mechanisms as the United Nations and the European Union's Common Security and Defence Policy (CSDP).

[19] UNPOL Policing: http://www.un.org/en/peacekeeping/sites/police/policing.shtml (accessed 10 May 2016).

[20] http://www.un.org/en/peacekeeping/sites/police/division.shtml (accessed 10 May 2016).

to peacekeeping operations, with international police taking on interim executive policing functions[21], provision of operational support, and advisory roles. The "Report of the Panel on United Nations Peacekeeping" (2000[22]) - commonly known as the "Brahimi Report" - further redefined and affirmatively positioned the police component within peace operations, influencing member states' approach to personnel contributions and professionalization.

Within the context of fragile and conflict afflicted states (FCAS), International Police Missions are an essential component in the promotion of peace, security, rebuilding and [eventual] normalisation.

In the KAIPTC Paper "Cultural Diversity in Peace Operations", the introduction states that,

> Peace operations should aim at the empowerment of peoples and be based on local traditions and experiences, rather than the imposition of foreign modes of conflict management and governance...

(Odoi, 2005, p. 3)

However,

> As the United Nations learned during the course of their earlier 'CIVPOL'[23] efforts in Bosnia-Herzegovina, Kosovo and Timor-Leste, one size does not fit all[24], but taking into account cultural differences and the way a given society is organised and

---

[21] Kosovo (UNMIK), Timor-Leste (UNMISET, UNMIT) – patrol service, investigations, crowd control etc.

[22] http://www.un.org/en/ga/search/view_doc.asp?symbol=A/55/305 (accessed 10 May 2016).

[23] CIVPOL: Civilian Police, a term used in UN Peacekeeping Operations from 1993 until 2007; renamed UNPOL (United Nations Police). The US still use the term CIVPOL to denote their programme.

[24] Hence the Brahimi Report, the subsequent formation of the "Offices of the Rule of Law and Security Institutions", and the greater role of specialist regionals organizations (e.g. EU-CSDP, OSCE, OECD), government development agencies, foundations (e.g. DCAF) and I-NGOs.

functions[25], the fundamental role and purpose of police remain the same…

(de Saint-Claire, 2014, p. 74)

That being said, it became apparent that,

> Duty-related conduct issues are as much related to culture as training. Problem solving entails changing this cultural mind-set through the demonstration of worth and benefit. The process takes time but can be achieved through practical training, familiarity with operational procedural requirements, positive reinforcement and oversight.

(de Saint-Claire, 2014, p. 75)

Given the global or regional representation that makes up an International Police Mission, this statement equally applies to deployed personnel as local law enforcement. 'Cultural Diversity in Peace Operations' (Odoi, 2005, p. 9) concludes that,

> Culture in peace-keeping operations is ordinarily understood as instrumental, as a tool that can be used to achieve one's ends. Instead of being regarded as the background or pre-condition of communication, cooperation and co-existence cultural understanding tends to be used as a reinforcement of the distinction between "us" and "them", instead of a common ground. Consequently, the challenge lies not only within developing effective training modules on cultural diversity, but also developing long-term strategies on cultural diversity.

By the early 2000's Cross-Cultural Awareness, Diversity and Working Relations training had become an essential part of the Mission pre-deployment curriculum, dealing with:

- Hierarchy and Status.

---

[25] For example, tribal and clan structures, traditional and customary justice etc.

- Groups vs. Individual.
- Time Consciousness.
- Communication.
- Conflict Resolution.

Initially much focused on "cultural shock"[26] rather than gaining an insight into the Host Nation's culture, customs and traditions. However, this changed over time with Mission-specific training providing an insight into conflict history, local customs and law, though quality, length, and course objectives varying greatly.

To support preparation and orientation, the United Nations Police (UNPOL) offers three Mission guidelines that 'touch' on cultural knowledge issues (mission impact), notably:

- Guidelines for United Nations Police Officers On Assignment With Peacekeeping Operations (DPKO, 2007[27])
- United Nations Police Handbook (DPKO, 2005[28])
- Police Capacity Building and Development (DPKO/DFS, 2015[29]),

as does "Europe's New Training Initiative for Civilian Crisis Management" (ENTRi),

- "In Control"[30]

Gearoid Millar (2014) neatly sums up ideal requirements in "An Ethnographic Approach to Peacebuilding: Understanding Local Experiences in Transitional States",

---

[26] 1. Honeymoon; 2. Initial Confrontation; 3. Adjustment Crisis; 4. Recovery; 5. Return Home.

[27] http://www.un.org/en/peacekeeping/sites/police/documents/
pkop_unpol_guidelines_062010.pdf

[28] http://www.un.org/ruleoflaw/files/Handbook%20on%20Policing%20in%20PKeeping
%20Operations.doc

[29] http://www.un.org/en/peacekeeping/sites/police/documents/Guidelines.pdf

[30] http://www.entriforccm.eu/assets/pdf/20160524FINALVersionforHomepage.pdf

The effect of peacebuilding interventions demands an understanding of the local and culturally variable context of intervention.

Security Sector Reform – "A Path to Normalisation"

The security sector can be defined as the structures, institutions and personnel responsible for the provision, management and oversight of security in a country. Security Sector Reform (SSR) is the process of rebuilding and reforming a state's security sector through monitoring, evaluation, review and implementation.

According to OSCE, SSR embraces the Human Dimension of the Security Sector: Rule of Law, Human Rights, Democratic Practice and Integrity – positively impacting the broader field of Human Security[31].

The mandated function(s) of a typical Police SSR Mission, may include:

• Monitoring and reporting.
• [Interim] Executive policing (incl. war crime investigations, formed police units etc.).
• Disarmament, Demobilisation, Reintegration (DDR).
• Refurbishment and re-equipping.
• Strengthening policy and procedural reform.
• Mentorship of senior police management.
• Skills transfer and training of frontline personnel (formed police units, investigations, organised crime, community policing etc.); and
• Public education and community outreach.

Some nations favour a "train and equip" approach, however developing a state's security sector is more sophisticated, involving the engagement of civil society, growing leaders, developing institutions and instilling professionalism. SSR programmes need to take a holistic approach, balancing local politics, policy, legitimacy, accountability, and interrelationships, between the government and its people (McFate, S.,

[31] Human Security is a holistic approach beyond traditional protective security, which also includes economic, water, food, health, welfare, and education.

2015). SSR (and Rule of Law) programmes also need to appreciate 'local want' and what local solutions already function well.

Case-in-point, in East Timor the United Nations Mission initially disparaged customary law due to its community-level administration and regional inconsistency (crime definitions and penalties), instead solely favouring the standardisation and usage of formalised legal mechanisms (TLLEP, 2013, pp. 26-27). Beyond the impracticalities of implementation, this went contrary to community practice, wishes, traditions and sense of legitimacy - creating discord in UN-community cooperation. The UN failed to understand that as a means to maintain community harmony Timorese customary law prioritises community and collective rights over those of the individual (Butt et al., 2009). Therefore, any offence against an individual is a wrongdoing against the entire community, and addressed that way (USAID, 2009). Although not formally included in the Constitution, customary law has since been granted backing and informal recognition as a broker for conflict management and local enforcement.

In Somalia's north, customary tribal councils are recognised by the regional authorities in Puntland and Somaliland to dispense justice and settle inter-tribal disputes. Western judiciary focuses on offender punishment and/or rehabilitation, but most often little thought is given to the victim; under Somali customary law (Xeer[32]) - a 'blood price' is extracted in the event of libel, theft, physical harm, rape and death, as recompense to the injured party. For example, if a married male was murdered, the entire family (or whole tribe) of the offender would be held liable to service the blood price - to ensure that the victim's wife could provide for her family in the long-term (two cows, a goat etc.). International development agencies[33] (for Rule of Law and SSR) working in both provinces quickly realised that in a country torn apart by 30-years of civil war, this system of dispensing justice works, significantly contributing to the easing of local strife and tensions - and

---

[32] *Xeer* is the set of rules and obligations developed between traditional elders to mediate peaceful relations between Somalia's competitive clans and sub-clans.

[33] Examples: USAID, GIZ, DFID etc.

should not be interfered with. That simple act of understanding gained international agencies acceptance, credibility and opened doors.

As stated in "Renegotiating the Contract",

> An interventionist force [...] which does not quickly gain acceptance and confidence of the people is likely to face insurmountable obstacles on its pathway to full reformation as valuable resources which could otherwise be directed towards state building will be required to suppress uprising and call into question the very legitimacy of the intervention itself.
>
> (Briant & Oram, 2014, p. 86)

SSR is most often undertaken utilising the Liberal Democratic agenda of rule of law, human rights, transparency, accountability and other Western-orientated governance mechanisms – some of which may seem imposed. The implementation of such mechanisms is an 'exercise in compromise' due to perceived compatibility issues with established local governance structures, customs, laws, or religion. However, the result of regime change[34], through popularist overthrow or international intervention[35], calls for a political process of inclusion, equal representation and justice. No other modern political system offers this except democracy. Although the Arab Monarchies[36] withstood the Arab Spring, the winds of change that swept through neighbouring countries also forced them to appease and modify domestic policy, granting more rights and freedoms to their citizens.

Fittingly, in the words of Winston Churchill (House of Commons, 11 November 1947),

> Many forms of Government have been tried, and will be tried in this world of sin and woe. No one pretends that democracy is perfect or all-wise. Indeed it has been said that democracy is the

---

[34] As witnessed during the Arab Spring.

[35] Iraq, Afghanistan, Libya.

[36] Arab Monarchies are deemed more legitimate based on 'descent'.

worst form of Government except for all those other forms that have been tried from time to time.

Clearly Security Sector Reform is both deeply cultural and political – requiring the active "buy-in" of the Host Nation - as it re-wires de facto authority structures and practices (McFate, S., 2015), necessitating four cultural knowledge areas:

- Organisational Culture (government and politics)
- Police Culture
- Nationalism
- Community Culture

Of course this raises the subtle question of whether cultural knowledge is a tool for cooperation, intelligence, or both – a dilemma likewise faced by Human Terrain System social scientists.

"Police need vs. community want" is the issue facing police officers in-mission and in their domestic duty stations, most often addressed through the "Community Policing" approach (a model extolled and exported in International Police Missions).

Part Three: Domestic Policing

Police are the public, and the public are the police.

Sir Robert Peel

In a domestic setting, the Human Terrain – the target population – are the communities in which police perform their work.

Policing the Human Terrain: Community Policing

The notion of professional policing was adopted by Sir Robert Peel, when appointed British Home Secretary in 1822, as a means to address 'crime prevention' whilst balancing 'public order' concerns[37]. Subsequently, in 1829 Peel established England's first full-time,

---

[37] Prior to the formation of the Metropolitan Police, 'public order' duties were carried out by armed soldiers.

centralised, professional police force[38] - London's Metropolitan Police. He is credited[39] for formalising the concept of "policing by consent", expressed through the "Peelian Principles" - a set of guidelines that laid the foundations for ethical law enforcement throughout the British Commonwealth, as well as the United States.

The seventh principle summarises policing by consent stating that,

> The police are the public, and the public are the police; the police being the only members of the public who are paid to give fulltime attention to duties which are incumbent on every citizen in the interests of community welfare and existence.

"A rationale of Community welfare": essentially the Peelian Principles place the interests of the community at the heart of policing, carried out by members of that community - individuals who live with and know the traditions, history and beliefs of that community.

Although definition and approach differ markedly across the world, in general terms Community Policing focuses on the police building ties and working closely with members of the communities within their area of responsibility. Conceptually, officers make their presence known and rely on community members to report any suspicious behaviour or tips on criminals in the area. This cooperative approach creates relationships and engenders trust. Attention focal points being: cause and prevention, problem solving, reassurance, local engagement and partnerships (de Saint-Claire, 2014, p. 69).

Pioneered in the United States in the late 1960's, the US Department of Justice defines community policing as,

> A philosophy that promotes organizational strategies that support the systematic use of partnerships and problem-solving techniques to proactively address the immediate conditions that

---

[38] The City of Glasgow Police was the UK's first, established in 1800.

[39] Peel did not write them himself, but rather collated previous works, presenting them as an ethical and procedural guideline.

give rise to public safety issues such as crime, social disorder, and fear of crime.

(COPS-USDOJ, 2014)

The UK's Neighbourhood Policing programme was influenced by the emergence of community policing in the US, similarly with the aim of reducing [fear of] crime and improve public confidence by engaging with communities, targeting their concerns and priorities by providing a visible and accessible presence. The result, known as "citizen focused policing", places the emphasis on community engagement in securing trust and confidence of local residents (Police Foundation, 2015, p. 3). The term 'community engagement' is used less in the US, as 'community policing' is the all-encompassing philosophy, reflecting elements of both 'citizen focus' and 'neighbourhood policing'.

A prominent form of Community Policing is "Problem-oriented Policing" (POP), which places a greater emphasis on research and analysis, crime prevention, as well as community and local business engagement in the reduction of community problems[40]. However, POP is noted to have limitations in the most deprived, unstable and crime-ridden communities, where police lack knowledge and understanding of the socio-economic/socio-cultural context (Police Foundation, 2015, p. 4) - the very areas where such information is required.

Community Policing: Challenges

As an exercise in true democratic policing, community engagement, trust building and mutual understanding, the benefits of community-police partnerships are clear, but as a definitive tool for crime reduction Community Policing remains statistically questionable (Police Foundation, 2015, p. 5).

What is clear is that police resources are directed towards 'popularist priorities' of the time, which over the last 15 years has been domestic security and terrorism rather than community concerns -

---

[40] The last decade has seen policing prioritise state security issues over community concerns; POP serves as a means for the public to wield greater influence in what issues the police should focus on.

which seems self-defeating as the radicalisation[41] process is often regarded as a result of situational factors: community disconnect, neglect, exclusion and alienation (Francis, 2012).

In the face of fiscal cut-backs and subsequent reduction in field personnel, 'rapid response' and technology[42] substitute for regular police presence and engagement. Contrary to known 'good practices', the result has been,

> Reactive rapid response servicing large geographic areas, necessitating the abandonment of foot patrols[43] [and similar], thus losing contact and familiarity with the various communities - and more especially first-hand knowledge of local problems. This lack of physical presence creates a "rift between the community and the police" (McMurtry & Curling, 2008: p. 34), and a belief - unfounded or otherwise - that police have become less concerned with preventive community issues. With police disengagement, and the conditions for trust being lost, over time marginalised communities begin to view random and sporadic police patrols as 'Big Brother' invasive monitoring and repression rather than preventive and protection measures. In response police themselves approach communities with an air of ambivalence – if not belligerence (as one would an enemy), leading to discriminatory policing tactics, e.g. racial profiling, stop-and-search tactics, intimidation, non-proportional use of force, noble cause corruption etc.
>
> (de Saint-Claire, 2014, p. 69)

---

[41] It has been argued that the term *radicalisation* is inappropriate given that radical means revolutionary and new, whereas extremist Islam is in fact arch-conservative and fundamentalism.

[42] For example: vehicle mobility, communications, electronic surveillance, CCTV, ANPR etc.

[43] In favour of patrol vehicles: fast moving, seeing little, rapid response, a psychological barrier between the police and pubic, requiring less personnel.

Needless to say, such measures prove counter-productive as they diminish faith in the criminal justice system, the impartial legitimacy of its agents – undermining the entire principle of 'policing by consent'.

Unlike Peel's London, more than often police officers no longer have their roots in the community in which they serve - further leading to a lack of community engagement and in-depth understanding of local issues, concerns and perspectives. This is compounded by two additional issues, throughout the West:

- A majority of police officers are Caucasian, from middle class backgrounds; whereas.
- Tension areas tend to be in lower socio-economic localities, characterised by high unemployment, low income, disenfranchisement, youth-at-risk, and immigrant communities.

Today's western metropolitan centres are truly ethnically diverse, but not necessarily a melting pot as ethnic groups tend to cluster amongst their own – often leading to an exaggerated sense of cultural identity and otherness. Therefore, policing in culturally and ethnically diverse communities poses particular challenges, most especially in terms of language and cultural barriers (Police Foundation, 2015, p. 6).

Addressing such challenges means:

- Initiating programmes of strategic inclusivity;
- Planning for [increasingly] diverse / multicultural communities; and
- Assuring that the needs of the vulnerable and hard-to-reach are met.

One thing is abundantly clear, in today's diverse societies cultural competence is the key to effective Community Policing, opening the doors to partnerships, two-way communication, trust, knowledge and understanding.

Nonetheless, a decade's worth of high profile incidents involving the Police Departments of Ferguson[44], Chicago[45], and London's Metropolitan Police Service (MPS)[46] have cast a contentious thematic spotlight on current methodologies employed, oversight mechanisms and approach to community relations – both in policy and practical application.

Case Study: The London Riots - Community Disconnect

Between 6 and 11 August 2011, thousands of people rioted throughout Greater London. The resultant unrest generated violence, looting, arson, and the mass deployment of police.

Protests began in the North London suburb of Tottenham, following the death of Mark Duggan - a local and alleged drug dealer - shot dead by police on 4 August 2011.

As an ongoing investigation, transparency over the circumstances surrounding Duggan's death was protracted and murky, with police quickly accused of a cover-up.

Multiple violent clashes with police followed, along with the destruction of police vehicles, a magistrates' court, public transport and dozens of homes, as well as vandalism and looting businesses within the protestors own communities. In an environment of poor or no police response, gangs of locals[47] took to the streets to defend their homes, families and community.

---

[44] Police shooting of Michael Brown, Ferguson, MO.

[45] For example: Homan Square, Laquan McDonald etc.

[46] Allegations of corruption, bribery, noble cause corruption, cover-ups, mishandling and manipulation of investigations, illegal phone-tapping, intimidation, non-proportional use of force, detention without charge, racial profiling (*ref.* Steve Lawrence Murder Case, 2010 Northumbria Police Manhunt, 2010 Student Protests, 2011 London Riots, 2009 G20 Summit Protests and Death of Ian Tomlinson).

[47] Described extensively by the British media as "vigilantes" (*ref.* Google: Daily Mirror, BBC, The Telegraph, The Guardian, The Week, Huffington Post (UK), The IB Times, The Independent etc.) https://www.google.de/search?q=london+riots, +vigilantes&ie=&oe=#q=london+riots,+vigilantes&start=10

In the aftermath some 4000 people were arrested, 2200 were formally charged. But the destruction and cost went well beyond material goods, damaging the relationship between the police and the communities it was sworn to serve and protect.

But of course Mark Duggan's death was not the true cause, merely the catalyst. It is important to note that unlike civil disorder from years before,

> There was no sense among the rioters of being part of a collective, no desire to transform society, just an inchoate, nihilistic desire to cause mayhem and to profit from the looting. The riots were not 'protests' in any way, but a mixture of incoherent rage, gang thuggery and teenage mayhem.
>
> (Malik, 2011)

Those who feel of little worth fear no consequence.

Beyond the aforementioned weak police response, root causes have been summarised as:

- Social deprivation.
- Economic inequality.
- High youth unemployment.
- Racial profiling.
- Moral poverty and opportunism (ref. aggravated robberies, looting, vandalism etc.).

Perhaps more than anything else, social deprivation leads to a lack of cohesion within a society itself – and social cohesion is the one psychological barrier that stops society from spiralling out of control.

Perspectives on Global Development 2012 (OECD, 2011), states that,

> A cohesive society is one that works towards the well-being of all its members, fights exclusion and marginalisation, creates a sense of belonging, promotes trust, and offers its members the

opportunity of upward mobility. While the notion of 'social cohesion' is often used with different meanings, its constituent elements include concerns about social inclusion, social capital and social mobility.

London's boroughs have large concentrations of both lower socio-economic and immigrant communities - communities which often display disproportionately low income, high unemployment, a largely unqualified workforce and disenfranchised youth. In examining London's immigrant groups[48], all have their own language, culture, perspective, and attitudes. As immigrants, integration and acceptance by the wider [host] community is slow, if not reluctant; similarly adopting local norms by these new groups are also sluggish, if not actively discouraged.

The London Riots exhibited a clash of two cultural types, represented by two unlike cultural groups: mixed lower socio-economic [groups] vs. an organisational culture - the "System", embodied by the police.

In the eyes of the British public, police ideally serve the interests of the community, performing their role in a 'transparent and accountable' manner. However, by those on society's fringes, London's Metropolitan Police were seen to personify the attitudes of white middle class England – a class and lifestyle the lower socio-economic groups can only hope to aspire.

White middle class England had the social expectation of the 'others' to fit-in and integrate. Those groups who did not (or could not) were looked down on, or treated with suspicion and fear. In London, those clearly of immigrant background, within the lower socio-economic areas, were frequently targeted by the police using 'stop and search' tactics. Such tactics were seen as hostile, racist and repressive – strengthening the idea that these groups and the immigrant community were 'outsiders' – of little worth or social standing.

What was not considered before or after the riots was how the police were seen as an organisation by those on society's fringes.

---

[48] Black, Asian, MENA, South-East and Eastern European communities.

Many immigrants originated from countries where police corruption, violence and victimisation are considered normal. Therefore, any police presence was viewed with distrust and fear, reinforced by MPS racial profiling and stop-and-search practices. However, other parties viewed the British police and justice system with disrespect, regarding it as soft and impotent[49].

Mark Duggan was shot during an armed police intercept as part of Operation Trident. Operation Trident targeted gun crime in London, with special attention to shootings relating to the illegal sale of drugs and crime in Afro-Caribbean communities. At the time it was not clear if Duggan had a criminal connection, nor was it clear if he had a gun, or indeed if he had actually shot at a police officer. But the lack of police transparency, past experiences of racial profiling, and suspicion that it was a police cover-up was enough to spark protest. With large elements of the community turning against them, the police did not know how to respond. The tactic of letting the situation 'burn itself out', and not provoking the crowd by keeping a discrete distance had the opposite desired effect: it reinforced the belief of police impotence, leading to an escalating of the situation.

After five days, and the deployment of over 44,000 police officers in London, the riots did eventually burn themselves out. But the financial and social costs were heavy. And community trust in the police – as an organisation and partner – disappeared as quickly as flat screen TVs during the looting.

In the aftermath the 'blame game' was played, but ultimately the riots were a monumental failure by government to re-connect with its constituencies and identify their priorities.

A bulk of the responsibility was shouldered by the Metropolitan Police Service (MPS) for lack of forewarning, poor preventative measures and weak response. However, immediately following Mark Duggan's shooting (prior to the riots), the MPS did attempt to gauge

---

[49] "What Caused the London Riots: A Failure in Police-Community Relations" (v.4), in "International Police Mission Training: Resource Book 2016", Simon de Saint- Claire (2016), (for National Police Agency of Japan).

the mood of the public by consulting community contact groups (IAG[50], KIN[51] etc.).

Such networks were established as part of 2005's Neighbourhood Policing Programme which also introduced Safer Neighbourhood Teams (SNT), consisting of dedicated police officers and Police Community Support Officers[52] (PCSOs). However, neighbourhood policing hasn't been a priority for a number of years, and due to budget cuts the employment of PCSOs has been in steady decline, with the MPS even "toying with scrapping them entirely"[53].

Therefore, it's interestingly to note that, beyond strategic and tactical measures, the Metropolitan Police Service report, "4 Days in August: Strategic Review into the Disorder of August 2011" identified five areas to improve concerning community engagement:

- Enhance Neighbourhood Police presence
- Key Individual Networks (KIN) - review, develop, examine alternative options
- Social Media - community interaction; counter-intelligence
- Stop and Search - revise attitude and method of encounter
- Youth Engagement - build and develop through Youth Ward Panels[54]

Case Study: The Chicago Model – a Template for Domestic HTS?

The London Riots were a short-term civil upheaval in response to social conditions, ultimately constrained by the social contract. Whereas Chicago - well-known as the most violent city in the US -

---

[50] Independent Advisory Group - members provide advice and guidance to the police on specific communities.

[51] Key Individual Network (KIN) members assist their local Safer Neighbourhoods team in identifying issues and understand the thoughts and feelings of the local community.

[52] Non-warranted uniformed field staff, focusing on local crime and anti-social behaviour.

[53] *PCSO's Facing Uncertain Future*", Iain Weinfass, Police Oracle, 1 June 2016 http://www.policeoracle.com/news/PCSOs-facing-uncertain-future_91999.html (accessed 1 June 2016).

[54] Youths become involved in setting policing priorities that matter to them.

demonstrates the social contracts[55] fragility, when an organisational culture fails to connect and engage.

> In the aftermath of the Ferguson, Missouri, incident and other highly visible force incidents, public trust and confidence in the police has been shattered in cities across the United States. As a result, many police departments have sought ways to restore police legitimacy through community policing initiatives, procedural justice training, and other strategies. In fact, many have turned to Chicago, Illinois, for direction, since the Chicago Police Department has been involved in such initiatives for several years.
>
> Superintendent Garry McCarthy / Prof. Dennis Rosenbaum, 2015)

In May 2011 Garry McCarthy was appointed Superintendent[56] of the Chicago Police Department (CPD), the USA's second largest non-federal police force. Based on similar social experiments with the New York and Newark (N.J.) Police Departments, he quickly transformed the CPD into 'America's laboratory of police science' - inviting in teams of criminologists, legal scholars, and social scientists, with the aim of reducing violence, reforming police methodology and engaging estranged communities[57]. To achieve this, he needed to transform CPD's culture from a force to a service: from warriors to guardians.

McCarthy's rationale was that,

> Crime strategy needs to focus on people, places, and things that are going to cause crime. And that's where the academics come in.
>
> (Weichselbaum, 2016)

---

[55] Ref. John Locke's *Second Treatise of Government*. US Constitution: powers from the consent of the governed.

[56] In Chicago Superintendent of Police is equivalent to Police Chief / Commissioner.

[57] Essentially a police-orientated form of the Human Terrain System.

His quest to reduce violence and engage Chicago's worst affected communities wasn't new, in 1993 the CPD implemented the city-wide *Chicago Alternative Policing Strategy* (CAPS) programme, in an effort to bring Chicago's diverse communities, police, and other city agencies together as a means to prevent crime rather than react after the fact.

To encourage mutual dialogue and cooperation,

> Eight or nine 'beat officers' are assigned to each of Chicago's 279 police beats. The officers patrol the same beat for over a year, allowing them to get to know community members, residents, and business owners and to become familiar with community attitudes and trends.[58]

Moreover, under CAPS, regular 'Beat Community Meetings', between community members and the police, are held to discuss potential problems, strategies and solutions. To support these efforts, in the late 1990's 'cultural diversity training' was introduced as a means to,

> Understand the impact that culture has on the administration of justice and the delivery of effective public safety service.
>
> (Vialpando, 2016)

Unfortunately, the training didn't translate well to actual police-public interaction.

Several years later the US Health Sector introduced "Cultural Competence"[59] as a tool to enhance service delivery, meeting the needs of both health profession and the people they serve.

Cultural Competence can be defined as:

---

[58] "*What is Caps*", http://home.chicagopolice.org/get-involved-with-caps/how-caps-works/what-is-caps/ (accessed 30 May 2016).

[59] Introduced in 2002, since increasingly embedded into US medical education curricula.

The ability of an individual to understand and respect values, attitudes, beliefs, and mores that differ across cultures, and to consider and respond appropriately to these differences in planning, implementing, and evaluating health education and promotion programs and interventions.[60]

The concept was quickly adopted by police agencies - including the CPD - as a means to recognise socio-cultural characteristics that define and influence the behaviour of different groups in society. From a field perspective, cultural competence skills could assist officers effectively communicate with the different ethnic groups in a way that would promote mutual understanding, thus reducing suspicion, confusion, antagonism or chances of conflict (Vialpando, 2016).

CAPS was further complemented in 2009, with the establishment of the National Network for Safe Communities[61]: a coalition of police chiefs, prosecutors, mayors, community leaders, service providers, street-based outreach workers, academics, ex-offenders, and others concerned about the impact of crime and current crime policies on communities (von Ulmenstein & Sultan, 2011).

According to their website[62], the National Network brings together jurisdictions from around the country that actively implement a two-prong strategy of reducing violence and eliminating drug markets.

National Network Co-Chair David Kennedy used Chicago to refine the Violence Reduction Strategy (VRS) programme – an initiative for preventing gang violence (Weichselbaum, 2016). VRS focuses on identifying key gang members using frontline intelligence and innovative new social network analysis techniques to identify target areas, as well as the group members at highest risk for violent victimisation or offending - and through home visits giving them individualised messages about their vulnerability, the help/options

---

[60] SHAPE America (Society for Health and Physical Education).

[61] Launched by the "Center for Crime Prevention and Control", John Jay College of Criminal Justice, NYC.

[62] National Network for Safer Communities: https://nnscommunities.org/ (accessed 2 June 2016).

available to them, and their legal risks. This approach is reputed to have reduced violence dramatically in 2013, (von Ulmenstein & Sultan, 2011), though the trend reversed dramatically in 2015 (Sanburn, 2016).

CAPS was revitalised in early 2013, with the programme decentralised and moved out to the 25 police districts it serves, with McCarthy declaring,

> Under the new initiative, each police district will be assigned a CAPS sergeant and two police officers, as well as a community organizer and a youth services provider. Four citywide coordinators will oversee community policing programs targeted at victim assistance, seniors, youth, and victims of domestic violence.[63]

Additionally, the CAPS programme capitalised on social media (incl. Twitter) and new website to encourage community [anonymous] reporting, participation and feedback.

However, despite CAPS upbeat mantra "Together, we are working to identify and solve neighbourhood crime problems [...] and to improve the quality of life in Chicago's neighbourhoods"[64], locals described CPD efforts as "too much policing, too little policing – both at the same time" (Weichselbaum, 2016). Even so, residents are not hesitant to call the police in times of need, but feel that the police have withdrawn so much that there is a pervasive atmosphere of mutual contempt and enmity; and when police do respond it is usually with disproportionate force. Too much Warrior, not enough Guardian, which seems at odds with the ideology behind CAPS and VRS.

Of course police officers are - by virtue of their profession – suspicious: as a result of their training, the nature of the work, the people who they deal with, and the simple cautious act of self-preservation (Millar et al., 2010). Although a generalisation, having

---

[63] NBC-CHGO, (8 January 2013) "*Emanuel, McCarthy Aim to Change CAPS*", http://www.nbcchicago.com/blogs/ward-room/Emanuel-McCarthy-Aim-to-Change-CAPS-186084182.html (accessed 2 June 2016).

[64] *bid.* 58.

regular contact with [alleged] offenders can sour one's view of human nature, influencing future interactions with the public, including stereotyping. Such suspicions, views and experiences tend to create a passive divide between police officers and elements of the community - with the result of a police esprit de corps-driven closed professional culture. However, the closed nature of such a culture excludes external stimuli, perspectives and experiences, with internal views looping.

With this in mind, CPD patrol officers assigned to impact zones – often 'rookies' – have adopted a pseudo-siege mentality. This stance is reflected in their belief that the idea of a guardian force implies passivity and weakness: "You don't stand guard in a war zone" (Weichselbaum, 2016) - an easily understood stance given the crime statistics.

In 2015 Chicago had a city-wide homicide rate of 17:100,000, compared with a national rate of 4:100,000; in the most violent districts, this rate was 62 (Iraq's rate was 20). To compound this record, there were over 700 gang factions across the city's 22 police districts, with the CPD confiscating more illegal weapons than in New York and Los Angeles combined (Weichselbaum, 2016).

It's little wonder that street rappers and film-makers[65] have rebranded Chicago "Chi-raq".

The so-called 'impact zones' (the CPD term for the deadliest areas[66]), where much of the violence occurs, could only be described as slums: run-down, impoverished, segregated (Black or Hispanic majorities), with over 25% unemployment, low income families, a largely unqualified workforce, and disenfranchised youth (Weichselbaum, 2016) - without any hope of a positive future. A hauntingly familiar tune.

By embedding HTS-style academic research teams, Superintendent McCarthy endeavoured to change police culture by changing the way

---

[65] Spike Lee's 2015 movie "Chi-Raq", inspired by gang-related violence in Englewood, Chicago.

[66] Example 'Impact Zones': 5th District (Calumet) - Riverdale; 7th District (Englewood); 9th District (Deering) - Fuller Park; 11th District (Harrison) etc.

they engage with society, making police approachable, with every encounter considered fair and cordial.

Additionally, through problem-solving and collaborative police relations with the community stakeholders, all parties can be open to the desired balance of warrior vs. guardian. In fact, in dire public safety situations communities welcome the 'warrior' – especially if said actions are considered legitimate and procedurally impartial.

One approach, promoted by Yale professors Tracey Meares and Tom Tyler, was to help develop a "procedural justice"[67] curriculum for the CPD, designed to overhaul officers' interactions with the public, focusing on attitude, approach and active communication, with the desired outcome of residents being more inclined to trust the police.

In "Why People Obey Law" (2006), Tom Tyler identifies five strategies that can be applied by police departments to enhance procedural justice:

- Voice (all sides of the story have been heard).
- Human touch (dignity and respect).
- Neutrality (the decision-making process is unbiased and trustworthy).
- Explanations (comprehension of the process and how decisions are made); and
- Helpfulness (police interest in your personal situation to the extent that the law allows).

In "Community Policing Revisited" (2016), Chapman and Martin state that these strategies are the fundamental components of a police-community partnership that successfully co-produces public safety. Underlying procedural justice is the idea that the police and criminal justice system must be seen to demonstrate its legitimacy to the public it serves (Tyler, 2006). Referencing London's Metropolitan Police Service 'stop-and-search' procedure, most individuals had no issue

---

[67] Procedural justice (aka procedural fairness) describes the idea that how individuals regard the justice system is tied more to the perceived fairness of the *process* and how they were treated rather than to the perceived fairness of the *outcome*.

201

with the legitimacy of the practice itself, but rather the approach, attitude and frequency.

When police officers make a visible effort to communicate and engage with members of the public - to serve the public - people become more cooperative (Millar et al., 2010, p. 5).

McCarthy was terminated from his position following Laquan McDonald's shooting by CPD Officer Jason Van Dyke (20 October 2014), and even though the city is still reeling from the fallout, McCarthy's legacy remains. Although deemed a failure in Chicago, the "Chicago Model" has been adapted by police departments throughout the country, with the US Department of Justice spending millions promoting its approach. On the heels of Ferguson, MO., President Obama even recommended that other cities should adopt Chicago's strategies (Weichselbaum, 2016).

As the dust settles in Chicago, US law enforcement authorities have come to realise that:

- Cultivating cultural competence fosters legitimacy, trust, partnership and common ground; and
- Cultural competency tools are an effective intelligence mechanism in their dealings with the ever changing dynamics of the Human Terrain - where challenges go beyond diversity issues, and into the realms of large scale civil unrest, gang culture, and the culture of violence.

The CPD became a grand experiment, utilising academics and scientific method to analyse and influence two disparate cultures: the police and their most problematic communities. There are many reasons why it didn't fulfil its promise in Chicago – but much had to do with the immobility of entrenched attitudes, impatience and politics.

On discussing events - the politics, the police, the street - McCarthy simply concludes that Chicago is a place where "culture trumps policy" (Weichselbaum, 2016).

Democratic Policing, Society and the Social Contract

An important function of the State is the provision of security and public order. To do so, the State claims sole monopoly in legitimate physical coercion within its given geographical and political jurisdiction. Police functions in a democratic society must:

• Have a position of independence relative to the state and be responsible towards the needs of citizens; and
• Be transparent, accountable, abide by the rule of law and human rights standards.

In autocratic and unstable states, policing is closely associated with maintaining the government - often 'securing order' through the misuse of force. Under these conditions law enforcement tends to have adopted a 'militarised'[68] approach, where normal civilian police duties (crime prevention) have been relegated to the much broader theme of State Security (public order)[69]. Such practices are seen as obstacles to well-functioning policing and community engagement (de Saint-Claire, 2014, pp. 60-1).

In liberal democracies, police are mandated to use that force proportionately against the public, when deemed necessary. And, on the whole, the public regard this arrangement as reasonable under the social contract - a theory which regards use of force as necessary to uphold law and order in the pursuit of maintaining a safe society[70].

Under the social contract individuals are understood to voluntarily surrender some of their rights to the State. Although government officials, police are seen as politically impartial in their enforcement role, themselves governed and restricted by specific rules and the

---

[68] Tactical uniform, automatic weapons, protective equipment, attitude.

[69] State Security issues are also being prioritised in liberal democracies, with police being militarised .

[70] The role of policing bodies in dictatorships or under military rule differs, as it is the role of State Security Forces to ensure/secure the power mechanisms of the government, rather than serve the public.

same laws[71]. Therefore, the social contract views police as a protective force against crime and social disorder.

This perspective is held widely by the public at large, and even under the lurking shadow of scandal (corruption, racism, disproportionate use of force, and abuse of powers), the police remain respected as both a public service and institution.

The social contract – and goodwill - is essentially the public's 'buy-in': a socio-political and cultural relationship that does not exist in international interventions.

The Dichotomy of Politics and Society: Case Studies of Immigration and Integration

The themes of immigration and integration have been touched on throughout this work, most specifically in relation to the socio-cultural friction leading up to the 2011 London Riots.

Most Western European countries have large immigrant communities, either as a direct result of [de]colonisation, guest worker programmes, [il]legal economic migration (per the last decade), or conflict - as is now being experienced with the Syrian refugee crises.

The refugee crisis - combined with equally vast numbers of economically-driven illegal immigrants from the Balkans and the Maghreb - have changed the political face of the EU, with nationalist and far-right groups beginning to influence mainstream governance[72], as witnessed in Austria (Freiheitliche Partei Österreichs, FPÖ), France (Front National, FN), Germany (Alternative für Deutschland, AfD), and Britain (UK Independence Party, UKIP) - where it also became a major argument of the 'Brexit' campaign.

---

[71] Social Contract Vision: http://www.activistrights.org.au/handbook/ch01s06s02.php (accessed 28 May 2016).

[72] To keep right-wing parties out of power, Incumbent mainstream governments compromise liberal policies in order to mollify nationalist sensitivities and insecurities.

Germany: Willkommenskultur (Welcome Culture)

Germany actively chose to champion the refugee cause. But even within Germany exist growing social dissonance and polarisation: the altruistic wish to help vs. the cultural and socio-economic unease combined with security concerns[73] resulting from the sheer number of so many foreigners - as publicly expressed through the right-leaning Pegida[74] protest movement.

With over 16 million immigrants[75], Germany has the second largest immigrant population in the world (UN DESA, 2015), and it's a country where one in five Germans identify themselves as having mixed ethnic heritage.

Despite these numbers, German culture remains relatively insular. Due to past mistakes[76] immigrant integration remains incomplete, with ethnic communities clustering amongst their own, where language acquisition is slow, and home traditions and differences[77] - often expressed through nationalism and religion[78] - become exaggerated. With a feeling of low social mobility and exclusion, youths and young men look for a fix to improve their standing, either through religious expression or a lifestyle of crime.

Crime committed by foreigners – resident and non-resident – is disproportionately high (and organised) compared to those committed

---

[73] Criminality (sexual assaults, shoplifting, burglary, organised crime) and the correlation between refugee numbers and the likelihood of a terrorist attack.

[74] UK: http://www.pegidauk.org/v1/; Germany: https://pegidaoffiziell.wordpress.com (accessed 10 June 2016).

[75] Through the "gastarbeiterprogramm" (Schonick, 2009), EU migration, illegal economic immigration, and the sporadic influx of refugees (Balkans conflicts of the 1990's; currently Afghanistan, Syria and Iraq).

[76] *Gastarbeiters* were always regarded as temporary migrants, therefore Germany did not establish structures to facilitate integration, nor did the Guest Worker (esp. Turks) make much effort to integrate.

[77] Food goods appearing in supermarkets, clothing (headscarf, burqa/chadri, niqab), gender roles, communications style s (volume, body language) etc.

[78] Mosques, Synagogues and Orthodox Churches are common meeting grounds.

by German citizens[79], with offenders typically of Turkish, Eastern European, South European, Moroccan, Syrian or Afghan origin (BKA, 2014). The German criminal justice system – orientated towards rehabilitation and reintegration over punishment – tends towards leniency, which translates to comparatively low risk of conviction or incarceration for foreign offenders. Realising that custodial sentences are less likely for transnational criminals without substantial evidence, police investigators are often more concerned with establishing criminal patterns (i.e. repeat offending) rather than making opportunistic arrests, in a bid to prove that such crime is being run as an ongoing business. Unfortunately, this approach is less than preventive, and does little for the victim(s).

Transnational crime and immigrant crime should not be viewed as synonymous. However, immigrant perpetrated repeat offences can be linked to third-party 'professional handlers' (supplier/receiver relationship). Such crimes - characteristically pick-pocketing, shoplifting, burglary, drug dealing, aggravated robbery, and sexual assault - pose their own unique set of problems, most especially concerning the position of criminal justice (ref. prosecution and incarceration), public perception and general acceptance of immigrant groups.

Due to Germany's complicated immigration laws, even the term 'immigrant' is not straightforward, as those born in Germany (to Gastarbeiters – guest workers) before 1990 are not eligible for German citizenship - but know no 'home' other than Germany (Bucerius, 2014). Due to fears of deportation – real or imagined – there is an inclination to 'live in the shadows'.

Refugees seek asylum, but may have no wish to live in the Host Nation beyond the period of crisis, whereas immigrants come to stay. Germany's approach is by granting successful asylum seekers permanent residency (incl. the right to work, access to education etc.), whilst those denied asylum are left in limbo.

---

[79] Statistics do not differentiate between ethnic Germans, Naturalised Germans, and children born in Germany to immigrant parents.

Throughout, acceptance and integration remain a challenge.

For the current wave of refugees and immigrants, the steps to asylum and integration are as equally long and arduous as the road they travel to reach Germany. In "A refugee with an axe, and Germany's open door could be slammed shut"[80], Konstantin Richter opines,

> Refugees who entered Germany had high hopes. Smugglers told them they'd prosper and find jobs instantly. Now they are languishing in asylum-seeker centres and struggling with bureaucracy, uncertain whether they can stay at all. Many of them are young men who are homesick, angry and frustrated, and extremists are deliberately visiting their homes because they know they are fertile ground for recruiting.

To appease public concern, and proactively integrate the refugee population, in May 2016 the German Government passed the "Meseberg Declaration on Integration"[81], aimed at clarifying asylum seekers rights and responsibilities. Of relevance to this contribution:

- Immigrants must understand and respect the foundations on which German society is built, its culture, values, and the laws of the land.
- Integration is a two-way process that involves the offer of government services, but equally an obligation on the part of incomers to make an effort.
- The guiding principle in the integration policy is justice - justice for those recognised as refugees, and justice for the German people.
- Learned from past mistakes, regional authorities will settle refugees, avoiding segregation, ethnic clustering, and the creation of immigrant ghettos.

---

[80] The Guardian, 22 July 2016, https://www.theguardian.com/commentisfree/2016/jul/21/refugee-axe-germany-train-open-door-migration (accessed 22 July 2016).

[81] https://www.bundesregierung.de/Content/EN/Artikel/2016/05_en/2016-05-25-meseberg-gabriel-merkel-mittwoch_en.html (accessed 18 June 2016).

- Zero tolerance policy on attacks on women, children and other vulnerable individuals, whether they are German citizens, asylum-seekers, or refugees.
- Failure for not meeting their obligations could result in the suspension of social allowances, downgrading of status, and in some [rare] cases deportation.
- Increasing the percentage of employees with a migrant background in German public authorities to enhance communication, cultural competence and understanding.

Such measures are deemed necessary as Germany's local population feels overwhelmed, economically punished[82], and seeing what they regard as the erosion of their way of life. Unfounded or not, with the steady rise in burglaries and sexual assaults, and threats to State Security - as experienced in Belgium and France - Germans are steadily feeling insecure with their growing immigrant population.

In the US context, proportionally immigrants – and the offspring of immigrants - are not the criminal or terrorist threat as commonly portrayed. According to the "Oxford Handbook of Crime and Criminal Justice" (2011),

'[M]ost second generation immigrants continue to enjoy lower crime rates than the native born population'.

In fact, US domestic terrorism is most often attributed to US citizens involved in right-wing (anti-government) and white nationalist (Hate Crime) groups[83].

The 'Handbook' continues, pointing out that,

---

[82] Paying for and/or subsidising immigrants, with [free] healthcare, lodging, clothing, monetary allowance – things the local populace are not entitled to or given lower priority.

[83] In a survey conducted by the 'Police Executive Research Forum' (2014), of 382 US law enforcement agencies: 74% reported anti-government extremism as one of the top three terrorist threats in their jurisdiction; 39 % listed Muslim extremism; followed by left-wing and eco extremism.

In stark contrast, research findings in European countries indicate that some second-generation immigrant groups have crime rates that drastically exceed those of the native-born population.

(Bucerius, 2011)

Referencing crime rates, European States statistically differentiate between nationalities, but not ethnicity[84]; however, as suggested by Prof. Sandra Bucerius, criminal investigation agencies do target specific ethnic groups over others. In an interview with "The Atlantic" (2015), Prof. Bucerius states her belief that immigrant groups engaging in criminal activities, experience higher than average social, economic and political exclusion (as echoed in the London Riots and Chicago's 'impact zones'). This background does not mean all immigrant groups will turn to crime, but rather that this recurring theme of marginalisation creates a risk factor.

What we can say is that - in some European countries – like Germany, the Netherlands, Belgium, or France, we see a disproportionate number of second-generation immigrants involved in crime who are likely Muslim.

(The Atlantic, 2015)

France

Liberté, égalité, fraternité: unlike the multicultural positions of Germany and the United Kingdom, the Constitution of the Fifth Republic (1958[85]) establishes France as a secular and democratic state, that holds equality among its peoples as inviolable. However, France takes this stance a step further regarding culture, ethnicity, religion, and gender - anything that distinguishes one community or individual identity from another - as a private concern, not an issue of State. Admirable as the

[84] Germany does not categorise immigrants by ethnicity, e.g. all ethnic groups originating from Turkey are Turks, irrespective if they are Kurds, Assyrians etc.

[85] https://www.legifrance.gouv.fr/Droit-francais/Constitution (accessed 14 June 2016).

intent of absolute equality is, ignoring individuality and difference creates its own problems.

In "How France Grew Its Own Terrorists" (2015), M.G. Oprea states,

> Although minorities should not be singled out by the State, neither should they be ignored. Refusing to acknowledge that they exist leads to alienation and creates parallel communities – just as the Britain's staunch multiculturalism has done.

Both approaches produce similar results: disaffected and isolated from mainstream culture.

Case in point, French Muslim youth are embracing their Muslim identity more aggressively and openly than their parents' generation. Those who strictly adhere to Islam believe their faith should regulate all aspects of their lives, including law, governance and public expression of faith. The French State's policy of not acknowledging such differences - and the total secularisation of society[86] - is by default alienating five million Muslims (7.5% of the population)[87].

Contrary to policy aims, the growing immigrant communities are far from integrated, having become a discontent Islamic sub-culture.

The 2004 law banning religious symbols in public schools[88] provoked national controversy as it was specifically seen as a ban on the Nijab (Islamic headscarf) – and an attack on Islam.

October-November 2005 saw widespread and prolonged rioting among the Arab-immigrant suburbs of Paris, Lyon, and Lille by socially estranged youth. In identifying underlying reasons, the aptly named

---

[86] Banning of religious symbols in public, headscarves.

[87] 70% of whom claim descent from the former North African colonies of Algeria, Morocco and Tunisia.

[88] Loi no 2004-228 du 15 mars 2004 encadrant, en application du principe de laïcité, le port de signes ou de tenues manifestant une appartenance religieuse dans les écoles, collèges et lycées publics https://www.legifrance.gouv.fr/affichTexte.do?cidTexte=JORFTEXT000000417977&dateTexte=&categorieLien=id (accessed 22 June 2016).

"The October Riots in France: A Failed Immigration Policy or the Empire Strikes Back?" (2006) states that,

> The French immigration experience is markedly different than those of other European countries, as France is tainted by colonial history, republican idealism, a rigidly centralized government structure, and deep-seeded traditions of xenophobia.

The article attributes and compares current French immigration policy to that of the colonial 'mission civilisatrice'[89],

> Rather than accept cultural differences, the French government demands that all its citizens adhere to a rigid and exclusive 'French' identity.

Authors Dr. Yvonne Haddad and Michael J. Balz emphasise,

> Government social structures meant to ease the disparity between social classes, such as public housing and education, generally do more to aggravate problems than to solve them; public housing is woefully inadequate and the education structure institutionalises the poor quality of schools in immigrant communities.

The result: stunted social cohesion, marginalisation, low social capital, rage and extremism – the latter of which is channelled through Islamism. Extremist Islam considers itself at war with Western Ideology - a view which appeals to young Muslims who wish to reject a Western culture and society they believe rejected them. This gives them raison d'être (Oprea, 2015), as expressed in the terrorist attacks on Charlie Hebdo (7-9 January 2015) and multiple locations around Paris (13-14 November 2015). Notably, by the end of 2015 over 1700 French citizens had joined ISIS as jihadi fighters (Soufan Group, 2015, p. 12).

---

[89] Civilizing mission: the rationale for colonisation, contributing to the spread of civilisation, in reference to the Westernisation of indigenous populations.

Young men (and women) who join Islamist movements often do so:

- Growing up in a country they believe has never wanted them.
- Feeling excluded from mainstream society.
- Over a sense of injustice or grievance (e.g. lack of equal opportunity, police racial profiling, frequent "stop and search" tactics).
- For a sense of belonging, group status and identity.
- Where the future appears bleak, searching for meaning in their lives.
- Believing that Islamic values should be implemented in all spheres of life.
- Where unemployment is high, the [comparative] standard of living is low.
- As becoming a jihadi fighter washes away their sins - an attractive offer to the faithful (Shelley, 2014).

Of the latter, it should be noted that crime and terrorism are not exclusive; in the absence of a sponsor, it's more than often criminal activity that funds domestic terrorism.

As discussed, based on past mistakes Germany is taking proactive steps to address such integration issues, including social and security concerns, whereas France is still coming to terms with ethnic disparity and domestic terrorism. The challenge, from both a government policy and policing point of view, is finding acceptable compromises, and understanding that ethnicity and culture strongly influence the way in which people engage, interact and respond. Integration and acceptance is a two-way street, based on the expectations of both host and immigrant communities.

Taking this a step further, generally speaking, the Criminal Justice System needs to appreciate that,

> Commonly held ethical values are a reflection of culture, and are not interpreted by each society in the same way. Nevertheless, many societies, lacking the West's legal institutional knowledge, have long held human dignity as their core principle.
>
> (de Saint-Claire, 2014)

What is acceptable practice in one culture, may be illegal in the West. "Policing a Diverse Society" (Clements, 2006, pp. 139-40) highlights entrenched cultural themes that can pose legal issues in Western society:

- Arranged and/or forced marriages.
- Honour-based crimes (e.g. killings).
- Modes of dress (e.g. burka, headscarf, Sikh turban and dagger etc.).
- Gender.
- Domestic violence.
- Female Genital Mutilation (FGM).
- Food and alcohol.
- Sexuality.
- Education.
- Corruption.

Dealing with many of these issues goes beyond the black and white of legal or illegal, right or wrong, requiring the 'buy-in' of leaders from within their own communities.

At the time of writing, a mother in Lahore, Pakistan, had proudly exclaimed to the streets how she had doused her own 17-year-old daughter with petrol, then set her alight for eloping with an ethnic Pashtun. By doing so her family honour was restored[90].

According to the non-profit crowd-funding site GlobalGiving[91], somewhere in the world a girl is violated with female genital mutilation (FGM) every 10 seconds, adding that,

> Communities practice FGM mostly for cultural reasons. Since it is such a powerful social norm, most families will have their daughters cut despite the health risks and harm.

---

[90] *Pakistan: Mother 'burnt her daughter to death' over marriage"*, BBC: http://www.bbc.com/news/world-asia-36479386 (accessed 1 July 2016).

[91] *"Female Genital Mutilation (FGM): What You Need To Know"* https://www.globalgiving.org/fgm/?rf=ggad_16&gclid=CNLKso_6yM0CFfYV0wodWtABLA (accessed 27 June 2016).

In Western society we could not think of something more barbaric than to mutilate one's own child, however,

> FGM is practiced under the belief that women and girls will remain pure and ensure a proper marriage.

The legal response is clear on such cases, but fighting a fixed belief is difficult, though not impossible. Such acts are preventable. Policing diverse communities – characterised by ethnicity, culture, identity, religion, and nationalism - is something than can only be addressed through insight, institutional knowledge and sensitivity.

But where and how to gain such foresight? In the ongoing battle to "win hearts and minds", engage, create partnerships and glean information, Community Policing is definitely the front line, but could be considered a tactical application rather than a strategic approach. Perhaps the place to start is by taking a leaf from Garry McCarthy's strategy book by adopting the Chicago Model, and inviting in teams of social scientists? Or view HTS as a workable template, drawing on instruction from the US Army's Human Terrain Team Handbook. Of course the British Military have regarded cultural knowledge as a backdrop to foreign deployment for over three decades, so conceivably "Culture and Human Terrain" (JDN 4/13) could provide some guidance? Or does the business world hold the answers through the utilisation of cultural intelligence and intercultural communication skills?

Part Four: "Looking Back to Move Forward"

To Review

This contribution sought to examine the rationale behind the establishment of the Human Terrain System as a cultural knowledge tool, and how such an approach could be applied to both international policing and domestic law enforcement.

Up until the early 2000's the US military had a very simplistic and limited understanding of the countries undergoing intervention/ assistance, thus impeding stability (esp. counter-insurgency) and capacity building efforts (donor nation non-consultative view of host nation wants). The Human Terrain System provided an effective tool for the military to gain a practical understanding of targeted cultural behaviour for application in intelligence, mission management, the subsequent decision making process and strategic planning – similar to the needs of any police operation.

Of course the role of the military, and that of civilian law enforcement are worlds apart. Police do not face an enemy; and any force dispensed is used proportionally. Moreover, unlike deployed soldiers, police officers are already on their 'home turf' – and have been empowered by the community to police that community (regardless whether that be on a city, state or national level).

In times past police officers were truly members of the community in which they worked – possessing in-depth local knowledge; nowadays an officer generally doesn't live in the area in which they police - that 'connection' and 'knowledge by association' is lost. Communities requiring 'specific police attention' are no longer homogenous, being instead a multicultural melting pot or ethnic cluster, characterised by low income, high unemployment, social deprivation and few prospects. In contrast, a majority of police personnel are 1.) white, and 2.) come from middle-class backgrounds i.e. not representational of the communities they police. Geographic, class and cultural differences invariably lead to a disconnect in engagement, communication, understanding and mutual objectives. Even so, domestic policing does 'attempt' to reflect the makeup, values and wants of society. To do so police employ a number of mechanisms to deal with the concerns of the communities in their charge, most notably through varying forms of Community Policing.

That being said, Community Policing faces challenges: personnel deficiencies, financial constraints, political prioritisation, and community assent/reception. Due to their diverse makeup communities can view police as friend or foe – or both, proving less than conducive towards police partnerships, mutual cooperation and the provision of information.

However, through our shared sense of values, the social contract guarantees that most members of society will customarily adhere to expected norms and surrender certain rights to the State in exchange

215

for its protection. As witnessed in Chicago, even [former] offenders will turn to the police when they themselves are victims of crime or in some cases to seek protection. The social contract works because it is accepted as an integral and essential part of a functioning society - meaning that society is 'open' to the idea of police cooperation. Cooperation means fostering and developing,

> Strong community networks, relationships and resources. Developing such relationships requires both ongoing efforts and constant renewal of relationships through clear communication and trust between local law enforcement multicultural community members.
>
> (Shusta et al., 2015, p. 275).

But as was clearly the case in London, Chicago and France, makeshift attempts at community "buy-in" proved less than successful.

Arguably neighbourhood-style policing, which prioritises community reassurance and involvement, has made little impact on crime prevention, reduction and investigation - which is the ultimate aim of such strategies.

Following "9/11", many countries explored and adopted an alternative approach,

> A strategic, future-oriented and targeted approach to crime control - broadly represented in the concept of "intelligence led policing" (ILP) - built around analysis and management of problems and risks, rather than reactive responses to individual crimes.
>
> (Maguire & John, 2006).

Intelligence-led Policing (ILP) involves the identification and targeting of high-rate, chronic offenders, and devising strategic interventions based on that intelligence. Taken further, ILP can be regarded as a

Framework for the management of policing priorities of all kinds: it can incorporate the perspectives of partner agencies and local communities, and can set parameters for reactive as well as proactive responses to crime. The structured use of analysis within the Model potentially takes full account of these factors, yet retains an essentially evidence based process of decision making and prioritisation, as well as a 'forward looking' focus on threats to community safety.

(Maguire & John, 2006).

The Royal Canadian Mounted Police regards that ILP,

Requires reliance on intelligence before decisions are taken, be they tactical or strategic. Tactical intelligence affects operations while strategic intelligence is used to set priorities, allocate resources within the organization and may influence public policy'[92].

As ILP increasingly utilises electronic surveillance and information technology, the focus moves towards data collection, analysis, interpretation and archiving. The question of 'how' police intelligence is being collected, processed and disseminated raises genuine legal concerns over privacy and data security (Taylor & Davis, 2010): the conflict of security vs. civil rights. This contrasts greatly to the relative acceptability of the methodology employed for the military intelligence cycle (ref. HTS). Regardless of whether information is collated by social scientists or highly trained tactical operatives, the fact that the Human Terrain System was essentially a military intelligence gathering and analysis mechanism should automatically raise doubts over its compatibility with the transparency and accountability associated with domestic policing. HTS was a tool used to exploit weakness, weaponising social science.

---

[92] RCMP: *Criminal Intelligence Program* http://www.rcmp-grc.gc.ca/ci-rc/index-eng.htm (accessed 26 June 2016).

By extension, taken to its full potential, Intelligence-led policing blurs the line between the role of 'State security' and 'domestic policing'; without sufficient oversight mechanisms exists the very real possibility of abuse of police power - an inevitable result of increased secrecy that surrounds intelligence (Brodeur & Dupont, 2006).

As an information gathering mechanism, Intelligence-led Policing is the closest model comparable to the Human Terrain System. Unquestionably ILP is an effective tool in addressing reducing crime (ref. repeat offending). However, ILP can only be regarded as 'part of a whole'; the importance of community partnership processes cannot be overlooked. ILP is a fact-based system that sets high-level priorities over local concerns. It ignores the human factor, community wants, and any underlying cultural aspect.

Looking beyond intelligence gathering, the overall concept of partnering with social scientists to design strategies of how to engage, establish common ground, build bridges and engender trust seems sound. This brings us closer to the Chicago Model.

Given time Chicago's "police science laboratory" would have yielded results if the city's politicians had been patient, and CPD field officers had committed to the concept - surrendering the warrior in favour of the guardian. Inspired by the Chicago Model, metropolitan centres throughout the US are preparing their guardians through policy, operational procedures, active management support, and training. Beyond preparation for the field, solid training changes the attitudes of police culture itself by demonstrating benefit and worth.

Effective policing isn't just about the number of officers on the streets, but how they are utilised. Cultural Competence is no different than any other required knowledge skill, it needs to be integrated as a core aspect of policing philosophy, through policy, management, training, and field operation. This means accurate needs assessment, developing community-policing strategies and active partnerships, assuring resources, and ensuring field officers are appropriately prepared and supported.

To ensure competence, Cultural Knowledge' orientation training should include:

- Intercultural communication.
- Cultural dimensions theory (Hofsteade).
- Local history.
- Demographics and ethnography.
- Multiculturalism, ethnic clustering and community relations.
- Ramifications of demographic and sociological changes.
- Behavioural influences.
- Culture and crime (e.g. honour crimes etc.).
- Community support entities (public and private).
- Public relations - enhancement through transparency and engagement.
- Conflict resolution skills.
- Overview on Islam (or other relevant religious groups).
- Role of gender in the community.
- Putting socio-cultural knowledge into competent practice.

The ultimate objective is to develop officers who can understand and adapt to the nuances of policing a pluralistic society, and who can adeptly use this knowledge in their daily work. Police officers are not social scientists, though often engage in 'on-the-spot' social work and mediation – and if the latter, they are doing something right.

There is no one singular 'cure-all' guide or system that can be customised for use in every environment, and that proves equally valid in international police missions[93].

As discussed, the purpose of an international police mission is to support a Host Nation in their transition from crisis/conflict/disaster to peace, stability and normalisation, through the provision of Security Sector Reform (SSR) and democratic policing programmes. Unlike deployed UN/NATO/AU soldiers, international police officers (IPOs) work closely with their local counterparts, as interim patrol officers, investigators, monitors, mentors and trainers. Due to this close daily contact natural working relationships develop.

---

[93] International, regional and bilateral - peacekeeping, peacebuilding, security sector reform.

Prior to deployment, cultural awareness, language, gender, HEAT[94] and mission-specific courses are compulsory within the broader 7-week pre-mission training programme[95], and are widely considered essential for in-mission communication, mutual understanding, building good working relations, and establishing fledgling trust (with 'internationals', counterparts and locals). Upon arrival, most IPOs are given an additional 3-5 day orientation briefing, which introduces the more practical aspects of their deployment (duties, accommodation, shopping, travel, personal security, health, cultural etiquette etc.).

Once deployed the "Status of Mission Agreement"[96] (SOMA) grants IPOs certain rights, privileges and immunities. Outside of their duty, this is necessary as, unlike military peacekeeping forces[97] barracked in secure camps, IPOs are normally accommodated directly in the communities in which they serve – sometimes as a boarder with a local family, sharing an apartment with a fellow officer, or renting a purpose-made housing container (depending on mission area, security issues [98] and accommodation availability). As a consequence of proximity, IPOs learn first-hand about the local people - their culture, their beliefs, their views, and their differences - simply by living among them. And the exchange is two-way, breaking down barriers and creating a foundation for understanding, if not trust. By virtue of simply living, shopping, socialising and working among the local population - these officers become familiar with their target Human Terrain, passively acquiring workable cultural insight. With such knowledge, officers are able to more readily implement viable SSR programmes and gain local 'buy-in'.

---

[94] Hostile Environment Awareness Training.

[95] Unfortunately, length, quality and content vary from donor country to country.

[96] Between the Host Nation and donor organisation or country.

[97] NATO, AU and/or UN Mission Troops.

[98] EUPOL were withdrawn from the community, and placed permanently in heavily guarded camps due to active security threats.

Lesson learned: Cultural Knowledge is best enabled by long-term immersion and regular first-hand contact with communities[99]. In a summary of his speech "Reflections on the Counterinsurgency Era" (2013), US General (ret) David Petraeus highlighted, "focus on the security of the people, by living with them in their neighborhoods", thereby enabling a better understanding of the population.

At an IPOs end-of-mission (usually after 12 months), there is often little time for formal information exchange during 'hand-over' with their replacement, however knowledge management[100] does exist. Upon their return home mission veterans attend a compulsory week-long debrief, which is the perfect opportunity to exchange knowledge, relate experiences, present issues, and add to the long list of 'lessons learned'. Following the 'cool-down' period, veterans are often utilised as pre-deployment trainers, bringing authenticity, relevance and understanding to course modules.

It would be fair to state that within an International Police Mission cultural knowledge is learned (prior to deployment) and acquired (in-mission). Therefore, one could conclude that a non-military Human Terrain System would be 'superfluous to need'. Given that a Police Mission cannot implement programmes unilaterally, and that local cooperation is imperative - any implementation of an HTS-type 'intelligence' programme would be met with suspicion, undermining the Host Nation's fragile trust and goodwill, endangering any prospect of further openness and active cooperation.

Conclusion: From 'Human Terrain System' to the 'Human Dimension of Policing'

Given a clearer understanding of purpose, compatibility and acceptability issues associated with the Human Terrain System, it becomes apparent that a more suitable approach to policing diverse communities is required.

---

[99] *Ibid.*15.

[100] The process of capturing, developing, sharing, and effectively using organisational knowledge.

Based on its successful adoption in several US cities[101] (Weichselbaum, 2016), the people-centred "Chicago Model"[102] could quite conceivably provide police and academic researchers with an effective means to address complex community, national and even international policing issues. At the organisational level, a Chicago Model framework would do well to integrate and adapt "Human Relations" methodology - the dynamics and interplay of people in groups, in particular within a professional context (e.g. police and community members). Originally developed for the business sector as a motivational and productivity tool in the 1930's[103] (Monahan & Fisher, 2010), Human Relations theory has become standard practice in organisational management and human resources.

The concept examines,

- The power of natural groups, in which social aspects take precedence over functional organisational structures;
- The need for reciprocal communication, in which communication is two-way; and
- The development of high quality leadership to communicate goals and to ensure effective and coherent decision making.

As an organisational policy "Police Human Relations" would incorporate "Cultural Competence" practice, repositioning police as a public service provider: from Police Force to Police Service. To paraphrase Abraham Lincoln, "for the people, by the people"[104].

---

[101] New York, Baltimore, Oakland (Calif.), Minneapolis, Pittsburgh, Gary (Ind.), Fort Worth (Texas), Stockton (Calif.), and Farmington (New Mexico) etc.

[102] Procedural Justice, Use of Force Model, Chicago Alternative Policing Strategy (CAPS), Violence Reduction Strategy (VRS), RespectStat (citizen feedback), research-based innovations etc.

[103] As part of "Observer Effect" studies; became the precursor to formal Human Resources.

[104] Fittingly, Lincoln's Gettysburg Address espoused rights, equality, freedom, reconciliation, and unity.

Quoting "Practical Strategies for Culturally Competent Evaluation" (CDC, 2014),

> Cultural competence is essential to fostering meaningful stakeholder engagement.

Drawing inspiration from the National Center for Cultural Competence[105], Police-orientated Cultural Competence would require:

- A defined set of values and principles that reflect behaviours, attitudes, policies, and structures that enable them to work effectively cross-culturally.
- The capacity to:
  - Value diversity,
  - Conduct self-assessment,
  - Manage the dynamics of difference,
  - Acquire and institutionalise cultural knowledge, and
  - Adapt to diversity and the cultural contexts of communities they serve.
- Incorporate in all aspects of policy-making, administration, practice and service delivery, systematically involving community partners[106].

> Cultural competence is a developmental process that evolves over an extended period. Both individuals and organizations are at various levels of awareness, knowledge and skills along the cultural competence continuum.
>
> (Cross et al., 1989 / NCCC).

The desired aim is to cultivate police officers' interpersonal skills in:

- Engaging, communicating and conveying information;

---

[105] Cultural Competence definitions, Georgetown University, Center for child and Human Development http://www.nccccurricula.info/culturalcompetence.html (accessed 1 July 2016).

[106] Community groups, special interest groups, local authorities, businesses etc.

- Developing sensitivity, interpreting emotion, reactions and body language;
- Being open (not assuming); and
- Mediation and conflict resolution.

Such skills provide officers with the ability and tools to engage and maintain appropriately compatible and mutually beneficial police-community relations. We must not lose sight that the ultimate purpose of any such strategy is to partner with the communities to prevent, reduce and investigate crime; but any form of partnership requires mutual knowledge, understanding, transparency and trust.

What has become abundantly clear is that to achieve effective community engagement, Human Terrain research and Cultural Competence practice should be actively integrated in all aspects of law enforcement.

Collective practices need a title work under and reference. Within the last five years, elements of the International Security Sector[107] have added "Human Dimension" to its lexicon, a term which references social attitudes, processes, interactions and behaviours – the 'science of human systems' (NAP, 2016). The Security Sector applies this 'human systems' framework to its application of rule of law, human rights, democratic practice and integrity[108] - all of which determines the conduct of democratic policing. Upon close scrutiny, the Human Dimension is a simple, self-explanatory catchphrase that accurately describes and encompasses all [of the above] recommended approaches, methodologies and models, whilst allowing for the flexibility of innovation and customisation: "The Human Dimension - a people-centred approach to policing diverse communities".

In conclusion, having examined the origins and purpose of the US Army's Human Terrain System, it is undoubtedly an ideal tool for military intervention - and potentially stability-orientated peacekeeping

---

[107] OSCE (57 participating States from Europe, Central Asia and North America); the United Nations, the US Army.

[108] Human Dimension mechanisms: http://www.osce.org/odihr/43666 (accessed 1 July 2016).

operations (Julardzija, 2011). Less so within a civilian setting, where any government programme requires public consent, legitimacy, transparency and accountability. In such a light, the Human Terrain System will always be viewed as an ethically ambiguous military intelligence gathering tool.

References

Briant, Nathan; Oram, David (2014), "Renegotiating the Contract: A re-examination of Social Contract Theory against the backdrop of modern day 'State reformation' post-crisis, and Police Integrity", in Hovens, J.L. (ed.) "Building Police Integrity: A Post-Conflict Perspective" (Netherlands Royal Marechaussee / EUPST, Amsterdam)

British Home Office (2011), "An Overview of Recorded Crimes and Arrests Resulting from Disorder Events in August 2011" https://www.gov.uk/government/publications/an-overview-of-recorded-crimes-and-arrests-resulting-from-disorder-events-in-august-2011 (accessed 28 May 2016)

Brodeur, Jean-Paul; and Dupont, Benoit, (2006), "Knowledge Workers or 'Knowledge' Workers?", in "Policing & Society" (Vol. 16, no. 1 (March 2006): pp.7-26) http://www.benoitdupont.net/files/sites/31/2015/07/BrodeurDupont_KnowledgeWorkers.pdf (accessed 26 June 2016)

Bucerius, Sandra, (2011) "Immigrants and Crime", in Tonry, Michael (ed.) "The Oxford Handbook of Crime and Criminal Justice" (OUP, USA)

Bucerius, Sandra, (2014) "Unwanted: Muslim Immigrants, Dignity, and Drug Dealing" (Studies in Crime and Public Policy, OUP)

Bundeskriminalamt (BKA): Police Crime Statistics 2014 - Non-German suspects by nationality http://www.bka.de/nn_194552/EN/Publications/PoliceCrimeStatistics/policeCrimeStatistics (accessed 18 June 2016)

Bundesministerium des Innern (BMI) - Asylum and Refugee Policy: Asylum Procedure Act (AsylVfG): http://www.bmi.bund.de/EN/Topics/Migration-Integration/Asylum-Refugee-Protection/Asylum-Refugee-Protection_Germany/asylum-refugee-policy-germany_node.html (accessed 18 June 2016)

Butt, S.; David, N.; and Laws, N. (2009), "Looking Forward: Local Dispute Resolution Mechanisms in Timor-Leste", Sydney Law School, Legal Studies Research Paper No. 09/33 http://ssrn.com/abstract=1401105 (accessed 5 June 2016)

Centres for Disease Control and Prevention (CDC), (2014), "Practical Strategies for Culturally Competent Evaluation", (Atlanta, GA: US Department of Health and Human Services) http://www.cdc.gov/dhdsp/docs/cultural_competence_guide.pdf (accessed 1 July 2016)

Chan, Janet B.L., (2008) "Changing Police Culture: Policing in a Multicultural Society", (Cambridge University Press)

Chapman, Brett.; and Martin, Eric (2016), "Ideas & Insights: Community Policing Revisited" in "The Police Chief", (Ed. 83 (March 2016): pp.44–46).

Clemens, Phil (2006), "Policing a Diverse Society" (Blackstone's, Oxford University Press, NY)

Community Oriented Policing Services, US Department of Justice (2014) "Community Policing Defined", http://ric-zai-inc.com/Publications/cops-p157-pub.pdf (accessed 27 April 2016)

Cross, T.; Bazron, B.; Dennis, K.; and Isaacs, M., (1989) "Towards A Culturally Competent System of Care, Volume I" (Washington, DC: Georgetown University Child Development Center, CASSP Technical Assistance Center)

de Saint-Claire, Simon (2014), "Shade of Grey in the Thin Blue Line: Determinates of Police Conduct" in Hovens, J.L. (ed.) (2014), "Building Police Integrity: A Post-Conflict Perspective" (Netherlands Royal Marechaussee / EUPST, Amsterdam)

Earley, P. Christopher (2002), "Redefining interactions across cultures and organizations: moving forward with cultural intelligence", in Staw, B.M, Kramer, R.M., (eds.), "Research in Organizational Behavior" (Vol.24, Elsevier)

Francis, Matthew (2012) "What causes Radicalisation? Main lines of consensus in recent research", Radicalisation Research: Guides http://www.radicalisationresearch.org/guides/francis-2012-causes-2/ (accessed 1 July 2016)

Geneva Centre for the Democratic Control of Armed Forces, International Security Sector Advisory Team (DCAF-ISSAT) (2016) "National Security Strategies", http://issat.dcaf.ch/Learn/SSR-in-Practice/Principles-in-Practice/National-Security-Strategies (accessed 6 May 2016)

Glenn, R.W., Panitich, B.R., Barnes-Proby, D., Williams, E., Christian, J., Lewis, M.W., Gerwehr, S., and Brannan, D.W., (2003), "Training the 21st Century Police Officer: Redefining Police Professionalism for the Los Angeles Police Department" (RAND, Los Angeles)

Hackett, Conrad, (2015), "5 Facts About the Muslim Population in Europe" (17 November 2015, Pew Research Centre), http://www.pewresearch.org/fact-tank/2015/11/17/5-facts-about-the-muslim-population-in-europe/ (access 18 June 2016)

Haddad, Yvonne Yazbeck; and Michael J. Balz, (2006), "The October Riots in France: A Failed Immigration Policy or the Empire Strikes Back?" in "International Migration" (2006: Vol. 44, no.2: pp.23–34).

Julardzija, Semir (2011), "Human Terrain System in Peacekeeping Missions" (Peace Operations Training Institute) http://cdn.peaceopstraining.org/theses/julardzija.pdf (accessed 28 June 2016)

Le Sage, Andre (2005), "Stateless Justice in Somalia: Formal and Informal Rule of Law Initiatives", (Centre for Humanitarian Dialogue) http://www.hdcentre.org/uploads/tx_news/166StatelessJusticeinSomalia.pdf (accessed 2 June 2016)

McCarthy, Garry F.; and Rosenbaum, Dennis P., (2015), "From CompStat to RespectStat: Accountability for Respectful Policing", in The Police Chief 82 (August 2015): pp.76–78

McFate, Montgomery, (2014) "Pax Britannica: British Counterinsurgency in Northern Ireland, 1969-1982" (Wilberforce Codex)

McFate, Montgomery; and Lawrence, Janice H. (eds.) (2015), "Science Goes to War: The Human Terrain System in Iraq and Afghanistan" (C Hurst & Co Publishers Ltd)

McFate, Sean, (2015), "Raising an Army: Ten Rules", from "The Modern Mercenary" (OUP)

McMurtry, Roy; and Curling, Alvin (2008) "Community Policing Strategies", The Root Causes of Youth Violence: A Review of Major Theoretical Perspectives, (Queen's Printer for Ontario, p.34)

Maguire, M.; and John, T. (2006) "Intelligence led policing, managerialism and community engagement: Competing priorities and the role of the National Intelligence Model in the UK", in "Policing and Society" (Vol. 16 no. 1, 2006: pp.67-85).

Malik, Keenen (2011), "Moral Poverty and the Riots" http://www.kenanmalik.com/essays/gp_riots_print.html (accessed 30 May 2016)

227

Metropolitan Police Service (2012), "4 Days in August: Strategic Review into the Disorder of August 2011": http://content.met.police.uk/News/MPS-report-into-summer-disorder/1400007360193/1257246745756 (accessed 30 May 2016)

Millar, Gearoid (2014) "An Ethnographic Approach to Peacebuilding: Understanding Local Experiences in Transitional States" (Taylor and Francis)

Millar, L., Braswell, M.; and Whitehead, J., (2010) "Human Relations and Police Work" (Waveland Press, Inc. Long Grove, IL.)

Monahan, Torin; and Fisher, Jill A. (2010), "Benefits of 'Observer Effects': Lessons from the Field", US National Library of Medicine, National Institutes of Health http://www.ncbi.nlm.nih.gov/pmc/articles/PMC3032358/ (accessed 1 July 2016)

National Academies of Sciences, Engineering, and Medicine, "Chapter 7: Human Sciences", in "2015-2016 Assessment of the Army Research Laboratory: Interim Report" (Washington, DC: The National Academies Press, 2016. doi:10.17226/21916) http://www.nap.edu/read/21916/chapter/9 (accessed 1 July 2016)

Odoi, Nana, (2005) "Cultural Diversity in Peace Operations", KAIPTC Paper, No.4 http://www.kaiptc.org/Publications/Occasional-Papers/Documents/no_4.aspx (accessed 10 May 2016)

OECD (2011), "Perspectives on Global Development 2012: Social Cohesion in a Shifting World" (OECD Publishing, Paris), http://dx.doi.org/10.1787/persp_glob_dev-2012-en (accessed 28 May 2016)

Oprea, M.G. (2015), "How France Grew Its Own Terrorists", (The Federalist) http://thefederalist.com/2015/01/16/how-france-grew-its-own-terrorists/?_sm_byp=iVV8rnWsR3rMv1kS (accessed 16 January 2015)

Petraeus, David H. (2013) "Reflections on the Counterinsurgency Era", (The RUSI Journal, Vol. 158, Iss. 4)

The Police Foundation (Longstaff, A., Willer, J., Chapman, J., Czarnomski, S., Graham, J.), "History and development", (2015) from "Neighbourhood policing: Past, present and future" http://www.police-foundation.org.uk/uploads/catalogerfiles/neighbourhood-policing-past-present-and-future---a-review-of-the-literature/neighbourhood_policing_past_present_future.pdf (accessed 21 May 2016)

Price, David H. (2009) "Human Terrain Systems, Anthropologists and the War in Afghanistan" (Counterpunch)

Price, David H. (2011) "Weaponizing Anthropology: Social Science in Service of the Militarized State" (AK Press)

Sanburn, Josh (2016) "Chicago Shootings and Murders Surged in 2015" (TIME), http://time.com/4165576/chicago-murders-shootings-rise-2015/ Schmidt, Patrick L. (2007), "In Search of Intercultural Understanding" (Meridian World Press)

Shelley, Louise I., (2014), "Dirty Entanglements: Corruption, Crime and Terrorism" (Cambridge University Press)

Shonick, Kaja, (2009) "Politics, Culture, and Economics: Reassessing the West German Guest Worker Agreement with Yugoslavia" in "Journal of Contemporary History", (Oct 2009, Vol. 44 Issue 4, pp 719-736)

Shusta, Robert M.; Levine, Deena R.; Wong, Herbert Z.; Olson, Aaron AT.; and Harris, Philip R. (eds.), (2015) "Multicultural Law Enforcement: Strategies for Peacekeeping in a Diverse Society" (6th Edition, Pearson / Prentice Hall)

The Soufan Group, (2015) "Foreign Fighters", http://soufangroup.com/wp-content/uploads/2015/12/TSG_ForeignFightersUpdate_FINAL3.pdf (access 19 June 2016)

Taylor, Robert W.; and Davis, Jennifer E. (2010), "Intelligence-Led Policing and Fusion Centers", in Dunham, R.G.; and Albert, G.P. (eds.) "Critical Issues in Policing: Contemporary Issues" (6th ed., (Long Grove: Waveland Press Inc.) pp.224-244)

Timor-Leste Legal Education Project (TLLEP), (2013) "Legal History and the Rule of Law in Timor-Leste" (Stanford Law School / USAID / The Asia Foundation) http://web.stanford.edu/group/tllep/cgi-bin/wordpress/wp-content/uploads/2013/09/Legal-History-and-the-Rule-of-Law-in-Timor-Leste.pdf (accessed 9 June 2016)

Tyler, T. R. (2006), "Why People Obey the Law", (Revised Edition, Princeton University Press)

UN DESA, Population Division (2016) "International Migration Report 2015: Highlights", (ST/ESA/SER.A/375) http://www.un.org/en/development/desa/population/migration/publications/migrationreport/docs/MigrationReport2015_Highlights.pdf (accessed 03 June 2016)

USAID (2009), "Fostering Justice in Timor-Leste: Rule of Law Program Evaluation" http://pdf.usaid.gov/pdf_docs/Pdacm677.pdf (accessed 9 June 2016) von Ulmenstein, Sibylle; and Sultan, Bonnie, (2011), "Group Violence Reduction Strategy: Four Case Studies of Swift and Meaningful Law Enforcement Responses" (Center for Crime Prevention and Control, John Jay College of Criminal Justice / COPS, US DOJ)

Weichselbaum, Simone (2016), "The 'Chicago Model' of Policing Hasn't Saved Chicago: why is everyone copying it" (Marshal Project / TIME): https://www.themarshallproject.org/2016/04/19/the-chicago-model-of-policing-hasn-t-saved-chicago (accessed 29 April 2016)

Chapter 9

Communication Peculiarities Between Believers of Islam and Public Servants

Dr Gediminas Bučiūnas

The author of this study researches the communication peculiarities with immigrants during the process of pre-trial investigation and legal proceedings. The study is based on author's personal experience, analysis of scientific literature about the religion of Islam and Muslim customs, interviews with citizens of the Islamic Republic of Afghanistan who worked in places such as the United Nations Assistance Missions in Afghanistan, the European Union Police Missions in Afghanistan, International Security Assistance Force (ISAF) and Afghanistan citizens who emigrated to Europe during the period of 2012 to 2014. This topic has not been touched at all in Lithuania, Latvia and Estonia. Communication with adherents of Islam has become particularly important in 2015 - 2016 due to the massive flow of immigrants from Asia and Africa to Europe. The arriving people bring their own customs - disregarding or not knowing those customs while performing public administration functions or criminal procedure actions (e. g. questioning a female (Muslim), using police dogs during a search) can provoke a negative reaction towards public servants and in some cases even induce radicalization of some parts of the population; of migrants. The author's suggestions concerning pre-trial investigation procedures and public administration will help reduce frictions between public servants who are responsible for maintaining public order and believers of Islam, as well as immigrants from the continents of Africa and Asia.

Introduction

There is a common misconception, that radicalisation is a phenomenon that only occurs in the religion of Islam. Islam has been labeled as one of the most aggressive religions in the world, even though there are no grounds to link it to aggression and radicalisation. The religious ideas themselves are not aggressive, but interpretation and absolutism can change them, especially when those ideas are seen as the only "true truth". Overall, there are a lot of cases of radicalisation among different social groups and adherents of a religion. One of the examples is a Norwegian right-wing extremist Anders Breivik, who has been found guilty for wilfully killing dozens of people[1].

In this era of digital technologies, ideas and information spread rapidly, a great example would be social networks and their part during the „Arab Spring" in Syria in 2011. Social networks are used by various extremist and terrorist organisations, including the Islamic Caliphate, in order to get young individuals to join their ranks and fight for their cause. The „Arab Spring" stirred North African and Middle Eastern countries such as Tunisia, Libya, Egypt, Syria and other Muslim states[2]. It led to the changes of non-democratic regime by both peaceful protests and armed clashes between supporters of the old regime and the forces supporting democratic changes in the country's governance. The increase of armed clashes forced many people from North Africa (Libya, Tunisia, Egypt) and the Middle East (Syria, Iraq, Afghanistan, Pakistan) to attempt an illegal entrance to Europe. According to the data of the European Commission, in the year 2014 more than 276 113 immigrants entered the European Union, mainly from Italy. This number is 138 percent larger than in 2013[3].

---

[1] Norway Mass Killer Gets the Maximum: 21 Years. http://www.nytimes.com/2012/08/25/world/europe/anders-behring-breivik-murder-trial.html?_r=0

[2] Christopher Philips Syria's bloody Arab spring. http://www.lse.ac.uk/IDEAS/publications/reports/pdf/SR011/FINAL_LSE_IDEAS__SyriasBloodyArabSpring_Phillips.pdf

[3] Irregular immigration. http://ec.europa.eu/dgs/home-affairs/what-we-do/policies/immigration/irregular-immigration/index_en.htm.

The vast majority of immigrants travelled by sea and land. They mostly took sailing boats, rafts from North Africa, Turkey to islands in the Mediterranean Sea belonging to Italy and Greece. After that they changed their course to Austria, Germany, the United Kingdom and Sweden.

The author will overview the peculiarities of communication with immigrants. People who arrive from war-torn countries could be mistreated or abused while public servants perform public administration procedures or public security functions, for example during asylum seekers related procedures.

The majority of immigrants from Asia and Africa share not only the same religion (Islam), but also strong communal-tribal relations, which is one of the main uniting origins of newly arriving persons from war-torn countries to the European Union states. Secondly, the countries from which the immigrants arrive usually differ from Europe, because they have very strongly rooted religious and traditional norms. This can be clearly seen when it comes to communication peculiarities while conducting public administration or juridical procedures with adherents of Islam. Some things that are considered normal for Europeans are not considered acceptable for people from other cultures, e.g. one should avoid maintaining direct eye contact with a female Muslim during interviews or surveys.

Among immigrants migrating from Africa and Asia to the continent of Europe, there might be criminals and suspects responsible for a certain crime in their country of origin, e. g. genocide, mass killings, some of them might have intentions to carry out terror acts in Europe[4]. International treaties and national law oblige European Union Member States to take action in order to prosecute such persons. In order to reveal the crime and its perpetrators, various proceedings are carried out based on the law acts and regulations of that particular state.

Each procedural investigative action is carried out in accordance with the criminal procedure act and forensic science rules. It should be kept in mind that suspects of criminal activity who are trying to enter

[4] Just wait...Islamic State reveals it has smuggled thousands of extremists to Europe. http://www.express.co.uk/news/world/555434/Islamic-State-ISIS-Smuggler-THOUSANDS-Extremists-into-Europe-Refugees

the European Union Member States territory for asylum are usually prepared for the unexpected and has a carefully prepared plan on how to behave in certain situations. One may refer to it as a „plan B". In a case where the European Union Member State public servant is unaware of the communication peculiarities with arriving immigrants regarding asylum or pre-trial investigation, an arriving suspect may take advantage of this situation by spreading his ideas and beliefs. Thus, knowing the traditions and religious beliefs of the arriving immigrants can help avoid conflict situations that may occur in the future.

Massive influx of refugees from Syria, Iraq, Pakistan and other Asian, African countries to Europe is one of the biggest challenge for migration and border guard services, other law enforcement agencies. State institutions should pay more attention to the „unwritten law" – actions of behaving that is usual among people of particular group carrying on interview during administrative procedures, pre-trial investigation, for example particularities of interviewing with Muslim female, searches at facilities where a Muslim female lives. It became object of this article – communication particularities between believers of Islam and public servants.

The author of the article wants to highlight specific features of asylum seekers interview, also, search, examination actions of facilities and interview during one of the criminal procedures stages – a pre-trial investigation. Findings of this articles will be useful for public servants who are performing or are going to perform their functions in the near future, also it helps public servants to cope with pre-conflict and conflict situations while performing public duties and prevents the spread of various interpretations about the behaviour of public servants.

Particularities of Interviews on Asylum Seeker Status and Interviews During Pre-Trial Investigation

Every research aims to achieve some objectives despite of its type and nature. For example, criminal investigation seeks to reveal crime, establish grounds for and conditions of criminal liability. A person shall held liability under criminal law for committing a crime. Only the court has the exceptional right to impose a criminal penalty. When studying natural phenomena, for example when researching the factors influencing climate change in different parts of the world, the most effective means of research instruments are used to achieve the results. Some research instruments are more suitable for investigating natural phenomena, others are more suited for social phenomena such as immigration and crime for example the murder is prohibited by law in Lithuania, France, Chad and Syria. One of the research instruments could be considered an interview. The interview procedure in criminal procedure is similar in Spain and Poland. The asylum procedure is regulated by international laws, national laws and post-legislative acts. Each European Union (EU) Member State has different requirements for the asylum seekers, however the interview is a required procedure in all EU Member States.

Criminal investigation is regulated by procedural laws. These laws can be separate acts or codes, which determine the order of actions taken during a search, examination or interview. The procedural law cannot outline all possible outcomes during the interview, it only draws general guidelines and conditions in order to carry out the investigative action. At first sight, it can be difficult to see the differences of interview for asylum in the Republic of Lithuania and the Syrian Arab Republic. The above mentioned procedure has a few common traits, but at the same time it is widely different due to religious and customary norms. Disregarding customary and religious norms can have negative consequences on the image of a country's state institutions. In addition it could frustrate the refugees and cause conflicts, spread radicalisation and violence. The asylum in the Republic of Lithuania is regulated by the Law on the Legal status of foreigners.

This law states that a foreigner or stateless person has the right to apply for asylum in the territory of the national border, in a territory that is subject to the legal regime of the border, in a territorial police institution or the Foreigners' Registration Centre. Public servants of the state must interview the asylum seeker immediately. The interview procedure is not fully regulated by the law, but the main guidelines of the procedural action are provided. A similar course of action is provided in the criminal procedure law.

A pre-trial investigation officer or prosecutor carries out the investigation of an offence according to the conditions provided by the law. It is up to the public servant to decide which investigative procedural steps are most efficient according to investigation tactics and other factors, e. g. testimony of a witness. Not every person can be a witness. Only those that know the particular circumstances or bearers of significant evidence are suited to be witnesses. It is stated in the 2002 14th of March law No. IX-785 art. 78 of the Code of Criminal Procedure (CPC) of the Republic of Lithuania. In 2014 a similar provision was adopted in the CPC art. 52, 64 of the Islamic Republic of Afghanistan and the Arab Republic of Egypt.

The CPC of the Republic of Lithuania[5], Chapter V, section one, art. 78-83 regulates who is suitable to be a witness. It also describes what type of persons cannot be witnesses, specifies the circumstances of witness questioning, peculiarities of personal testimonies and describes the rights and duties of a witness. Article 183, 185 of the same procedural law overviews the peculiarities of victim and witness questioning. A similar procedure is described in the CPC articles 58-64 of the Arab Republic of Egypt[6] and the Islamic Republic of Afghanistan. The previously mentioned laws of criminal proceedings only provide the general guidelines regarding the participants of the interview.

An interview as a research tool is used during the investigation of criminal offences of Lithuania, Afghanistan and Egypt. The conditions and applications of this method has similar conditions and peculiarities in the previously mentioned countries and one of the arising questions is what are the main differences? Searching the answer for this question the author of the study begins with scientifically formulated recommendations while carrying out interviews. One of the recommendations is to keep a direct eyes contact during the interview. The author of the article suggests that it is only a general recommendation. A conclusion can be made that blindly relying only on

---

[5] The Criminal procedure code of the Republic of Lithuania. Official Gazette, 2002, Nr. 37-1341.

[6] Criminal procedure code of 1971. http://www1.umn.edu/humanrts/research/Egypt/ Criminal%20Procedures.pdf

the rules formulated by forensic science is not a suitable approach. Certain issues can be encountered while performing public administration and public order functions without the knowledge of an immigrant's country of origin, history, cultural features, moral and ethical values.

The worst case scenario is the disregarding of customary and religious norms of migrants origin country. This can result in violence and violence-promoting movements in the continent of Africa or Asia. In order for asylum interviews to be more effective, it is not enough to know the peculiarities of inspections, searches, the Constitution and the national Criminal Procedure Act and pre-trial investigation. A person should also have a minimal knowledge of the Quran, which regulates in details the daily Muslim life (how often one should pray, marriage, divorce, family matters and etc). In some countries, the priority of religious norms is enshrined in the Constitution. For example in article 3 of the Constitution of the Islamic Republic of Afghanistan it is stated that law cannot contradict with the religion of Islam[7].

A researcher of customary law, Thomas Barfield from Boston observed that customs exist as an informal source of law and are quite often used in social regulations that do not include positive law and religious law norms.

This is especially important to know when performing the functions of public administration or separate procedural investigative actions on adherents of Muslim regardless of their procedural status.

The Framework Convention for the Protection of National Minorities states that a democratic society should not only respect the ethnic minorities and their culture, but also create the right conditions for their expression, perseverance and development[8]. The Republic of Lithuania signed the above mentioned Convention and ratified it in accordance with the law. It has become an integral part of the Republic of Lithuania's legal system. This law act has a big influence on the

---

[7] The Constitution of Afghanistan. http://www.afghanembassy.com.pl/afg/images/pliki/TheConstitution.pdf

[8] Framework Convention for the Protection of National Minorities. http://www.coe.int/en/web/conventions/full-list/-/conventions/rms/090000168007cdac

criminalistic methodology in the process of actions governed by the CPC regarding national minorities.

Forensic science provides recommendations in detail on how to conduct interviews of a suspect or a witness. While preparing or improving an already existing methodic of interview conduction in criminal procedure, we have to pay attention to the main options which are set up in the Framework Convention for the Protection of National Minorities. It guides us forward to customary law and unwritten rules. A lot of Eastern European scholars and practitioners highlight the importance of keeping eye contact during an interview procedure in their publications, articles, handbooks on conducting interview. It is pointed out that an interviewer should establish direct eye contact with interviewees and maintain it during the interview procedure. First of all, it helps to read interviewee's thoughts, predict his/her behaviour during the interview. Secondly, to control the situation during the interview and to receive valuable information from the body language of an interviewee. Finally, to construct interview trends, evaluate the quality of informations or even catch moments/situations where an interviewee is trying to avoid uncomfortable questions.

The "Direct eye contact" interview model was and is widely spread amongst law enforcement agencies officials. The „direct eye contact" model experiences impact from challenges of the 21st century - migration processes in Europe, especially undocumented (illegal) migration. This model should be modified according to new requirements brought by the new times. Arriving migrants from Asia, and Africa come with their own customs, habits to European countries. Some habits, customs are widely different from most populations of European Union Member States, especially those arriving from the East and Middle European countries. For example, in the Muslim society „direct eye contact" model during communication, interview is not welcome, especially if a male tries to establish direct eye contact or to keep on direct constant eye contact with a Muslim female. This behaviour of public servants can be accepted amongst some Islam religion followers as unacceptable behaviour or even worse, as an insulting act towards a Muslim female, targeting the spiritual values of Islam.

The author of this article conducted a survey amongst people who had emigrated from the Islamic Republic of Afghanistan to Europe. The author of the survey asked respondents a question: Can knowledge of Muslims customs, basic knowledge of Islam faith facilitate interview procedures? The respondents answered that a good knowledge of Muslim (not only) customary law, history of migrants origin country, their relations with Islam religion is a welcoming idea. It helps to avoid misunderstandings during administrative procedures between public servants and migrants, to decrease tension, to build bridges of understanding between new migrants and local population and to change state's image. The Law on Public Service demands from public servants to be tolerant and impartial. For example, Article 3 part 2 paragraph 8 of Law on Public service of the Republic of Lithuania states: „exemplariness. A public servant must duly perform his duties, constantly improve, as well as to be a person of integrity, tolerant, respectful and orderly." [9]

To sum up, it is not recommended for public servants to establish and keep a direct eye contact with a female belonging to Islam faith during the interview procedure.

Examination and Search Specifics

Another action quite often used in the pre-trial investigation is a search, which is regulated by the Republic of Lithuania Code of Criminal Procedure Article 207. Forensic science by the research of object divides search into: the area of residential and non-residential premises, a separate facility that might have lots of useful information about the crime. A similar action - inspection is regulated by the Islamic Republic of Afghanistan CPC. The investigation of this action in the Islamic Republic of Afghanistan has its own peculiarities. In most Muslim countries, females have separate rooms to which can access only those males that are associated with the female by blood or legal ties, eg., husband, brother, son. The neglect of this unwritten prohibition, which for centuries passed on from generation to generation, can be interpreted as an attack on women's honour.

---

[9] Law on Public service the Republic of Lithuania. *Official Gazette, 2002, Nr. 45-1708.*

According to local customs, the honour of a woman must be defended, and at defence of their measures range is quite wide. This should be taken into account during the investigation and other actions, such as search. It means that only a female servant can carry out the inspection (of rooms) or search where Muslim women live.

In the examination (of rooms) or a search of Muslim people, a very sensitive issue is the use of police dogs in order to look for significant objects. This is a very big problem of the investigation carried out on the adherents of Islamic religion and in their living quarters, cult buildings - mosques, religious schools. Muslims treat dogs as unclean animals, and their presence inside the room is not a tolerable thing[10]. British Police Chiefs Association recommends to place shoes-pads on the dog's paws when using police dogs for inspection or searches in Muslim houses of worship or home[11]. Another important point is to respect the holy book of Islam - the Quran. This book, its copies, or its individual parts can not be folded, placed on the ground, torn, burned or damaged in other ways. These actions shall be regarded as the greatest disrespect for both the Islamic religion and its adherents. As an example of what the consequences may be contrary to this advice, the author provides a case that occurred in 2012. There was a worldwide outrage in Muslim communities with outbreaks of violence in various parts of the world after a case in which pastor Terry Jones from US Florida planned to burn the Quran[12]. To sum up, during an inspection/examination (of rooms) or a search, the Muslim Holy book - Quran cannot be folded, placed on the ground, torn, burned or damaged in other ways. Considering the religious attitudes of the Islam adherents and their customs, the appropriate choice of tactics in the public administration functions or procedural investigative process will guarantee that the Muslim people's values will not be insulted.

---

[10] Unclean animal. http://en.wikipedia.org/wiki/Unclean_animal

[11] Police sniffer dogs to wear bootees during house searches to avoid offending Muslims. http://www.dailymail.co.uk/news/article-1032449/Police-sniffer-dogs-wear-bootees-house-searches-avoid-offending-Muslims.html

[12] Pastor weighing plans to burn Qurans amid U.S warnings. http://www.cnn.com/2010/US/09/07/florida.quran.burning/

Conclusions

• It is not recommended for a public servant to establish and keep direct eye contact with a female belonging to the faith of Islam during the interview procedure.

• During an inspection (of rooms) or a search, the Muslim holy book - the Quran cannot be folded, placed on the ground, torn, burned or damaged in other ways. Considering the religious attitudes of the Islam adherents and their customs, the appropriate choice of tactics in the public administration functions or procedural investigative process will guarantee that there Muslim people's values will not be insulted.

• Only a female servant can carry out an inspection (of rooms) or a search where a Muslim female lives.

References

The Constitution the Republic of Lithuania. Official Gazette. Nr. 33-1014.

The Framework Convention for the protection of national minorities. Official Gazette. 2000-03-08, Nr. 20-497.

The Criminal procedure Code of the Republic of Lithuania. Official Gazette. 2002-04-09 Nr. 37-1341.

Law on Legal status of foreigners. Official Gazette, 2004, Nr. 73-2539.

Law on Public service . Official Gazette, 1999, Nr. 66-2130.

The Constitution of Afghanistan. http://www.afghanembassy.com.pl/afg/images/pliki/TheConstitution.pdf

Criminal procedure code of the Islamic Republic of Afghanistan. EUPOL-AFGHANISTAN, 2014.

Dogs in the Islamic tradition and nature. Encyclopaedia of Religion and Nature. New York: Continuum International, 2004.

Thomas Barfield. Afghan customary law and its relationship to formal judicial institutions. United States institute for peace. Washington D. C. 2003.

The customary laws of Afghanistan. http://www.usip.org/sites/default/files/file/ilf_customary_law_afghanistan.pdf

Burda, R., Kuklianskis, S.,Interview during pre –trial investigation stage. Mykolas Romeris University. Vilnius, 2007.

Burda, R. Kriksciūnas, R. Latauskiene, E. Tactics and methodics of criminalistics. Mykolas Romeris university. Vilnius, 2004.

Jupp, J. Legal transplants as tools for post-conflict law reform: justification and evaluation. Cambridge Journal of International and Comparative Law (3)1 p. 381–406, 2014.

Kurapka, E., Malevskij, H, Palskys, E.Basics of forensic science. Mykolas Romeris university. Vilnius, 1998.

Best practices for building investigative capacity in developing or post-conflict countries. Research memorandum. International network for promote the rule of law. July 2012. USA.

Quran Translated by Jakubauskas, R., Geda, S. Vilnius, Kronta, 2010.

Аверьянова, Т. В., et al. Криминалистика. Москва, 1999.

Балашов Д. Н., Балашов Н. М., Маликов С. В. Криминалистика. Москва: Инфра-М, 2010.

Белкин, Р. С. Курс советской криминалистики. Т. 1: Общая теория советской криминалистики. Москва: Академия МВД СССР, 1977.

Chapter 10

Investigating the Public Perception of Door Supervision in the Night-Time Economy

John Akerele

Door supervision, a sector of the private security industry has been plagued with issues of misconduct, violence, aggression and criminality. The introduction of the Security Industry Authority (SIA) was a means to regulate and improve the reputation of door supervisors. Years after regulation, door supervision is still criticised for aggression, violence and unprofessional conduct. A plethora of academic literature has centred on how regulation has affected door supervisors, with no insight from the general public's perception. The primary aim of this small-scale study is to provide an insight into the perception of door supervisors with regards to the general public. A quantitative design was utilised, featuring an online questionnaire. Findings indicate that the general public is not aware of the regulation and changes made within door supervision. Despite negative perceptions or experiences encountered, door supervisors are found to increase safety. With more customer focused SIA training and increased media awareness of the improvements, this could alter the reputation of door supervisors in a positive way.

Introduction

The past decade has seen the rapid growth of the private security sector into an integral part of the commercial realm (Walker, 1999; Button, 2002). Encompassing various subdivisions of the security sector, private security has progressed to become an extended fragment of the public policing family (Wakefield & Gill, 2009). Despite this progression, the private security sector experienced issues regarding regulation and organisational structure.

The Security Industry Authority (SIA) was established in order to regulate the private security sector under the terms of the Private Security Industry Act 2001 (SIA Annual Report, 2010-2011). As one of the designated sectors of private security, door supervision over the years has been associated with negativity and scrutiny from the government and the general public. Indeed, a considerable amount of academic research has highlighted a number of behavioural issues which have damaged the image of door supervision (Walker, 1999; Winlow, 2003; Hobbs, Hadfield, Lister & Winlow 2005; Pratten, 2007; Roberts 2009).

Regardless of the regulation of door supervisors, little research has concentrated on the public's opinion of the occupation. Door supervision has received negative media coverage, associated with aggression and violent incidents, contributing towards the adverse image of door supervisors (Winlow; Hobbs; Lister; Hadfield, 2002). This is also supported by a growing number of academic literature focused on violence and aggression in the night-time economy (Walker, 1999; Roberts 2009). The main aim of this research literature is to gain an insight into the perception of door supervisors, from the outlook of the general public. This research entails a brief literature review and a methodological outline on the perception of door supervisors. The findings of this research will be systematically presented, explained and end with a discussion of viable recommendations. This research can also be used as a benchmark for other similar studies.

Issues Regarding Door Supervision

Over time, the night-time economy has become a place where patrons come to socialise and be entertained. Door supervisors, the guardians of the night-time economy became more prominent, with the evolution of the late-night dance culture (O' Mahoney, 1997). The major role of the night guardians is to uphold a constitutional public safety duty, which can extend to access prevention and removal of individuals who

244

display unruly behaviours (Licensing Act, 2003). When these situations are managed incorrectly, this negatively affects the public image of door supervisors.

Labelled as bouncers, some door supervisors have abused this privilege of the role and engaged in criminal activities (Morris, 1998; Budd, 2003; Green & Plant, 2007; Roberts 2009). Despite this vital job role, door supervisors have managed to captivate the public, the media and academic researchers in a negative way (Winlow, 2003). The factors below depict the problematic areas facing door supervision.

Door Supervisors and Factors Affecting Public Perception

When working within an environment where people are under the influence of alcohol and other prohibited substances, violence and aggression are a valid part (Graham & Wells, 2001; Graham & Wells, 2003). Despite the role to ensure safety and reduce violence, door supervisors have been accused of violent behaviour, aggression and illicit sales of drugs, which has resulted in criminal convictions for some door supervisors (Winlow et al., 2002). A door supervisory role requires the ability to challenge and control the surroundings, which will not be easily accepted by most night-time patrons (Van Brunschot, 2003).

> Many local crime networks brought an increased number of criminal histories, and so reputations, to an occupation that already, by nature, tended to utilise men of local notoriety.
>
> (Lister, Hadfield, Hobbs & Winlow, 2001).

The quotation above indicates that there is a general assumption that door supervisors are from notorious or corrupt criminal backgrounds by default (Lister et al., 2001; Livingstone & Hart, 2003). This lack of integrity has tarnished the perception of door supervisors and the profession as a whole. Doors supervisors have experienced difficulty being classified as a profession in its own right. Comparing door supervisors to another profession such as a police officer, the profession is not as respected (Abrahamsen & Williams, 2006). This could be affiliated to the lack of academic certification courses for door supervisors and the lack of a cohesive voice within the private security sector as a whole (Pratten, 2007).

The media have documented incidents involving door supervisors, leading to negative media portrayal overall (Seiter, 2006). Negative representation via the media can have dire effects on the public's opinion, as the media can at times be influential. Using headlines such as *"Control freak and his reign of terror: Pumped full of steroids, sword-wielding club bouncer Moat"* (Daily Mail, 5 July 2010) can cause misconceptions. The headline was in reference to Raoul Moat, who previously was a bouncer but current profession was as a tree surgeon. When negative incidents occur, door supervisors are quickly seen as thugs and bullies (Anthias, 1999). This could be associated with the way films portray door supervisors, as big muscular men throwing patrons out of venues with headlocks (Monaghan, 2002). All these negative stereotypes have an effect on the public's perception and such misconceptions encourage 'bouncer' stereotypes (Messerschmidt, 1999; Monaghan, 2002).

In some countries, door supervision can be viewed as an expansion of the policing family giving them access to body arms and official power (Button, 2003; Wakefield, 2003). However, in countries such as the United Kingdom, door supervisors do not have any official power or legal authority to use physical force on a patron. Mopas and Stenning (2001) clarify that patrons usually comply with rules and regulations of a venue as a trade-off for gaining access and remaining in the venue.

Unlike official police officers that rely on legitimate use of physical force, door supervisors tend to use the following strategies to maintain authority:

- Symbolic rules and regulation conferred by night-time venues.
- The use of a statutory power of arrest.
- Use of physical appearance such as size, strength and uniforms to deter unlawful conduct.

As a profession, door supervisors do not have any special powers, but have the same common law code as citizens e.g. citizen's arrest. With the increase in lawsuit and court costs, employers often discourage using physical force except in legitimate self-defence situations (Van Brunschot, 2003; Mopas and Stenning, 2001).

Previous research has highlighted that door supervisors also find it difficult to adequately protect themselves when confronted with violence (Finney, 2004). There have been cases involving the use of force on a patron where door supervisors have been arrested and prosecuted (Perkins, 2008; Button, 2007). Hobbs, Hadfield, Lister, & Winlow, (2005) noted that door supervisors would prefer the support of the police in some situations, however, it is often found the police are hesitant and unaccommodating to attend to violent incidents within a venue.

Door Supervisors in Perspective

There is an increasing amount of literature that supports the concept that the night-time economy is a common place for aggression and violent behaviour (Grahams & Wells, 2003; Roberts 2009). The investigation of door supervisors arose from research pertaining to alcohol, aggression and violence in the night economy. This developed inadvertently as door supervisors were noted as a contributing factor to aggression and violent incidents (Finney, 2004). The two terms 'aggression and violence' have attracted the interest of academic scholars in investigating the nature of door supervisors (Winlow; Hobbs; Lister; Hadfield, 2002).

With regards to the academic world, door supervisors are perceived to be an out-group of the night-time society and are not easily accessible for research studies. This has resulted in difficulties in investigating door supervisors. Many studies have adopted different research methods such as ethnographic research approach in order to examine the traits and characteristics of door supervisors more closely.

Table 10.1 Related Literature and Research Methods

Author	Journals/Books	Research method
Roberts (2007)	Bar aggression in Hoboken New Jersey: Don't blame the bouncers!	Observation (researcher status unknown by participants)
Perkins (2008)	Taking it on the Chin; Violence Against British Door Supervisors	Interview
Flynn (1997)	Regulating The Privatisation of Policing	Interview and questionnaires
Michael (2002)	A Sense of Security?	Questionnaires
Rigakos (2002)	The New Parapolice	Observation (researcher's status known by participants)
South (1985)	Private Security and Social Control	Observation (researcher's status unknown by participants)
Adu-boakye (2002)	Private Security and Retail Crime Prevention	Observation (researcher's status unknown by participants)
Wakefield (2003)	Selling Security – The Private Policing of Public Space	Observation (researcher's status known by participants)
Graham, La Rocque, Yetman, Ross, and Guistra (1980)	Aggression and barroom environments	Observation (researcher status unknown by participants)

Button (2007) noted that it has been difficult to research door supervisors within close proximity, as door supervisors tend to be suspicious of researchers. As evident from Table 1, most research has investigated door supervisors using an observational method, which can sometimes be deemed as deceptive because participants are not usually aware they are being investigated. Despite all the research on door supervisors, no academic literature has focused on what the patrons think about door supervisors.

Regulation and Door Supervisors

Over time, the misconduct and unprofessional behaviour of door supervisors has led to a negative perception of the profession. This prompted regulation and the rebranding of door supervision as a whole (Walker, 1999; Button, 2002).

Reporting to the Home Secretary, the duties of the SIA in the door supervision sector includes; enforcing licensing acts on all door security personnel and assisting security companies on assessing security criteria. These regulations were put in place to tackle the issues within door supervision. In order to be approved as a licensed door supervisor, all individuals must be ready to undergo the following process.

Licensing

The license application fee for door supervision is £220 for a three-year licence. After achieving the SIA approved training course, the next stage is applying for a licence. This would feature an identity check and criminal record check. There are rules of conduct that the door supervisor must adhere by, this includes displaying license badges whilst at work (Lister et al., 2001).

SIA Approved Training Courses

These training courses are not delivered by the SIA, however, the SIA have endorsed training organisations to train and award certifications. The door supervisors training course briefly centers on four stages; common module, specialist module, conflict management and physical intervention module. Sometimes these courses extend to basic first aid training (Lister, Hadfield, Hobbs & Winlow, 2001; Pratten, 2007).

Arguably, the SIA training course can be classified as insufficient training, due to its inability to completely prepare individuals for the reality of the job role (Hobbs, Winlow, Hadfield & Lister, 2005; Pratten, 2007).

Criminal Record Checks

This was introduced to reduce criminality in relation to applicants who had committed serious offences and would be rechecked every 3 years. This, in addition to identity checks confirms the demographic and identity of applicants. The SIA has the power to fine, suspend, revoke and convict door supervisors in light of misconduct (The Security Industry Authority 2008; Pratten, 2007).

Prior to regulation, door supervisors were deemed to have a negative image and perception (Finney, 2004). Over the years, criminality, aggression and violent behaviour have been attributed to door supervisors as a profession (Pratten, 2007). Roberts (2007) noted that there are other factors such as alcohol intoxication on the part of the patron that contributes to aggression and violent incidents as well.

The introduction of the SIA has rebranded door supervision as a profession, adding structure and accountability for criminal offences within the sector. After the establishment of the SIA, there has been a growing number of academic research on the effect of regulation on door supervision, however, there is no research focusing mainly on the public perception of door supervisors. The public perception of door supervisors can be used to gauge the impact of regulation on the image and reputation of door supervision.

Methodology

In order to investigate the public perception of door supervisors, a questionnaire was implemented to ascertain attitudes, opinions and general knowledge; regarding door supervisors in the United Kingdom. The questionnaire was directed to 100 individuals, however, 60 respondents successfully completed this over a period of three weeks. Table 2 features a breakdown of the demographics of the respondents in relation to gender and age.

Table 10.2 Breakdown of Age and Gender.

Age	Female	Male	Total
18-20	3	5	8
21-29	13	8	21
30-39	4	9	13
40-49	4	6	10
50-59	1	6	7
60 or over	0	1	1
TOTAL	**25**	**35**	**60**

The research showed that the demographic of most respondents were between the ages of 21-49 (73%), were employed and most likely to be either White British/Other (38%) or Black British - Afro/Caribbean (32%). The targeted respondents were the general public with a focus on patrons of the night-time economy. A convenience sample was used to obtain a wider response, however, due to this random selection of respondents, the findings cannot be generalised to the rest of the population. Recruitment for the participants occurred on social networking websites such as Facebook, Twitter and online forums, where a standardised link requesting participation was posted.

Due to the advantage of an online questionnaire, participants came from a range of places within the United Kingdom. Online recruitment was preferred due to the difficulties researchers previously had recruiting participants in person (Mopas & Stenning, 2001). All respondents participated on a voluntary basis and consented to this. Online presence of the questionnaire also reduced experimenter bias and demand characteristics thus improving the reliability of the data.

Participants were able to access the questionnaire at any time and within the comfort of the participant's own environment. The online questionnaire was also cost and time effective. The questionnaire reduced geographical issues, increased the variety of respondents and was preferable to interviews for these concepts (Campion, Palmer &

251

Campion, 1997). However, such an online questionnaire research design did not allow for the control of extraneous variables within the respondent's environment, which could skew the results slightly. The questionnaire was also limited by the dependence on retrospective recollection, which can sometimes be flawed. In order to ensure participants did not randomly answer; the questions and formats were randomised to initiate thought.

Measures

The questionnaire enclosed 17 questions, featuring a range of rating scales, multiple choice, closed and open questions. The open question format was used to gain an understanding of why the participants chose particular options. This helped ensure that participants were not randomly selecting options without much consideration.

The online survey contained a randomising function for each question to ensure that repeated formats appeared different and would require some thought. The questionnaire aimed to investigate the impact of the media on the image of door supervisors; how much factual knowledge was actually known by the public about door supervisors regarding regulation. Themes included how experiences impacted the opinion of door supervisors from a personal and external standpoint. The questionnaire focused on:

- The overall opinion of doors supervisors.
- The underpinning knowledge; was it factual or opinionated in relation to door supervisors.
- Personal experiences and the perception of door supervisors.
- Whether media influence was a factor in the image of door supervisors.

The validity of questionnaires as research collection instruments has been heavily debated; this centres on the trade-off between validity and reliability (Bryman, 2012; Johnson & Turner, 2003; Stanton, 1998). However structured questionnaires provided a large element of reliability as the participants responded to the exact same questions, so there is no inconsistency (Robson, 1993). The first part of the questionnaire focused on demographical information. The second part of the questionnaire focused on contextual background questions for example, how frequently the respondents went out. This was important because if an individual went out regularly they are likely to have encountered more experience with door supervisors. The third part of the questionnaire centred on placing the media in context and ascertaining any media influence. Lastly, the final part of the questionnaire concentrated on door supervisors, experiences, opinions, potential knowledge and behaviour.

All rating scale questions within the questionnaire presented words that needed to be classified on a 5 point rating scale in relation to door supervisors, the media or experiences. The 5 point rating scale consisted of 1= Always 2=Mostly 3=Neutral 4=Occasionally and 5=Never. The answers were contingent on the respondent's understanding and thoughts of door supervisors or the perception of door supervisors in the night-time economy.

Respondents were treated fairly according to ethical regulations and were free to withdraw from the questionnaire at any time, with no penalty (Zimbardo, 1960). All respondents were provided with consent forms at the beginning of the online survey, which presented details of the research and ethical rights to participate freely. Anonymity, confidentiality and privacy were preserved in accordance with the Data Protection Act (1998). Respondents were not harmed physically or psychologically and there was no deception within the study (Milgram, 1963). Respondents were also provided debriefing statements with contact details, should the participants need to contact the researcher for any reason.

Findings

In order to completely understand the responses given, respondents answered three situational questions to establish context. Respondents were asked how often they went out in order to contextualise their opinions of door supervisors. The research found that 60% of the respondents went on a night out, once a week or every fortnight. This ensured that respondents had experiences of door supervisors within the night-time economy.

The questionnaire also focused on media impact and social networking. Respondents were asked what mediums of social media were used to stay informed and how often they used social media. The research found that 50% of respondents used social networking sites extremely often, mostly on sites such as Facebook and Twitter. People who frequently go on nights out, have a higher chance of social networking more frequently, a significant positive correlation indicated this relationship $r(n=60)= .479, \ p< .00^{**}$. People who go out regularly may want to capture the moment with photos or merely keep in touch with friends.

This relationship could be due to technologies such as application software that facilitates uploading videos, photographs and sharing thoughts with friends online (Cheung, Chiu & Lee, 2011). The thoughts shared could be positive or negative, notably, experiences that are negative would be easier to circulate (Cheung, Chiu & Lee, 2011).

Potential Media Influence

The use of the online questionnaire provided the chance to perform analysis on the public perception of door supervisors. The research suggests that the media have made an impact on the perception of door supervisors on the whole, as highlighted by Pratten (2008).

The questionnaire was able to explore the assumption of media impact. Participants were questioned about their perceived notions of media depiction of door supervisors, using a categorical rating scale ranging from very positive to very negative. Only a small amount of participants (15%) rated the media perception of door supervisors as very positive or positive. This was largely overshadowed by over two-thirds of participants (75%) that deemed media perception of door supervisors to be very negative or negative. The findings suggest the general public are aware that door supervisors have received bad press from the media over time.

It has been assumed that the media are able to sway and influence the general public depending on the headlines produced. The media provide an ability to create awareness of topics that can sometimes deviate from an individual's daily life. Comprehending the public's stance on the media was crucial in finding out the criteria that are considered against any new headlines provided by the media on door supervisors.

The questionnaire set out to examine this by using keywords and a rating scale. A t-test was conducted on the data to find the statistical significance of the test.

Table 10.3 The Respondent's Perception of the Media

	Media Perception				
Word	Mean (2dp)	SD	T Value	DF	P Value
Truthful	2.75	0.88	24.32	59	P<.001
Oppressive	2.38	1.04	17.70	59	P<.001
Influential	2.13	1.02	16.26	59	P<.001
Helpful	2.42	1.06	17.62	59	P<.001
Biased	1.93	1.02	14.64	59	P<.001
Impartial	2.73	1.15	18.45	59	P<.001
Informative	2.45	0.98	19.33	59	P<.001

The analysis was statistically significant; this indicates that the findings are statistically reliable; the public finds the media to be always or sometimes influential (65%), informative (57%) and helpful (55%). The findings indicate the general public are aware that the media can be influential to an extent but they are also aware that the media are not always accurate and can be biased at times.

Only 10% of participants believed the media have never been biased, contrasting with 72% of participants who believed that the media were always or had at some point been biased. This was supported with low ratings for the media being truthful and high ratings for the media being oppressive (60%). Such findings provide further insight into the public and the media, highlighting that the public understands the nature of the media.

The public is aware that despite the media presenting news, this may not be in an impartial manner and can sometimes even be in a victimising approach. It is important to note that the stance of the news reports may vary from different news outlets. Despite the negative depiction of door supervision within the media, the media publicise reports and increase awareness overall. However, the media alone cannot account for the bad reputation of door supervisors.

Public Experiences of Door Supervisors

The impression an individual forms following an experience has a considerable influence on future opinions (McCombs, 2002). Experiences can impact the manner an individual perceives something, this can be altered by positive or negative experiences. Public perception is particularly susceptible to this notion. Positive recent occurrences with the Police were found to increase and improve the image of the constabularies (Gallagher, Maguire, Mastrofski & Reisig, 2001).

Within door supervision, literature by Roberts (2009) depicted door supervisors as carrying out unprofessional practices. This, in turn, could affect the way patrons perceive door supervisors. Participants were asked to rate the overall experience of liaising with door supervisors. The findings presented interesting results as over half of the participants (59% cumulative amount) had described their experience with door supervisors as either very negative or negative. Again a reduced number of participants (26%) defined their experience with door supervisors as very positive or positive. Only a few participants (15%) felt the experience with door supervisors was neutral and not deemed to be negative or positive.

To ascertain if there had been any media influence that could have impacted on experiences with door supervisors, a Pearson correlation analysis was used. This was done to discover if there was a relationship between an experience with a door supervisor and the perceived media perception of door supervisors r(n=60)=.386, p=0.78 (n.s). The non-significance of the Pearson correlation analysis indicates, that there is not an established relationship between the two variables.

The questionnaire sought to find whether experiences of friends or family could influence an individual, 50% had been influenced by friends or family. Within the 50% sample of these respondents, 57% of those had been influenced negatively, with 43% of respondents being positively influenced. These figures demonstrate how bad reputations can be sustained and affected by social influence. The findings support the notion that people who have negative experiences with door supervisors are likely to have a bad perception of door supervisors (Gallagher, Maguire, Mastrofski & Reisig, 2001).

Door Supervisors in Closer Focus

Door supervisors have the responsibility of confronting challenging behaviours and advising intoxicated patrons of rules and regulations, which can sometimes go wrong (Livingstone & Hart 2003). Bearing this in mind, the public perception of door supervisors can indicate how successful the regulation of the door supervision sector has been.

Door supervisors are deemed as an out-group of society. This means that people have difficulty understanding the profession, as there is little insight into the legal power and regulation awareness (Winlow et al, 2001). The questionnaire assessed the perceptions of the general public on the image, attitude and behaviour of door supervisors.

Table 10.4 Depicting Factors Affecting the Perception of Door supervisors

Factors Affecting Perception of Door Supervisors

	Mean	SD	T Value	DF	P Value
Helpful	2.77	(1.18)	18.10	59	P<.001
Professional	2.80	(1.25)	17.22	59	P<.001
Intimidating	2.50	(1.30)	14.80	59	P<.001
Friendly	2.95	(1.30)	17.49	59	P<.001
Threatening	3.00	(1.23)	18.81	59	P<.001
Violent	4.07	(1.13)	27.80	59	P<.001
Well presented	2.42	(1.07)	17.36	59	P<.001
Approachable	2.82	(1.15)	18.86	59	P<.001

The results from the t-test show high levels of significance, which indicate that the factors above have a substantial impact on the perception of door supervision. The high level of statistical significance is pertinent in this investigation. The important elements show that there is a varying opinion on the perception of door supervisors. Door supervisors are viewed as occasionally violent however, door supervisors were found to be intimidating and threatening.

The elements of violence could be due to the fact that a large number of door supervisors have experienced threats of violence, with some door supervisors being repeated victims of violence (Perkins, 2009). It is interesting that door supervisors are observed as threatening by the public, as door supervisors themselves have experienced threats from the general public (Roberts, 2007). Despite this, intimidation, violence and low levels of approachability indicate that door supervisors do not have a positive image or to some extent reputation. This could have a large influence on the perception of approachability. Average levels of helpfulness and friendliness have not helped. This could be explained, as door supervisors are a physical deterrent for disobedience within venues.

Overtime, intimidation is an attribute that assists this and could explain why door supervisors are seen as unapproachable and unhelpful. Door supervisors were largely well presented (67%), with respondents interestingly deeming them as professional (47%). The findings depict a noteworthy contrast; in relation to how threatening and intimidating door supervisors can be and still remain approachable, helpful and welcoming. Door supervisors were sometimes friendly and helpful to a certain extent; most importantly violence was not mainly associated with door supervisors, this mirrors the successful regulation of the use of force, only when necessary (Perkins, 2009).

Contrary to general assumption and previous literature (Lister et al, 2001) door supervisors were perceived to be professional. This is a reflection of characteristics infused by the SIA (Button, 2008). Door supervision as a sector has become more professional, as a direct result of businesses viewing security as a fundamental feature rather than a supplementary section.

Door Supervisors and Safety

Regardless of the perceived negative experience door supervisors were found to increase safety (83%) at venues, which implies that door supervisors are fulfilling their aim. The findings can be linked to Robert (2009) who stated that the mere presence of a door supervisor increased safety within the night-time economy. The purpose of door supervisors at a venue is to ensure order and safely diffuse potential violent incidents. Security regulations in the night-time environment are laid down as a deterrent to patrons. Throughout the findings, door supervisors were perceived to largely increase safety. This, unfortunately, does not explore the issues that door supervisors' face within the role, which could impair the service patrons receive.

When establishments and clubs have financial difficulties, costs are normally cut from the security budget, often resulting in one-man door supervision. Not only is a lone door supervisor dangerous to personal safety, it is also less of a deterrent than two or more door supervisors being present. A lone door supervisor is more likely to be selective of patrons who enter their environment, which sometimes can cause arguments between the patron and door supervisor thus reinforcing further negative perceptions.

The Effect of the Bouncer Stereotype

Door supervisors are still commonly known as bouncers, a term synonymous with bad practice. Even so the reputation of 'bouncers' supersedes them. This is evident in the media, which has been plausible due to the previous unprofessional conduct of door supervisors (Winlow et al., 2003). Door supervision is an occupation that demands integrity due to the nature of the role. Integrity and trustworthiness have not been consistently demonstrated to the public by door supervisors (Graham & Wells, 2001; Green & Plant, 2007). The SIA is making an indisputable effort to rebrand the private security sector, with a focus on the door supervision sector. Regardless of this, there have been no documented attempts to reiterate this to the general public.

Despite this, 53% of respondents used the term bouncer, only 20% used the term doorman and 27% used the appropriate term of door supervisor. There has been little effort by the media to note the new improvements and circulate this widely. More awareness and customer service training for door supervisors is needed to reduce bad attitudes and overall approach.

Awareness of Door Supervisor Regulation and Rules

It was crucial to investigate assumptions the general public had in regards to door supervisors. Door supervision as a profession is largely portrayed as not having a regulatory body, with very little consequences for unprofessional behaviour (Maguire & Nettleton, 2003). The questionnaire focused on the subject of rules and regulation within the sector, in order to gain an understanding of preconceptions. It is also important to note that door supervisors, apart from being regulated by the SIA, must also adhere to the establishment's management and protocol, which may cause some undesirable characteristics. The findings stated 53% of respondents believed a criminal record check was required, to become a door supervisor. This contrasted with 47% of respondents who were not aware this was a standard requirement. Criminal record checks and identity checks prevent offenders from carrying out roles of trust, to instil confidence in the general public (Button, 2008). Over half of the respondents were aware of the need for a criminal record check, however, an element which increases confidence requires greater awareness as it helps to confirm the integrity of the sector. In regards to mandatory SIA licensing, the respondents were not well informed that door supervisors require a license to work. 53% of respondents believed that door supervisors could work without a license, with only 47% of respondents answering correctly.

As aforementioned, in order to be licensed, a lengthy character assessment is carried out. This features an identity check, a criminal record check and successful completion of the SIA approved training course, all at the cost of £220 (The Security Industry Authority, 2008). SIA licences must be renewed every 3 years. At that point, extensive character and criminal checks will be carried out again. This indicates the public are not aware of the SIA and the regulations put into place to improve the sector of door supervision. The misconception of the door supervision sector when it comes to the general public extends to the use of force and a door supervisor's rights.

This is an issue that has been deliberated, as what should determine the use of force? Prior to regulation door supervisors were able to use force, with no restrictions and normally no training on how to do so safely. Door supervisor's work in a setting where there are alcohol consumption and intoxication. Patrons could at any time become aggressive or violent (Roberts, 2009; Budd, 2003). A surprising 72% of respondents believed that door supervisors could use force on patrons, whenever they preferred. This is an interesting finding and provides a reason why the negative image of door supervision is unfailingly present.

Door supervisors have been given appropriate SIA regulated training to manage the use of force, which is only used in extreme circumstances. In order to prevent serious harm or fatality to night-time patrons, door supervisors are taught methods of physical intervention and safety. Where excessive force is being used inappropriately, there can and have been incidents in which door supervisors have been prosecuted (Maguire & Nettleton, 2003). In addition, the SIA are able to revoke and suspend licences in relation to the improper use of force or criminal activity. Door supervisors are an imperative instrument of control within the night-time economy, helping to thwart violence and safeguard patrons (Finney, 2004). Despite this, the general public is not aware of the measures and regulations put in place by the SIA to restore trust, safety and ensure good practice within this profession. This needs to be promoted.

Conclusion

Door supervisors indisputably carry out a challenging role, which is perceived negatively at times. There has been an attempt to remove negative imagery, amend bad practice and the overall image, although, the results indicate that to a certain extent it has been overlooked or ignored. The findings of this study are interesting and raise many thought-provoking questions about door supervisors and the image that eludes them. The study provides insight into an un-researched area of door supervision.

Providing evidence that to some extent, door supervisors are poorly perceived due to an uneven composition of negative media influence. There was a lack of knowledge of improvements on SIA regulations and door supervisor's personal attitude.

It is also apparent that the general public is not entirely aware of the regulation schemes that have been imposed by the SIA, to door supervision. The results indicate that awareness needs to be created to advise the public that door supervision, as a profession has been regulated. Respondents had limited knowledge about door supervision as a profession and what the job entails, however, a person's personal experiences in relation to door supervisors can affect public perceptions. To tackle this issue, more awareness on SIA changes are needed and customer service training for door supervisors may possibly reduce the bad impressions overall. Despite this, door supervisors are still seen as safeguards of the night-time economy (Morris, 1998; Roberts, 2009). The research indicates that more work needs to be done to improve the perception of door supervisors. To amend this, the SIA will need to advertise the new changes door supervision has undergone, which in turn will boost the profile of door supervisors. The research design was able to provide interesting results, however, due to the small sample size, there could be some issues with generalising. The high drop out rates limited the potential sample size. If this research were to be repeated, the recruitment period would be extended and a design that featured more participants would be adopted, to increase the sample power.

In addition, a mixed methodology design and other methods of participant recruitment would also be considered. Looking at the aim and objectives of this research study, the relevant research literature on door supervision and the methodology used were thought about. A regional comparison of the public perception of door supervisors would be noteworthy, to compare differences. Most importantly the study presented a chance to have an overview of door supervision, looking at the stance prior to regulation, after regulation and the public perception. The Table 10.5 next page takes into consideration these details.

Table 10.5 An Overview of Door Supervision and Image

Features	Before Regulation	SIA's Intention after Regulation	Public Perception after Regulation
Use Of Force	Freedom to use force with no regard or little consequence	Force is only used an extreme last resort Severe regulation to avert misconduct: Licences can be revoked or suspended Door supervisors can be fined or even convicted.	A large consensus believes door supervisors have freedom to use force with no regard or real consequences
Training	No training No qualifications required	SIA approved training qualification	Some awareness of training Not widespread
Licencing	No licence required	Compulsory licence by regulation Renewed every 3 years	Some awareness that a license is required Public not aware of stringent requirements
Regulation	No regulatory body	Regulated by the SIA	Not particularly aware of the SIA
Professional conduct	Lack of conduct	Professional	Improving professional conduct Still evidence of unprofessional conduct
Corruption	Excessive level of criminality Illegal activity	Low levels of criminality Criminal record check Identity check	Not aware of criminal record checks Implied level of criminality Lack of trust for door supervisors

The Table 10.5 displays the journey of door supervision, starting before regulation and the attempts to improve the reputation. Furthermore, the table indicates that despite the changes, the general public are not cognisant of the new changes. There is a slight difference between the regulation features and the public's current perspective. This provides an excellent indication of the ever-present negative reputation of door supervisors, from the public's view there appears to be little improvement. Knowledge and understanding are fundamental in depicting change, otherwise it can go ignored as seems to be apparent within the Table 10.5. As aforementioned, until the public are conscious of this regulation change, there is little evidence the perception will change.

Emphasising the stringent requirements needed to become a door supervisor and the clear standard for acceptable behaviour will make a difference. In conclusion, experiences are important and can be long lasting. Despite efforts to improve, the SIA must work to change this in regards to door supervision as a whole. Regulation has already been implemented to undergo a change process, however, this change needs more awareness in order to make a significant impact on the general public and their perceptions.

References

Adu-boakye, K. (2002). Private Security and Retail Crime Prevention: Ethnographic cases Study of Retail Shops in Portsmouth: Portsmouth University.

Peräkylä, A., Antaki, C., Vehviläinen, S., & Leudar, I. (Eds.). (2008). *Conversation analysis and psychotherapy*. Cambridge University Press.

Babbie, E. (2004). Laud Humphreys and research ethics. *International journal of sociology and social policy*.

Bryman, A. (2001). *Social research methods*. Oxford: Oxford University Press.
Bryman, A. (2012). *Social research methods*. Oxford university press.

Button, M. (2003). Private security and the policing of quasi-public space. International journal of the sociology of law.

Button, M. (2011). The Private Security Industry Act 2001 and the security management gap in the United Kingdom. Security journal.

Button, M. (2007). Security Officers and Policing: Powers, Culture and Control in the Governance of Private Space. Abingdon, Oxon, GBR: Ashgate Publishing Group

Carlen, P. (2010). A criminological imagination: Essays on justice, punishment, discourse. London: Ashgate.

Cheung, C. M., Chiu, P. Y., & Lee, M. K. (2011). Online social networks: Why do students use facebook?. Computers in Human Behavior.

Comte, A. (2006). A *general view of positivism*. Kessinger Publishing, LLC.

Comte, A. (1988). *Introduction to positive philosophy.* Hackett Publishing Company Incorporated.

Cowton, C. J. (1998). The use of secondary data in business ethics research. *Journal of Business Ethics.*

Creswell, J. J. (2003). *Research Design Qualitative, Quantitative, and Mixed Methods Approaches.* Handbook of mixed methods in Social & Behavioral research.

Creswell, J. W. (2008). *Research design: Qualitative, quantitative, and mixed methods approach.* Sage Publications, Incorporated.

Fay, J.J (2005). *Contemporary Security Management.* Boston: Butterworth-Heinemann.

Fernie, S. (2011). *Occupational licensing in the UK: the case of the private security industry.* Oxford University Press.

Finney, A. (2004). *Violence in the night-time economy.* London: Home Office

Flynn, P. (1997). *Regulating The Privatisation of Policing*: Essex University.

Graham, K., La Rocque, L., Yetman, R., Ross, T. J., & Guistra, E. (1980). *Aggression and barroom environments.*Journal of Studies on Alcohol.

Graham, K., & Wells, S. (2001). *Aggression among young adults in the social context of the bar.* Addiction Research & Theory.

Graham, K., & Wells, S. (2003). Somebody's gonna get their head kicked in tonight:Aggression among young males in bars—A question of values? British Journal of Criminology.

Hepburn, A., & Potter, J. (2006). Discourse analytic practice. Qualitative Research Practice. Concise Paperback Edition.

HM Government (2001). *The Private Security Industry Act 2001. London: Office of Public Sector Information.* http://www.opsi.gov.uk/acts/acts2001/ukpga_20010012_en_1 (Accessed 5th July 2016).

Hobbs, D., Hadfield, P., Lister, S., & Winlow, S. (2005). *Violence and control in the night-time economy.* European Journal of Crime Criminal Law and Criminal Justice.

Hobbs, D., Winlow, S., Hadfield, P., & Lister, S. (2005). *Violent Hypocrisy Governance and the Night-time Economy.* European journal of criminology.

Lister, S., Hadfield, P., Hobbs, D., & Winlow, S. (2001). Accounting for bouncers: occupational licensing as a mechanism for regulation. Criminology and criminal justice.

Lister, S., Hadfield, P., Hobbs, D., & Winlow, S. (2001). *'Be Nice':* the training of bouncers.

Livingstone, K., & Hart, J. (2003). The wrong arm of the law? Public images of private security. *Policing & Society.*

Lorenz, J., Rauhut, H., Schweitzer, F., & Helbing, D. (2011). *How social influence can undermine the wisdom of crowd effect.* Proceedings of the National Academy of Sciences.

Maguire, M. (2000), 'Researching 'Street Criminals': A Neglected Art', Roy King and Emma Wincup (eds.) *Doing Research in Crime and Justice* (Oxford: Oxford University Press).

Monaghan, L.F. (2002) Regulating 'Unruly' Bodies: Work Tasks, Conflict and Violence in Britain's Night-Time Economy. *The British Journal of Sociology.*

Mopasa, M. S., & Stenning, P. C. (2001). Tools of the trade: The symbolic power of private security-an exploratory study. *Policing and Society: An International Journal.*

Messerschmidt, J. W. (1999). Making bodies matter: Adolescent masculinities, the body, and varieties of violence. *Theoretical criminology.*

Michael, D. (2002). *A Sense of Security? The Ideology and Accountability of Private Security Officers.* PhD Thesis: London School of Economics.

Milgram, S. (1963). *Behavioural study of obedience*. Journal of Abnormal and Social Psychology.

Morris, S. (1998). *Clubs, drugs and doormen*. Home Office, Police Research Group.

O'Brien, K., Hobbs, D., & Westmarland, L. (2008). Negotiating violence and gender: security and the night-time economy in the UK Springer New York.

O' Mahoney, B. (1997) So This Is Ecstasy? Edinburgh: Mainstream Publishing

Perkins, A. (2008). T*aking it on the Chin: Violence Against British Door Supervisors.* Leicester University.

Pratten, J. D. (2007). Securing the doors: bouncers and the British licensed trade. *International journal of contemporary hospitality management.*

Prenzler, T., & Sarre, R. (2008). Protective security in Australia: Scandal, media images and reform. J*ournal of Policing, Intelligence and Counter Terrorism.*

Rapley, T.J. (2004). Interviews. In Seale C. Gobo G., Gubrium J.F., Silverman D. (eds) Qualitative Research Practice. London: Sage

Rigakos, G., S. (2002). *The New Parapolice.*   University Toronto: Toronto Press.

Roberts, J. C. (2007). Barroom aggression in Hoboken, New Jersey: don't blame the bouncers!. *Journal of drug education.*

Roberts, J. C. (2009). Bouncers and barroom aggression: A review of the research. *Aggression and Violent Behavior.*

Roberts, L. D., Breen, L. J., & Symes, M. (2013). Teaching computer-assisted qualitative data analysis to a large cohort of undergraduate students. *International Journal of Research & Method in Education.*

Shilling, C. (2001). Embodiment, Experience and Theory: In Defense of the Sociological Tradition. *The Sociological Review.*

Seiter, E. (2006). Stereotypes and the media: A re-evaluation. J*ournal of Communication*

Solan, S.M., & Tiersma, P.M. (2004). *Speaking of crime: The language of Criminal justice.* Chicago. University of Chicago Press

South, N. (1985). Private Security and Social Control: The Private Security Sector in the United Kingdom, Its Commercial Functions and Public Accountability. *Middlesex Polytechnic.*

Stockwell, T. (2010). *Operator and Regulatory Best Practices in The Reduction of Violence In And Around Licensed Premises:* A Review Of Australian And Canadian Research. Centre for Addictions Research of Bc: University of Victoria

The Daily Mail. (2010, July 5). *Control freak and his reign of terror: Pumped full of steroids, sword-wielding club bouncer Moat thought he was irresistible.* Retrieved November 21, 2013, from http://www.dailymail.co.uk/news/article-1292023/Raoul-Thomas-Moat-Pumped-steroids-bouncer-thought-irresistible.html#ixzz2sbkFyp7y.

The Security Industry Authority (2008). *Licensing Statistics.* London. http://www.the sia.org.uk/home/licensing/stats_2.htm (Accessed: 17 July 2013).

Toomela, A. (2008). Variables in psychology: a critique of quantitative psychology. *Integrative Psychological & Behavioral Science.*

Tomsen, S. (2005). 'Boozers and Bouncers': Masculine Conflict, Disengagement and the Contemporary Governance of Drinking-Related Violence and Disorder. *Australian & New Zealand Journal of Criminology.*

Wakefield, A. (2003). *Selling Security – The Private Policing of Public Space.* Cullompton: Willan

Wakefield, A. (2001). *The Private Policing of Public Space:* University of Cambridge

Wakefield, A. and Gill, M. (2009). When security fails: the impact of human factors on the deployment of retail security personnel. *Journal of Policing, Intelligence and Counter Terrorism.*

White, A. (2010). *The Politics of Private Security: Regulation, Reform and Re-Legitimation.* Basingstoke: Palgrave Macmillan

White, A. (2013). The impact of the Private Security Industry Act 2001. *Security Journal*

Winlow, S., Hobbs, D., Lister, S. and Hadfield, P. (2001). 'Get Ready to Duck: Bouncers and the Realities of Ethnographic Research on Violent Groups', *British Journal of Criminology,* Special Issue. Methodological Dilemmas of Research.

Winlow, S., & Hall, S. (2006). *Violent night: Urban leisure and contemporary culture*. Berg.

Chapter 11

The Perils of Accurately Measuring Fraud and Corruption: Is it Only Worth Doing When Public Money is at Stake?

Peter Stiernstedt

Public scandals regarding fraud and corruption involving mind staggering sums being intentionally diverted, dissolved or just simply lost, are reported one after the other. The significance of the problem is acknowledged by academics and institutions alike, with ongoing efforts to battle its detrimental effects from supranational initiatives, via nation state policy and corporate codes of conduct, down to individual ethics and morals. On a global level, measured in the trillions, fraud and corruption are arguably some of the most costly crimes to society. Thus to effectively combat fraud and corruption, most stakeholders, if not all, would like to know the range of fraud and corruption in their own vicinity and the only way to know the extent of anything is to measure and compare. An effort that require a unified definition of the sometimes rather elusive concepts of fraud and corruption. Without such definition measurements will still be possible, but eternally confined to the specifics of the definition used at that particular measurement at that particular time and place. Nonetheless it argued that fraud and corruption could and should be fought in any arena, public or private. It is not only morally correct but also demonstrably economical to do so given that measurements are done accurately. It may not be easy but few things worthwhile are. Hence, equipped with the proper tools, fraud and corruption can be sufficiently measured.

Public scandals regarding fraud and corruption involving mind staggering sums being intentionally diverted, dissolved or just simply lost, are reported one after the other. The significance of the problem is acknowledged by academics and institutions alike, with ongoing efforts to battle its detrimental effects from supranational initiatives, via nation state policy and corporate codes of conduct, down to individual ethics and morals. On a global level, measured in the trillions, fraud and corruption are arguably some of the most costly crimes to society (eg. Hameed, Magpile, & Runde, 2014; Gee & Button, 2015). The economic impact becomes even more eminent when adding to this equation the elusive financial aspects implicated by fraud and corruption. The private sector has learned this lesson the hard way in a number of incidents resulting in everything from insolvent banks to new regulatory legislation (Friedrichs, 2010). At first glance fraud, and even more so corruption, appears expensive and time consuming to measure accurately. Lets take the time to give the apparent problem a, often so crucial, second glance in an attempt to critically evaluate the title statement and analyse recent research findings on the matter of measuring fraud and corruption. By approaching the statement in reverse order a number of key elements can be identified. The first element is that of measurement, supposedly only being worthwhile when public money as opposed to private money is at stake. The second relates to the cost of time and resources to actually perform the measurement that are tied to the third element, the level of accuracy achieved. What is the economical validity of those three elements from the perspective of recent research?

The first element involving the attributes of public versus private money is perhaps the one most easily understood, at least intuitively. Private organisations can in a sense be seen as self-regulatory with regards to fraud and corruption. Too much of either and the organisation's success will be haltered at best and toppled at worst. In essence only private organisations with low levels of fraud and corruption will prevail, but evidently this is not the case.

Rather the opposite, with today's societal borders between public and private organisations becoming increasingly smudged (Palmer, 2008; Jeffares, Sullivan & Bovaird, 2009). Fraud and corruption in particular tend to gravitate towards large concentrations of monies such as financial institutions, insurance companies and public private partnerships. Those are large and important actors in the play called modern society, whose actions seriously effect both the overall plot and consequently the all the extras - the you's and me's of society. It would therefore be myopic, with regards to fraud and corruption, to make any significant distinction between the two when it comes to whether or not to measure. A typical organisation looses in average 5-6% of its revenue to fraud annually (ACFE, 2012; Gee & Button, 2013; 2015). It is in the collective interest of society as a whole, public functions, private services and individuals alike, that fraud and corruption are kept to a minimum.

This argument is furthered by the fact that fraud and corruption reach far beyond economical aspects into those of ethics and moral. Carrol and Buchholtz (2011) argues that business ethics cannot be separated from the full range of external and internal stakeholder concerns. This elevates the concept of measuring fraud and corruption above and beyond mere compliance. Having said that, the layers of compliance mechanisms are growing at companies across the world. This may seem to make sense, and from certain points of view it probably does, as a method of preventing unethical behaviour by increasing the number and strength of rules designed to curtail it. However, one of the more unsettling, unintended and unanticipated, consequences of this narrow focus of anti-fraud and corruption as compliance is a checkbox mentality that may give the illusion of reducing risk without really doing so. Moreover, as discussed by Rea, Kolp, Ritz and Steward (2016), a compliance-focused approach to fraud and corruption in an attempt to eliminate unethical behaviour can, unless treated with care, limit an organisation's ability to take intelligent risks.

Thus to effectively combat fraud and corruption, most stakeholders, if not all, would like to know the range of fraud and corruption in their own vicinity and the only way to know the extent of anything is to measure and compare. An accurate measurement allows for both absolute and comparative analysis and subsequently the ability to make an informed decision on how to proceed. As the title statement suggests there are challenges to this, and the first question becomes, is it feasible to do such measurement from a time and resource perspective? Before answering that question and continuing to the second element of the statement it is helpful to define and outline the differences between fraud and corruption. There is no single accepted definition for either fraud or corruption, but the former can in its simplest form be condensed to any crime that uses deceit as its primary means of achieving gain and/or causing loss. Corruption, similarly simplified, is the abuse of power. In relation to the time and resources needed to perform the actual measurement it is acknowledged that a more case specific and detailed definition is required (Smith, 2001).

Nonetheless, research shows that properly defined measurement can be investment effective. A good example of such are the Public Expenditure Tracking Surveys, used to assess the wastage, fraud and corruption in expenditure (Reinekka and Svensson, 2006). The surveys look at what happens to the original money that was allocated for a project as it travels through different layers of bureaucracy to ultimate delivery. The idea is to uncover the attrition in funds that includes fraud, corruption, error as well as bureaucracy and inefficiency. A variation of the Public Expenditure Tracking Surveys is the Frontline Provider Survey or Quantitative Service Delivery Survey. These assess front-line services against the expectations from the funding provided, showing that even when funding reaches the service point, other factors can further add to the attrition to the original funds. There is also Fraud Loss Measurement, a mechanism to measure fraud that is growing in many organisations (Button, et al., 2012). It is used as an assessment of a statistically valid sample of transactions within a given population to determine whether they are fraudulent, an error or correct. The financial cost of fraud report 2013, repeated in 2015, based on some 300 fraud loss measurement exercises, comes to three clear conclusions (Gee & Button, 2013; 2015):

- Losses to fraud and error can be measured cost effectively.
- It is likely that losses in any organisation will be at least 3%, probably more than 5-6% and possibly more than 10%.

• With accurate measurements losses can be reduced significantly.

Dispensing with the notion of dividing public and private money in relation to fraud, as well as taking into account the potentially substantial benefits of reduction, it is clear that measurement is both time and resource effective. When it comes to corruption the case is not as easily made. In theory, if the risk of getting caught and penalties for corruption increased the problem would be solved (Persson, Rothstein & Teorell, 2013). In practice, however, corruption is elusive by nature as it stretches all the way from unethical to illegal, and obviously combinations of both. There is also a socio-cultural aspect to corruption as different countries have varying conceptions of human nature and cultural characteristics (Albrecht & Albrecht, 2009). While long-term democracy supports a lower level of corruption, the political instability of many countries has the reverse effect (Pellegrini, 2008). Corruption is a global problem and of all the issues faced by society it is one of the most difficult to properly address (Johnson & Sharma, 2004; Schwartz, 2011). Detrimental in many ways as corruption does not only include the commonly associated bribery, but also nepotism, favouritism, misappropriation of funds and even extortion.

The deleterious effects do not end there as corruption, on an organisational level, also hurts the reputation of both the organisation itself and its host entity, not to mention the effect on the organisation's innocent constituents. All put together the negative effects of corruption outweigh most concerns for investment of time and resources if measurements are done with such accuracy that countermeasures can be effectively applied. Even in view of the assumption of time and resource effectiveness, the element of accuracy must be achievable for measurement to be viable. In the book Measuring corruption (Sampford, Shacklock, Connors & Galtung, 2006) several approaches to measuring corruption are presented. One is a general description of how to measure corruption developed by Transparency International, their approach follows the concept of the measurement chain. Designed to embed corruption research tools in a governance framework the measurement chain consists of five steps:

- Identifying the optimal measurement tool for the distinct purpose.
- Adapting the tool to local and specific conditions.
- Implementing the tool.
- Processing and communicating the results.
- Evaluating the impact of the measurement.

Even if not universally applicable without contextual adaptation, the point is that there are evidently tools available to measure both fraud and corruption. Thus, the subsequent question becomes: can a degree of accuracy be ascertained? The accuracy, and equally importantly the statistical validity, of these measurements are important to fully understand the problem. Currently corruption is predominantly measured by perceptions based composite indices such as Transparency International's (2016) Corruption Perceptions Index [CPI]. Not without critique in both methodology (Knack, 2006) and application (Andersson, 2009) it remains influential in putting the issue of corruption on the international policy agenda. Interpreting the CPI can also be a challenge with limited specificity as to the type of corruption measured, i.e. perceived. Progress over time may consequently be biased by changes in the perceived importance of corruption through media coverage or changes in corruption awareness (and expectations).

Further, just because a country perceives its domestic public sector clean, does not mean that it is not linked to corruption elsewhere. An example is Sweden, coming in third from the top in the latest CPI (2016), thus almost (but just almost) corruption free. Yet, TeliaSonera a part state owned telecom giant was allegedly paid millions of dollars in bribes to secure business in Uzbekistan - a country that comes in at place 153 in the 2015 CPI (see eg. Milne, 2015 and Dyfvermark, 2015).

Incidental anecdotes notwithstanding, more tangible attempts at measuring corruption also have its drawbacks. For example, measurements cannot be limited to detected incidents of fraud and corruption, as no crime has 100% detection rate. Just adding together detected incidents significantly underestimates the extent of the problem. This also imparts the predicament that if detection goes up, does that mean that there is more crime or that there has been better detection; equally, if detection falls, does that mean that there is less crime or worse detection? There is, nevertheless, a solution to this presented by Gee, Button and Basset (2010) by a methodology for accurate measurement exercises. The methodology is rather straightforward but, as most other statistically valid processes, implies the use of a professionally qualified statistician. To ensure adequate accuracy, the proper use of statistics is crucial to both the initial selection of a statistically valid sample and to the final estimation. The final estimation gauges the nature and extent of losses based on the findings from examination of that sample. Originally designed for measuring fraud, the methodology by conceptual proximity is also fully applicable to corruption. Each loss measurement exercise consists of six stages as follows:

• Scope - understand and prepare.
• Organise, train and communicate.
• Review data sample.
• Determine the presence of fraud and corruption.
• Statistical analysis.
• Reporting.

The scope of this discussion does not allow for further exploration of the methodology but it makes a clear case for fraud and corruption being plausible to measure accurately. Despite this many, if not most, organisations do not believe themselves to be subject to neither fraud nor corruption and therefore presumptuously do not measure the possible occurrence. On the other hand, organisations treating fraud and corruption as any other cost that can be measured and reduced may still be relatively small, but those who do can testify to the ensuing competitive advantage (Button & Gee, 2013; 2015). As a result of these advantages the means to measure is coming to par with the needs to measure. There is, however, one big hurdle yet to overcome to align research, business and legislative activities for effective measurement. The evaluation presented here uses simplified, borderline simplistic, definitions of the concepts of fraud and corruption.

The rationale for the underlying behaviour is completely glanced over and If one would like to take it yet another level of abstraction the question of understanding the fundamental drivers of fraud and corruption must be answered. One such attempt is the fraud triangle developed by Cressey in the 1950-ies (1950; 1953). Looking at how it has squirmed under the pressure scrutiny turning out everything from more or less conceptually forced constructs like 'The new fraud triangle (Kassem & Higson, 2012) to cautions of general application (Schuchter & Levi, 2015). The latter pointing at opportunity as a universal precondition of acts defined by others as fraud. A concept that research into the perception of corruption most likely will find as well, potentially providing a focus shift in how fraud and corruption are dealt with. A shift that does not necessarily move all instrumental emphasis from one thing to the other, as in move a limited field of vision from one place to another, but rather to widen the field of vision and incorporating a largely neglected part of anti-fraud and corruption work. Nevertheless, on the level of critical assessment presented in this paper the logic and cogency of the reasoning do not suffer from lighter definitions. However, in a more applied scientific approach the first fundamental step to further the possibilities of measuring fraud and corruption would be to adopt a commonly recognised definition of the two. Without such definition measurements will still be possible, but eternally confined to the specifics of the definition used at that particular measurement at that particular time and place.

In conclusion, fraud and corruption could and should be fought in any arena, public or private. It is not only morally correct but also demonstrably economical to do so given that measurements are done accurately. It may not be easy but few things worthwhile are. Hence, equipped with the proper tools, fraud and corruption can be sufficiently measured. The justification is based on the widely accepted management principle that an activity cannot be managed if it cannot be measured. By understanding the baseline of fraud and corruption - how much, in what areas, with what consequences - the necessary responses can be formulated. If nothing else, at a structural level, an example of a holistic bottom-up model for such response is described by Button (2008), taking into account specific conditions confinement referred to as nodes. Not singled out for its universalism in detail but rather as an example of encapsulating much of what current research indicates in terms of anti-fraud and corruption framework viability. Secondly, reliable measurements are also vital to understanding the degree of impact for various solutions. Be it from external consultants or internal auditors, the organisation can only develop countermeasures based on the measurements it got compared to set goals and standards. Evaluation and revision of the countermeasures from a time and resource efficiency perspective will provide organisational resilience. It is important to remember that there are no one-size fits all type remedies and that the ubiquity of fraud and corruption within the organisation itself may stifle the best-laid plans. This pushes for the behavioural and institutional understanding of the drivers and incentives that needs to be built into the governance of any anti-fraud and corruption policy framework.

Thirdly, as an umbrella rationale covering organisations, governments and individuals alike, is that of creating and maintaining a good reputation. Credibility is an asset that is as hard to quantify, as it is easy to loose and corruption certainly and effectively erodes confidence (Clausen, Kraay & Nyiri, 2011). If moral and ethics lie at the heart of any anti fraud and corruption framework it must arguably foster an environment of trust. In any case, as derived by the reasoning in this paper it is not necessarily time consuming or expensive to accurately measure fraud and corruption, nor does it just apply to when public money is at stake.

Rather the analysis points to economical, organisational and societal benefits to fighting fraud and corruption everywhere and at all levels. A first step towards winning that fight should be to enable accurate measurement by adopting a common definition. If not, those charged with anti-fraud and corruption tasks will be conducting a guessing game where the risk of being precisely wrong is larger than being broadly right.

> The greatest trick the devil ever played was convincing the world that he did not exist.
>
> Charles Baudelaire - Le spleen de Paris (1869)

279

References

ACFE. (2012). Report to the Nations on Occupational Fraud and Abuse 2012 Global Fraud Study Retrieved from http://www.acfe.com/uploadedFiles ACFE_Website/Content/rttn/2012-report-tonations. pdf

Albrecht, C., & Albrecht, C. (2009). International ethics, fraud and corruption: A cross-cultural perspective. *International Journal of Cross Cultural Management*, 16, 237–326.

Andersson, S., & Heywood, P. (2009). The Politics of Perception: Use and Abuse of Transparency International's Approach to Measuring Corruptionpost_758 746..7. *Political studies*, 57(4), 746-767.

Baudelaire, C. (1869). *Le Spleen de Paris* [Paris Spleen]. Paris: n.p.

Button, M. (2008). *Doing Security - Critical Reflections and an Agenda for Change*. New York: Palgrave Macmillan.

Button, M., Lewis, C., Shepherd, D. & Brooks, G. (2012). *Measuring Fraud in Overseas Aid: Options and Method.*

Button, M., & Gee, J. (2013). *Countering Fraud for Competitive Advantage: The Professional Approach to Reducing the Last Great Hidden Cost* Chichester: John Wiley & Sons.

Carrol, A. B., & Buchholtz, A. K. (2011). *Business & Society: Ethics, Sustainability, and Stakeholder Management* (8th ed.). Mason: South-Western Cengage Learning.

Clausen, B., Kraay, A., & Nyiri, Z. (2011). *Corruption and Confidence in Public Institutions: Evidence from a Global Survey.* The World Bank Economic Review, 25(2), 212-249.

Cressey, D. R. (1950). The criminal violation of financial trust. *American Sociological Review*, 15(6), 738–743.

Cressey, D. R. (1953). *Other people's money: A study in the social psychology of embezzlement.* Glencoe: The Free Press.

Dyfvermark, J. (2015, May 27). *Azerbaijan center in new Telia corruption scandal.* Retrieved May 2, 2016, from http://sverigesradio.se/sida/artikel.aspx? programid=2054&artikel=6174707

Friedrichs, D. O. (2010). *Trusted Criminals: White Collar Crime in Contemporary Society* (4th ed.). Wadsworth: Cengage Learning.

Gee, J., & Button, M. (2013). *The financial cost of fraud report 2013.* London: BDO LLP.

Gee, J., & Button, M. (2015). *The financial cost of fraud 2015: what the latest data from around the world shows.* London: PKF Littlejohn.

Gee, J., Button, M., & Basset, P. (2010). *Fraud loss measurement* Retrieved from http://www.port.ac.uk/departments/academic/icjs centreforcounterfraudstudies/documents/filetodownload, 127550,en.PDF

Hameed, S., Magpile, J. & Runde, D. (2014). *The costs of corruption: strategies for ending a tax on private-sector-led growth.* Washington, DC Lanham, MD: Center for Strategic and International Studies Rowman and Littlefield.

Jeffares, S., Sullivan, H., & Bovaird,T. (2009). *Beyond the Contract - The Challenge of Evaluating the Performance(s) of Public-Private Partnerships.* Paper for the annual conference of International Research Society for Public Management, (IRSPM). Copenhagen.

Johnson, R. A., & Sharma, S. (2004). About Corruption. In R. A. Johnson (Ed.),*The Struggle Against Corruption: A Comparative Study.* New York: Palgrave Macmillan.

Kassem, R. and Higson, A.W., 2012. The new fraud triangle model. *Journal of Emerging Trends in Economics and Management Sciences*, 3 (3), pp. 191 - 195

Knack, S. (2006) 'Measuring Corruption in Eastern Europe and Central Asia:A Critique of the Cross-Country Indicators', World Bank Working Paper 3968.

Milne, R. (2015, September 17). *TeliaSonera set for Eurasia exodus in wake of corruption claims* - FT.com. Retrieved May 02, 2016, from http://www.ft.com/intl/cms/s/0/846663e0-5d19-11e5-97e9-7f0bf5e7177b.html#axzz47UNyIapu

Palmer, S. (2008). Public functions and private services: A gap in human rights protection. *International Journal of Constitutional Law*, 6(3-4), 585-604.

Pellegrini, L. (2008). Causes of Corruption: A Survey of Cross-Country Analyses and Extended Results. *Economics of Governance*, 9(3), 245-263.

Persson, A., Rothstein, B., & Teorell, J. (2013). Why Anticorruption Reforms Fai— Systemic Corruption as a Collective Action Problem. *Governance*, 26(3), 449-471.

Rea, P., Kolo, A., Ritz, W., & Steward, M. D. (2016, April 29). *Corporate Ethics Can't Be Reduced to Compliance*. Retrieved May 02, 2016, from https://hbr.org/2016/04/corporate-ethics-cant-be-reduced-tocompliance?utm_source=twitter

Reinekka, R. And Svensson, J. (2006) 'Using Micro Surveys to Measure and Explain Corruption', *World Development*, 34 (2), pp. 359-370.

Sampford, C., Shacklock, A., Connors, C., & Galtung, F. (Eds.). (2006). *Measuring Corruption*. Aldershot: Ashgate Publishing Limited.

Schuchter, A., & Levi, M. (2015). Beyond the fraud triangle: Swiss and Austrian elite fraudsters. *Accounting Forum*, 39(3), 176-187. doi:http://dx.doi.org/10.1016/j.accfor.2014.12.001

Schwartz, M. S. (2011). *How to Minimize Corruption in Business Organizations: Developing and Sustaining an Ethical Corporate Culture*. In R. J. Burke, E. C.

Tomlinson & C. L. Cooper (Eds.), *Crime and Corruption in Organizations*. Farnham: Gower Publishing Limited.

Smith, R. G. (2001). *Defining, Measuring, and Reporting Fraud Risk Within Your Organisation*. I.I.R. CONFERENCES - Applying Risk Management to Implement a Proactive Fraud Prevention Strategy in Financial Services. Sydney.

Transparency International. (2016). *Corruption Perceptions Index 2015* R. Beddow (Ed.) Retrieved from http://www.transparency.org/cpi2015

Chapter 12

Fraud is Difficult to Define

Fabiana Maggie Ferraro

The issue of the definition of fraud has been vastly debated in the academic and legislative arena. Deeply entwined with the much broader concept of "lying", the efforts in defining the notion of "fraud" have often been hindered by a natural overlap of the theoretical concept of fraud, or deception, and its legal counterpart. This research starts distinguishing between the different approaches to fraud from a philosophical perspective and from the legislative point of view. Proposing the element of "deceit" and "dishonesty" as a leading premise of our discussion, this observation suggested that one of the most noticeable difficulties in defining fraud resides in the far-reaching spectrum of behaviours and actions involving dishonesty. From a purely legislative point of view, the most striking challenge arising from this analysis has been the dilemma of proving the component of dishonesty, especially in the modern corporate and financial world. The present legislative gaps in fraud-related regulations both in the UK and in the US seem to be the most apparent proof of the lack of a univocal and generally accepted interpretation of fraud.

In order to thoroughly discuss the assertion presented in the paper, it is opportune to investigate both the literature and past and present legislation in reference to the complex concept of fraud. Being not just a legislative matter, fraud has also been part of academic and philosophical studies: in 1983 Sutherland started to address the concept of fraud in his "white collar" crime theory (Levi, 2013, p. 183). From then on, both the academic writing on fraud and practitioners' contribution have been considerably prolific and have often stepped in the legislative production process (Doig, 2006, pp. 1-2). In this context, the issue of the difficulty in defining fraud has led to consistent limitations in terms of clear, effective law enforcement, as well as in terms of a realistic quantification of the problem (Tunley, 2014, pp. 2, 3). The primary purpose of this essay is therefore to discuss this issue providing evidence in reference to key UK and US legislation and according to past and present academic research on the subject of fraud.

In the attempt of determining the complexity of the definition of fraud, it is probably important to distinguish between the theoretical concept of fraud, and fraud as a legal notion. In fact, while the former potentially includes an ample variety of behaviours which are not always defined as fraud in accordance with the law, the latter specifies a precise definition of the acts constituting fraud (Smith, Button, Johnston, Frimpong, 2011, p. 15). From a theoretical perspective, fraud can be regarded as a general, comprehensive type of conduct which inevitably involves dishonesty and the use of a deceptive modus operandi in order to achieve an illegitimate advantage. The element of deceit is therefore the discriminating factor that defines and distinguishes a fraudulent behaviour from a rightful conduct (Reichel, Albanese, 2013, p. 120). In terms of legislation, the theoretical definition of such conduct had led to shape regulation in many ways in different parts of the world: while some countries, like the United Kingdom and the United States, have determined a specific crime of fraud, other countries have encompassed the key element of dishonesty in a wide range of other criminal offences. According to Reichel and Albanese therefore, the reason for such difficulty in defining fraud resides in the far-reaching spectrum of conducts involving dishonesty (Reichel, Albanese, 2013, pp. 120-1).

Cho and Lau observe that a first commonly accepted and contemporary definition of fraud was given by Dilhorne in Scott v Metropolitan Police Comissioner [1975] AC 910. Here, the concept of "conspiracy to defraud" was regarded as an agreement characterised by the dishonest intention to commit actions which will inevitably cause an injury to the person or his/her rights (Cho, Lau, 2012, pp. 56-7). Commenting on this assertion, Cho and Lau recognise the extent of the uncertainty in the definition of dishonesty, noticing that sometimes, especially in a competitive business environment, it can be very difficult to discern between a malevolent intention and maybe a more subtle, aggressive commercial practice (Cho, Lau, 2012, p. 57). Trying to outline the traits of such malicious conduct, Kirwan, citing Weldy, highlights that dishonesty is a conjoint merging of the intent to cause harm and at the same time of having a profit (Kirwan, 1994, pp. 185-6). As a consequence, it is the sole element of dishonesty that defines fraud as a criminal act: in this context it is reasonable to maintain that there is no judicial, authoritative definition of "dishonesty", which inevitably leads to such ambiguity in the definition of this offence (Law Commission, 2002, p. 14). In 1982, the Court of Appeal in R v Gosh, attempted to address this problem stating that a certain behaviour can be deemed as dishonest according to the standards of honest and reasonable people (Law Commission, 2002, p. 40).

In this context, the problem of a lack of a clear-cut, unequivocal definition of fraud was addressed several times by the UK legislators, in an effort to fill in the gap left by the existing legislation on the identification and prosecution of fraud. For example, the 1994 Law Commission Report no. 228 tried to carry out a review of the so called "offences of dishonesty", examining several existing acts like the Forgery and Counterfeiting Act 1981 and the Theft Act 1968 and 1978 (Law Commission, 1994, p. 7). It is worth noticing how the paper, and later other academics, emphasise the impact of the use of advanced technology on the crime of fraud, which arguably renders it more difficult to define (Wilson, Wilson, 2007, p. 36). Interestingly, the authors stress the importance of *proving* the crucial component of dishonesty: in the modern capitalist system in fact, the direct or indirect loss which derives from personal gains in the commercial sphere is not necessarily criminal (Law Commission, 2002, p. 14). In this light Levi, investigating the presence of long-firm fraud in the modern capitalistic world, suggests that for instance the exploitation of credibility is an essential component of capitalism, and it can credibly lead to the occurrence of long-firm fraud (Levi, 2008, p. lxxix). These considerations about the ambiguous nature of the concept of fraud, especially if placed in the context of the contemporary financial world, seem to contribute to the assumption that fraud is indeed a complex and multifaceted concept that is not always easy to define.

This interpretational uncertainty later led to a cardinal development in the legislation of criminal fraud in the UK: the Fraud Act 2006 abolished the so called deception offences previously regulated by the Theft Acts 1968 and 1978. Contrasting with the concept of deception in fact, the essential principle underpinning this new offence is misrepresentation (Farrell, Yeo, Ladenburg, 2007, p. 22). This totally new perspective also allowed courts to proceed with prosecution in those cases where the use of machines was involved, and thus no longer required the presence of a human mind in the process of deception (Farrell, Yeo, Ladenburg, 2007, p. 23). Although these innovations have undoubtedly eluded technicalities, they also have been criticised for depending too much on the idea of dishonesty, and the appropriateness of tests for the verification of a dishonest intent has been much debated (Campbell, 1984, p. 349; Steel, 2000, pp. 46-7). In terms of definition of the concept of fraud however, it seems rather obvious that the Fraud Act does not provide a clear, unequivocal interpretation of fraud, but it is instead concerned with how fraud is committed and by what means, in order to tackle this wrongful conduct with different measures. Another very interesting perspective on the difficulties in the definition of fraud, and on their impact and repercussions on the law-making process, is given by the rather provocative proposition advanced by Druzin and Li. Stating that the element of dishonesty seems to feature the heart of society and human relationships, they explore several philosophical presumptions aimed at defining the action of "lying" (Druzin, Li, 2011, pp. 530-61). In order to present the difficulties in defining fraud, and to investigate the effects on the jurisdictional system analysing the relevant legislation, they also stress the difference between the mere act of lying and deception. In fact, while lying is a plainly univocal action, deception involves by its very nature a multiplicity of behaviours, both implicit and explicit (Druzin, Li, 2011, pp. 565). Analysing lying in the form of fraud in reference to relevant UK and US legislation, Druzin and Li agree that fraud is indeed difficult to define, and its definition can change according to the statute used to prosecute such offences, depending on the case (Druzin, Li, 2011, pp. 549). Considering in particular The Fraud Act 2006, § 5, and Title 18, Chapter 47 of the U.S. Code Part I, they argue that both these key pieces of legislation only consider damage in the form of monetary loss and are thus predominantly concerned only with financial and proprietary deprivation. The consequent perception therefore, is that the clearest definition of fraud that can be found in reference to current legislation has an exclusively economic nature, and that law is arguably failing to address any other harmful repercussion of such conduct (Druzin, Li, 2011, pp. 549-50). On the whole, it seems safe to affirm that these "gaps" in the American and British key legislations suggest a compelling indication of the difficulty in defining the act of fraud.

In conclusion, this overview of the academic research on fraud, and the overall analysis of the relevant pieces of legislations, seem to suggest that fraud is rather difficult to define. Taken together, these insights indicate that there is a salient discrepancy between the theoretical concept of fraud and its legal definition. Specifically, the theoretical definition of the concept of "dishonesty" appears to be undoubtedly clear and undebatable. On the other hand, investigating the concept of fraud from a jurisdictional point of view, it is safe to assume that although it is easy to define dishonesty, which is the inherent characteristic of fraud, it is not equally easy to define fraud as a legislative matter. The current regulation tends to be substantially concerned with the operating modalities of frauding, rather than with determining a decisive, univocal interpretation of fraud. Several efforts have been made to reasonably widen the present definition of fraud in order to keep up with the new technological requirements in the modern world, and in spite of some arguable weaknesses in the current legislation, there is certainly room for further research to tackle the various unanswered questions on the controversial and intricate issue of defining fraud.

References

Campbell, K. (1984). The Test of Dishonesty in *R. v. Ghosh. The Cambridge Law Journal, 43*(2), 349-360. Retrieved from: http://journals.cambridge.org/abstract_S00081973001112632.

Cho, C.K., Lau, C. (2012). *Practical Approach to Prevention and Detection of Fraud. Guidebook for internal control professionals.* USA: South Eastern Publishers.

Doig, A. (2006). *Fraud.* Uffculme, Devon, GBR: Willan Publishing. Retrieved from http://www.ebrary.com.

Druzin, B.H., Li, J. (2013). The Criminalization of Lying: Under What Circumstances, If Any, Should Lies Be Made Criminal? *Journal of Criminal Law and Criminology, 101*(2), 529-574. Retrieved from: http://scholarlycommons.law.northwestern.edu/jclc/vol101/iss2/5/.

Farrell, S., Yeo, N., Ladenburg, G. (2007). *Blackstone's guide to the Fraud Act 2006.* New York: Oxford University Press.

Kirwan, C. (1994). Mischief or "manifest intent"? Looking for employee dishonesty in the uncharted world of fiduciary misconduct. *Tort & Insurance Law Journal, 30*(1), 183-194. Retrieved from: http://www.jstor.org/stable/25762478.

Levi, M. (2008). "The Phantom Capitalists: The Organization and Control of Long-firm Fraud". Aldershot: Ashgate Publishing Ltd.

Levi, M. (2013). *Regulating Fraud: White-Collar Crime and the Criminal Process.* London: Routledge.

Reichel, P., Albanese, J. (2013). *Handbook of Transnational Crime and Justice* USA: SAGE Publications.

Scott v Metropolitan Police Commissioner [1975] AC 819. Retrieved from: http://www.bailii.org/uk/cases/UKHL/1974/4.html.

Smith, G., Button, M., Johnston, L., Frimpong, K. (2011). *Studying Fraud As A White Collar Crime.* Basingstoke: Palgrave Macmillan.

Steel, A. (2000). The appropriate test for dishonesty. *Criminal Law Journal(24)*, pp.46–59. Retrieved from: http://papers.ssrn.com/sol3/papers.cfm?abstract_id=1030225.

The Law Commission. (1994). *Criminal Law: Conspiracy to Defraud* (Law Commission No. 228). Retrieved from http://www.bailii.org/ew/other/EWLC/1994/228.pdf.

The Law Commission. (2002). *Fraud. Report on a reference under section 3(1)(e) of the Law Commissions Act 1965* (Law Commission No. 276). Retrieved from http://lawcommission.justice.gov.uk/docs/lc276_Fraud.pdf.

Tunley, M. (2014). *Mandating the Measurement of Fraud: Legislating Against Loss.* Basingstoke: Palgrave Macmillan.

Wilson, G., Wilson, S.J. (2007). Can the General Fraud Offence 'Get the Law Right'?: Some Perspectives on the 'Problem' of Financial Crime. *Journal of Criminal Law, 71*(1), 36-53. Retrieved from: http://irep.ntu.ac.uk/R/?func=dbin-jump-full&object_id=183822&local_base=GEN01.

Chapter 13

Mutual Multi-Disciplinary Learning as a Pathway to Better Organisational Security

Jerry Hart

Since the early 1990s, there has been a significant growth in the number and range of training and education options for those wishing to enter the security world. However, the apparent strategy of developing security as a new specialist profession has had – and in the author's view, will continue to have – a limited impact on improving the management of security within organisations. This chapter argues that this type of security failure is at least partly because of the near absence of the subject from the teaching of mainstream management. Consequentially, security is insufficiently integrated into decision-making, operations and culture and all too often summoned only as a reaction to security failure. This chapter explains the development of a new approach to identifying and understanding security risks that also facilitates inter-disciplinary learning, enabling security professionals to tap into other areas of expertise while sharing their own knowledge and perspectives with non-security colleagues.

Introduction

In the early 1990s, I was privileged to study and work with Professors Martin Gill, Adrian Beck and others who pioneered the study of security management in higher education. The MSc in Security Management & Information Technology at what was then the Centre for the Study of Public Order (CSPO) at the University of Leicester (UK) soon established itself at that time as a world leader in the research and teaching of this evolving subject.

CSPO presented the subject and *discipline* of security as a combination of *criminology* (understanding the causes of crime), *management theory* (understanding organisations and delivered in partnership with the University's thriving MBA programme) and *information technology* (using data analysis techniques and technology developed within the broader social sciences). This was a robust and innovative approach that provided intellectual pathways to further development of the subject of security in terms of theory, practice and its wider significance to organisations and wider society.

At the time of writing and with around 23 years experience of working in security, I am now reflecting on the implications of the fact that, while we security students sat in on MBA lectures, there was no option for MBA students to join us in criminology class. As far as I know, no MBA student opted to research a security-related theme for their dissertation, and I wonder what affect – if any – spending time with fellow postgraduates who specialised in security had on their perceptions of the subject in their subsequent management careers. I suspect that more could have been achieved in this regard.

Of course, we can accept that MBAs and similar courses can't cover every aspect of management. Security is a 'specialism', as are accounting, finance, human resources and procurement disciplines. Yet most of these specialisms regularly crop up within a notional 'core' definition of management and therefore in the 'core' curricula of MBA programmes, while security management does not.

I didn't have time to conduct an exhaustive study for this chapter, but scanning and word-searching the prospectuses of the top five MBA programmes in each region[1] defined by *The Economist's* 'Full-Time MBA Ranking' found no mention of the word 'security'. However, references to other specialist functions, such as 'human resources' and 'finance' are abundant. Yet one of the founding fathers of modern management theory listed the provision of security ('protection of

---

[1] Asia & Australasia, Europe, North America and the Rest of the World.

property and people') as one of six key activities of industrial organisations (Fayol, 1916[2]).

Security *is* a core discipline, so what are the consequences of its absence from mainstream management education?

Perhaps it isn't a problem, so long as something is in place to help ensure the competence of specialists. Having access to experienced and educated security professionals within their management ranks undoubtedly benefits organisations. However, I suggest that this is no guarantee of achieving better security because of the realities of communication and prioritisation within most organisations. In truth, there are many barriers to the specialist security voice making itself heard – especially when it attempts to speak proactively about risks that have not yet manifested themselves in actual incidents.

This is sometimes the fault of the security specialist, who may appear to be 'peddling fear', in negative ('*pull back*') contrast to business development and other professionals who may argue for positive ('*push forward*') risk-taking to advance the organisation's mission. However, resistance to the security message may also be a consequence of a lack of awareness and indeed a 'knowledge gap' on the part of generalist managers who possess only lay understanding of security.

So how might we address this gap? Personally, I have sought to do so in the workplace by running security risk awareness seminars and workshops for colleagues, writing explanatory guidelines and consultation documents and by simply engaging with managers informally and exploiting any opportunity to share knowledge and promote my subject and its benefits. All of these approaches have their place, but the most exciting and likely to be most enduring results have come from a new approach that I have evolved while conducting research for my doctoral thesis.

---

[2] Fayol, H. (1916) *Administration Industrielle Et Générale*, http://mip-ms.cnam.fr/servlet/com.univ.collaboratif.utils.LectureFichiergw?ID_FICHIER=1295877017978, accessed 07 April 2015.

Business Process Security Analysis

My Doctorate in Professional Studies (DProf) research at the University of Middlesex sought to develop a new, multi-disciplinary approach to security risk assessment. Tagged 'Business Process Security Analysis' (BPSA), it seeks to identify and assess security risks at the *process level* but in the context of a whole system.

The research involved studying the structure, dynamics and perspectives of workers on a wide range of industries (including mining, oil & gas, automotive, pharmaceutical & manufacturing) in many territorial settings and security risk environments in more than thirty countries.

Many traditional approaches to security risk management advocate *enclosing* systems within a hard perimeter, such as ancient city walls and the defence-in-depth design of military fortifications. The problem with the resulting designs is that they can inhibit the free movement that many commercial or similarly interactive systems require in order to work (e.g. *shoppers want to enter the shop*). They also have limited effect in defending against internal threats (e.g. *employees need to access the workplace*).

BPSA formalises an approach to help lower or even dismantle such defences and focus protective efforts on those parts of the system that are most critical and/or vulnerable. Its theoretical foundations draw from a combination of General Systems Theory, Management Theory and Criminology.

The development of General Systems Theory is credited to Bertalanffy and his 1925 doctoral thesis. It presents an alternative to the reductionist approach of classical science – knowing more and more about less and less – which Bertalanffy argues may limit our understanding of the *whole*. Put simply:

> In order to understand an organized whole we must know both the parts and the relations between them.
>
> Bertalanffy (1972, p. 411[3])

---

[3] Bertalanffy, L von (1972) 'The History and Status of General Systems Theory', *The Academy of Management Journal*, December Vol 15 (4), 407-426.

Bertalanffy tells us that the early Greeks sought 'in the experienced world, an order or *kosmos* which was intelligible and, hence, controllable by thought and rational action' (ibid, p. 407). He proposes that General Systems Theory is 'a contemporary expression of perennial problems which have been recognized for centuries' (*ibid*).

According to Bertalanffy, the reductionism of scientific method – the focus on the activities and function of individual cells or 'elements' (the term coined by Kuhn, 1974) within a system – as opposed to a more holistic inclusion of the 'coordination of parts and processes' (Bertalanffy, 1928, p. 8[4]) had become a barrier to understanding systems as 'organised entities' (Bertalanffy, 1972, p. 410) in their own right.

He argues that, beyond simply forming the basis for understanding systems, his theory has the potential to unify the diverse perspectives offered by different disciplines:

> General systems theory, then, consists of the scientific exploration of "wholes" and "wholeness" which, not so long ago, were considered to be metaphysical notions transcending the boundaries of science. Novel concepts, methods, and mathematical fields have developed to deal with them. At the same time, the interdisciplinary nature of concepts, models, and principles applying to "systems" provides a possible approach toward the unification of science.
>
> Bertalanffy (1972, p. 415)

General Systems Theory therefore presents a 'natural fit' for anyone seeking to develop and manage multi-disciplinary approaches to problem-solving.

---

[4] Bertalanffy, L von, (1934) *Modern Theories of Development*, trans Woodger, JH (1934) Oxford: Oxford University Press; New York: Harper Torchbooks, 1962. German original: *Kritische Theorie der Formbildung.* Berlin: Borntraeger, 1928. 8.

Kuhn (1974[5]) developed the theory to include a series of complex definitions of the functions and interactions between system elements. These include:

Table 13.1 Functions and Interactions

Detector	The function that perceives and receives information
Selector	The rules or value system that determines decision-making and interpretation of the information received
Effector	The function that carries out the selected action or behaviour demanded by the selector

Kuhn's model allows for only two types of interaction:

Table 13. 2 Two Types of Interaction

Communication	The transfer of information between elements
Transaction	The transfer of energy or matter between elements

Kuhn's framework is morally neutral as 'transactions' may involve commodities, such as goods or services, but they may also involve 'bads' in the form of contributors to or elements of security risks. Hence, the 'detector' may be the offender, the 'selector' may be his or her perception of a criminal opportunity and the 'effector' the operational means of executing the threat.

Applying these principles in conjunction with various types of management theory allows the analyst to track risks from the initial opportunity or 'chink in the armour' that facilitate their emergence, to their eventual manifestation as acts of deliberate harm. It also facilitates evaluation of the effectiveness of the organisational control function that should be configured to deter, detect or delay such behaviours.

---

[5] Kuhn, A (1974) *The Logic of Social Systems*, San Francisco: Jossey-Bass.

Writing in 2005, Skyttner further highlights the importance of the relationships between system components:

> What we need to understand is not the behaviour of individuals parts but rather their orchestration. Often, our goal must not be to understand what things are made of, but rather how they are compounded and work together in integrated wholes.
>
> Skyttner (2005, p. v[6])

Management theory offers a body of knowledge and a range of analytical tools to help achieve this understanding. For example, McKinsey's 7-S framework[7] (Waterman & Peters, 1980[8]) is a recognised example of an enduring model that facilitates a comprehensive perspective on seven dimensions of organisation, all of which can possess vulnerabilities that offenders may exploit.

Similarly, Quality Management is a management philosophy that also has a particular affinity with General Systems Theory, in that both entail visualising organisations and activities as systems, comprising interlocking processes that engage in converting raw materials and information into products and services that are fit for purpose. Quality is 'an outcome – a characteristic of a product or service provided to a customer, and the hallmark of an organisation which has satisfied all of its stakeholders' (Charter Quality Institute, 2015[9]). Quality management is the series of activities, functions and disciplines that enable an organisation to deliver quality. This involves the application of a range of measures including those to minimise waste, both of material and effort, enable continuous improvement, and to ensure that customers

---

[6] Skyttner, L (2005) *General Systems Theory: Problems, Perspectives, Practice*, Singapore: World Scientific Publishing.

[7] Strategy, Structure, Systems, Skills, Style, Staffing & Shared Values.

[8] Waterman, R. H., Peters, T. J., & Phillips, J. R. (1980) 'Structure is not organization' *Business Horizons*, 23(3), 14-26.

[9] Chartered Quality Institute (2015) 'What is Quality?' http://www.thecqi.org/The-CQI/ What-is-quality/, accessed 25 June 2015.

pay for the product or service they have asked for and not the failings of the supplier or provider's management system.

Security is an attribute of quality because its absence causes defects and other forms of non-compliance that must be paid for – either by the producer or by the consumer. Quality management therefore empowers the security function:

> All non-conformances are caused [...] Anything that is caused can be *prevented*.
>
> Crosby (1984, p. 7[10]) (emphasis added)

An obvious example is theft – the direct cost of retail crime in the UK in 2013 was £511 million[11] – while a less obvious one may be cyber crime – estimated in the same year to cost up to US$100 billion per year in the US alone[12]. The impact of these losses is felt and funded to varying degrees by all stakeholders.

The principles of quality management – especially when combined with the systems approach discussed above – provide a coherent, rational and recognisable structure for identifying where security risks, like other potential defects, may occur at the process level and how they might affect subsequent processes and the system as a whole.

The third disciplinary pillar of BPSA is criminology – the study of the causes of crime. As a practitioner working within a private, albeit very large, organisation, my focus has to be on controlling the situation wherein crime may occur, rather than trying to change the values and governance of the wider societies outside. Situational Crime Prevention Theory and associated approaches have all provided an invaluable toolkit in terms of identifying and closing down opportunities for offenders. However, social crime prevention theories are also

---

[10] Crosby, P (1984) *Quality Without Tears*, New York: McGraw-Hill (1995 Edition).

[11] British Retail Crime Survey (2013), cited on http://www.kingdom.co.uk/articles/effect-of-retail-crime-on-businesses.aspx, accessed 21 June 2015.

[12] Center for Strategic & International Studies (2013) *The Economic Impact of Cyber crime and Cyber Espionage*, http://www.mcafee.com/uk/resources/reports/rp-economic-impact-cybercrime.pdf, accessed 10 June 2015.

useful, especially in terms of understanding the consequences of a lack of investment in personnel, employee engagement and other routes towards achieving a contented workforce.

Figure 13.1, next page, shows a simple example of how a BPSA is mapped, in this case presenting the plant operations and laboratory analysis at a gold mine. Ore is processed in a roughly clockwise direction from the Ball Mill Feed (top left) until it is refined into bullion. Samples are taken at key points and transferred to an analytical laboratory for testing. Among other things, lab testing provides an indication of the likely quantity and quality of precious metals that will be produced by the refining processes.

Although the entire physical area occupied by the system was surrounded by a military grade perimeter fence with strict access controls enforced by armed guards, opportunities for internal theft and tampering exist throughout.

While most precious metal content is in fine grain form, embedded in the surrounding ore, occasional gold nuggets may be found which can be stolen for sale to external processors for several hundred dollars. To the untrained eye, some sampling points appeared to comprise nothing more than fast moving torrents of muddy water, but placing a mesh basket in the flow may yield a significant reward. Collaboration with process experts helped identify such opportunities and informed recommendations for enhanced physical security and surveillance.The refinery is an area of the plant that is subject to exceptionally high levels of security, because it is here that bullion is produced and even a few drops of molten liquid can be collected, accumulated and sold for considerable sums. However, this was found to have vulnerabilities at key points, even though all employees were subject to a separate access and egress control regime. This included a full body search and prohibiting the entry or removal of any tools or other equipment unless under strict supervision. Repeated participant observation in the access and egress management processes revealed various human flaws, such as predictable search behaviours by guards or opportunities to request certain exceptions.

The comments in *italics* in the diagram concern security risks, while those in **bold** refer to security controls.

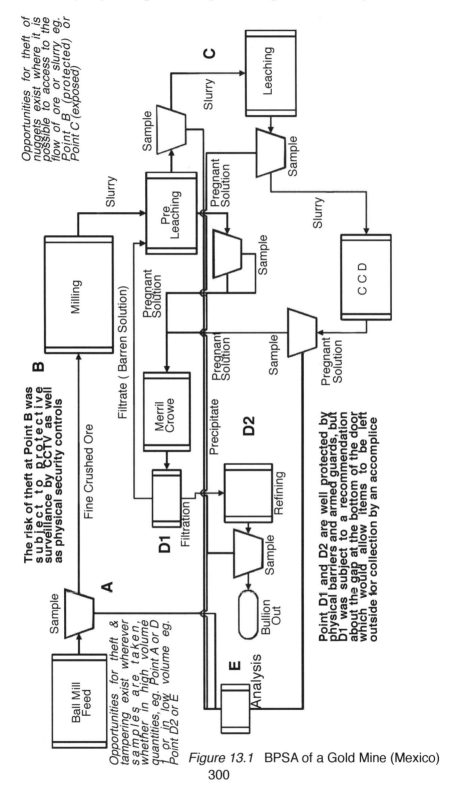

Opportunities for theft of nuggets exist where it is possible to access to the flow of ore or slurry eg. Point B (protected) or Point C (exposed)

The risk of theft at Point B was subject to protective surveillance by CCTV as well as physical security controls

Opportunities for theft & tampering exist wherever samples are taken, whether in high volume quantities, eg. Point A or D1 or in low volume eg. Point D2 or E

Point D1 and D2 are well protected by physical barriers and armed guards, but D1 was subject to a recommendation about the gap at the bottom of the door which would allow items to be left outside for collection by an accomplice

Figure 13.1 BPSA of a Gold Mine (Mexico)

300

In addition, the system shown was managed by several different departments within the mining company structure. Further analysis in collaboration with plant and laboratory experts revealed how the hierarchical management structure inhibited 'horizontal' communication between the different functions and departments. Such communication should enable information sharing about how vulnerabilities in one part of the system can create opportunities for offenders to exploit in subsequent processes.

Mutual Multi-Disciplinary Learning

Each setting – whether geographic or thematic – requires expertise and knowledge that I did not possess at the outset (and will continue to acquire *ad infinitum*). I had never worked in a gold mine, sea port, oil refinery or test laboratory before, so my specialist security knowledge was at risk of being too abstract, too theoretical and unable to create a positive impact on the security risk management of operations and facilities.

This deficit was corrected by access to another essential resource in the form of expert personnel at all levels of the organisation. These seasoned practitioners knew a lot about how some risks manifested themselves in some parts of their systems, but lacked the technical knowledge of risk and security – especially important concepts, such as crime displacement – to manage them effectively. I needed insights into the technical specifics of operations and they needed to better understand how to integrate security.

From an informal start, these collaborative interactions are now taking on a semi-formal status as product offerings being marketed to external clients as part of a quality auditing package. Multi-disciplinary teams are deployed to one or more facilities and collaborate, exchanging knowledge and perspectives and otherwise engaging in mutual learning, which they also share with client personnel.

The emerging knowledge fusion is captured in reports, which are then re-cycled into technical governance advice and training packages to enable wider dissemination.

Multi-disciplinary teams have become a common feature in other fields, especially healthcare (e.g. Fletcher, 2008[13]). It contrasts with uni-disciplinary working in which experts are grouped together in departments, rather than organised as multi-disciplinary teams in response to the characteristics of the problem they are seeking to treat. While uni-disciplinary approaches have some benefits – not least the opportunity to share diverse knowledge and perspectives within the same discipline – there is no reason why these should be forfeited if an organisation adopts a flexible multi-disciplinary approach to organisation and resource allocation. The team we assembled to conduct the audit and review referred to in Figure 13.1 provides a good example, as it comprised:

- A process engineer and mineral data specialist.
- A mine and product plant engineer.
- A geochemistry analysis specialist.
- A QHSE (laboratories) specialist.
- A security risk management specialist (myself).

I worked with all four colleagues to identify the processes that made up the whole system, the relationships between them and any associated risk factors. During a post-operation review we were all in unanimous agreement that we had learnt a great deal from each other which would change the way we worked in future. Crucially, my four colleagues stated that they had learnt a range of new concepts and techniques related to security that had raised their awareness, not only of security risks, but of how treating such risks could benefit the overall quality and efficiency of the system under scrutiny.

Conclusion

This chapter has presented the practical and theoretical basics of BPSA and how it has led to a more collaborative approach to information sharing and mutual multi-disciplinary learning and problem-

---

[13] Fletcher, M (2008) 'Multi-disciplinary team working: building and using the team', *Practice Nurse*; British Nursing Database pg. 42.

oriented collaboration in my organisation. I have argued that this offers at least a partial solution to the lack of formal understanding of security risk management encountered in many organisations which are likely to be a causal factor in many security failures. The approach can be adapted to any industry or setting and applied to promote awareness of any other disciplines that are not commonly included in mainstream management training and education.

Name Index

Subject Index

315